to my sisters and brother

CHILDREN AND JUSTICE

DECISION-MAKING IN CHILDREN'S HEARINGS AND JUVENILE COURTS

by

STEWART ASQUITH

1983

EDINBURGH UNIVERSITY PRESS

© Stewart Asquith 1983
Edinburgh University Press
22 George Square, Edinburgh

Set in Linoterm Trump Medieval
by Speedspools, Edinburgh, and
printed in Great Britain by
Redwood Burn Ltd, Trowbridge

British Library Cataloguing
in Publication Data
Asquith, Stewart
Children and justice
1. Juvenile courts—Scotland
I. Title
344.1105'8   KDC947
ISBN 0 85224 429 0
       0 85224 466 5 (paperback)

CONTENTS

ACKNOWLEDGEMENTS

Though ultimately the responsibility for this book is my own, it would be more than ungrateful to ignore the help and support a number of people kindly offered me in the writing of it. Directly involved in my doctoral thesis, on which the book is based, were Professor Neil MacCormick and Dr Alex Robertson. I am pleased to be able to say that the supervision they provided in those earlier days formed the basis of close and continuing friendships. My colleagues in the Social Administration Department at the University of Edinburgh have lived through the writing of this book with me, and Mike Adler in particular was able to provide the support and encouragement necessary for me to complete it. Chris Clark read the earlier drafts of some chapters and his comments rightly made me rethink and rework some sections. A large part of the work in the Department of Social Administration is with postgraduate students, and I want here to assure them that the contribution they make is important and is respected. Their presence has meant that, again through discussion with them, some of the ideas presented here had to be reworked considerably. I am grateful to them for that. The set of hieroglyphs that posed as a manuscript was typed largely by Valerie Chuter and Jackie McGeachie.

PART ONE

CONCEPTUAL GROUNDWORK

Chapter One

CHILDREN
AND JUSTICE

In the 1960s in the United Kingdom a welfare philosophy was accepted as providing the appropriate paradigm for dealing with children who commit offences. Changes in the systems of justice for children, introduced in Scotland through the 1968 Social Work Act and in England through the 1969 Children and Young Persons Act, were premised upon meeting the needs of children – whether they had committed an offence or were 'in need' for other reasons. However, in England the juvenile court was retained (though further restrictions were imposed on the prosecution of children and young persons). The changes in Scottish juvenile courts were of a more radical nature: a totally new form of proceedings known as the Children's Hearings was introduced. In place of a modified version of criminal court, children in need of care (because of an offence or for other reasons) are now dealt with in a hearing akin to an administrative tribunal.

This book compares the practical accomplishment of juvenile justice within these two different organisational and administrative structures – the juvenile court in England and the children's hearings in Scotland. There are two parts: the first offers a conceptual analysis of the development of juvenile justice in recent times and of the philosophical assumptions behind different approaches to delinquency control. The second part uses this conceptual groundwork, in presenting an empirical comparison of decision-making by magistrates in an English juvenile court and panel members in a Scottish panel. The English juvenile court and the Scottish Hearings system have both been subjects of a substantial amount of research, but there have as yet been few attempts to provide a detailed sociological comparison of the pursuit of justice in the respective systems.

There are now demands for further changes in juvenile justice not only in the United Kingdom but also elsewhere in the world. The philosophy of welfarism, which was the common currency of delinquency control in the 1960s, has itself now become subject to considerable criticism, as has been the move away from judicially based proceedings in the hearing of cases involving delinquency. Indeed, as will be argued later, the demand for organisational and administrative change is conceptually linked to current dissatisfaction with welfarism as the basis of programmes for dealing with children who commmit offences.

The demand for change is not a new phenomenon in relation to justice for children. Children have always posed conceptual and philosophical problems for the criminal law by virtue of their age and status of dependency on adults. And in the absence of agreement as to how children who offend should be dealt with and to what end, systems of justice for children have taken different forms both cross-culturally and over time. Indeed control of delinquency, almost by its very nature, is subject to continual modification and review as the legal and social status of children is defined and modified in the light of available knowledge – and belief – about the kinds of influences children are subjected to in the course of their development.

In many western industrialised countries this process of review continues, with the demand made for further modifications both in relation to currently held philosophies of delinquency control and consequently to the existing organisational and administrative arrangements that characterise juvenile justice in particular countries. Within the United Kingdom this has taken the form of a demand for a 'return to justice' for children, and recommendations made in other countries are premised upon principles similar to those of the 'justice movement' (see Morris et al. 1980). The attack on welfarism has generally been composed of two main arguments, directed at both the philosophy and practice of juvenile justice.

The first is that children's rights receive insufficient protection in systems based on a welfare philosophy for a number of reasons. *Theoretically*, the critics argue (Morris et al. 1980), welfarism is based on philosophically unsound principles in as much as it is not possible to identify objectively definable criteria which can be employed to explain delinquent behaviour nor to inform the measures to which children are subjected in their 'best interests'. In short, if we do not really know what we are doing with children we should not hide behind an empty rhetoric of therapy when what is being exercised is a form of social control. Semantic and linguistic devices conceal the ambiguity and confusion which is seen to be at the very roots of welfarism. *Practically,* the justice movement deplores the absence of sufficient legal and judicial safeguards in a system of justice based on welfare principles and in that respect its claims are reminiscent of the arguments made in relation to the infamous Gault and Kent cases which fostered a policy of 'constitutionalist revisionism' in the United States in the 1960s (see Faust and Brantingham 1974). The 'return to justice' as currently conceived, then, includes arguments in favour of a court hearing, of allowing judicial review of decisions, and of providing for legal representation. Children could then have the safeguards commonly available to adults caught up in the criminal justice system. It is no surprise then to find that the Scottish system of juvenile justice in which hearings take the form of administrative tribunals comes in for particular comment and criticism along these lines. Indeed, there has more recently been empirical evidence that even the minimal statutory requirements which should govern children's hearings in Scotland are in practice often being ignored (Martin, Murray and Fox 1981).

The second is that measures imposed on children should be offence-oriented rather than child-oriented and that children can therefore be legitimately punished for what they have done. The advocacy of children's rights and of punishment are in fact, in the terms of the justice movement, conceptually linked; only in a system in which children are punished for what they have done can their rights best be protected. Within a welfare philosophy children can be subjected to indeterminate measures which may appear inconsistent with the measures inflicted on children who have committed *prima facie* similar offences. Accordingly, the main proponents of the justice movement include amongst their principles the proposal that measures should be determinate, proportional (to the offence) and consistent (with other offences). Needless to say these in themselves provide for a decision-making process that is, in theory at least, more structured and restrictive than that manifested in a welfare system where wide discretionary powers are available to decision-making personnel. An unashamedly retributivist philosophy underpinning a legally and judicially oriented form of decision-making is seen as the most appropriate, and most just, basis for a system of juvenile justice.

An interesting feature of such arguments is the extent to which they have been voiced in other countries. In Canada, in recognition of the belief that children should have the same protection as adults, the Solicitor General has recommended

(1981) that children should be dealt with by judicial proceedings, involving legal representation, in which children should be punished for offence behaviour in acordance with strict guidelines. This is parallel with the principles of consistency and proportionality proposed by Morris et al. (1980). The 'return to justice' also involves a return to retribution. And in Northern Ireland, the Black Committee (1979), whilst accepting the need for determinate measures of a retributive nature, has rejected both the English juvenile court and the Scottish hearing system as appropriate forms of hearings for offence cases. Instead, it has recommended that, since 'justice' and 'welfare' are not readily reconciled within a single administrative structure, there should be two courts: a Welfare Court with jurisdiction only over decisions about the needs of children and a Criminal Court to hear cases involving offence behaviour. The intriguing feature of such a proposal is that children who offend and who may also be in need will require to appear before both hearings. Whatever the practical problems, the recommendations are made on the basis of doubt about the appropriateness of dealing with offenders by measures based on welfare considerations (see Adler 1981). Very similar proposals have also been made in the Republic of Ireland by the Task Force set up to inquire into child law and related services.

One of the implications of the 'return to justice' movement is that children are to be treated in the main as responsible for their behaviour and this is a feature of the changes recommended for England, Canada, Northern Ireland and the Republic of Ireland. It has also meant that issues about the age of criminal responsibility (ten in England and eight in Scotland at present) are again being discussed. The effect of the development of welfarism in the 1950s and later in the United Kingdom was that there was increasing pressure to raise the age of criminal responsibility. If however children are to be liable to punishment they have to be capable of criminal responsibility. The implication of this is that where systems of juvenile justice are based on a welfare philosophy the age of criminal responsibility may have to be lowered otherwise the punishment of children who offend could in some cases bear all the hallmarks of injustice. Thus, in Finland, where juvenile justice was recognised as epitomising the practical realisation of the welfare approach, arguments have been made in favour of lowering the age of criminal responsibility (Joutsen 1981). Indeed this is logically required since it is also proposed that children be punished much along the lines of the recommendations made in the other countries earlier considered.

There are of course a number of differences in detail in the proposals made for further modification to juvenile justice by these different bodies and individuals. However what they have in common is the commitment to punishment (as opposed to welfarism) as the means for dealing with children who offend and to judicial proceedings (as opposed to what are seen to be wide discretionary powers available within administrative forms of decision-making and a juvenile court in which attempts are made to promote the welfare of children). The common argument is that only within a system in which children are punished in accordance with strict guidelines can justice truly be said to be done.

There is then considerable international interest at present in both the philosophy and the actual practice of juvenile justice with a number of countries about to produce legislative statements. And in Scotland with its unique form of juvenile justice, the lack of total commitment to welfarism and the 'Hearings' system devoid of appropriate powers prompted a Consultative Memorandum inviting comment on proposals to introduce amongst other things such 'radical' measures as 'fining' of parents and children.

The attempt to reconcile welfare and more legalistic approaches to dealing with children who commit offences is of course not new and the history of juvenile justice has been described as a process of compromise between the two (Morris and McIsaac 1978). The 1968 Social Work (Scotland) Act and the 1969 Children and Young Persons Act in England both introduce proposals which reflected the commitment at that time. And though the systems that evolved from the respective legislation were very different, as will be discussed in more detail below, with the retention of the juvenile court in England and the establishment of a tribunal form of hearing in Scotland, both are nevertheless the outcome of a common movement to penal reform which had its roots in the last century (see Boss 1967). There are of course several histories of the development of justice for children in the United Kingdom and it is not the intention to present a detailed history here. Nevertheless, there are crucial elements in the evolution of juvenile justice systems which it would be more than unwise to ignore. This is for two reasons. First, the juvenile justice systems introduced by the 1968 and 1969 Acts were both offered as solutions to the basic conflict of the juvenile court – the need to reconcile welfare and judicial considerations within a single administrative structure. Secondly, the arguments which served to legitimate particular developments in the past have considerable relevance for current debate over the appropriateness of the systems that are in existence at present. Many of the proposals for a 'return to justice' are based on principles that have been well rehearsed a number of times before.

The Juvenile Court: a basic conflict

Developments in juvenile justice in many countries have their roots in the English 1908 Children Act. Quite apart from the very fact of the establishment of separate courts for juveniles, an important feature of the Act was the assumption of jurisdiction over both civil and criminal matters. This was to have important implications for the later development of the juvenile court, which in terms of its two areas of jurisdiction increasingly reflected the greater emphasis placed on the welfare of children who appeared before the court whether for having committed an offence or for some other reason. Consequently, delinquent and other children could be subjected to similar measures and committed to the same institutions. In particular in England, the 1933 Children and Young Persons Act – containing as it does the requirement to have regard to the welfare of the child – has been the source of much controversy about the nature and philosophy of the juvenile court. Wootton states in reference to the Act:

> Nevertheless, behind the clear and simple language of this statute there lurks a fundamental conflict which threatens to become the subject of acute controversy and perhaps to crack wide open the structure that has been so carefully built upon the foundations laid 53 years ago. (1959, p.678)

The conflict to which she refers is that contained within a system of juvenile justice whose principles are derived from criminal justice in its application to adults, and subject therefore to the rules of evidence and criminal procedure, but which at the same time is expressly required to have regard to the welfare of the children who are the subjects of decisions within it. This is of course the crucial dilemma of juvenile justice, and as such has been the focus of considerable comment. Cavenagh, for example, explicitly and concisely states the position of critics of a court-based system of juvenile justice: 'The practical difficulty in submitting child offenders to the criminal jurisdiction was, as they saw it, that the extent of a child's social need and the gravity of his offence were not necessarily in proportion to each other' (1967, p.65). And later, commenting on the similarity of the proceedings for delinquent and non-delinquent children she states that 'the procedure for dealing with non-criminal cases is in many ways similar to that for trial on a criminal charge though no question of criminal responsibility is involved' (1967, p.89).

Nor had the apparent incongruity of adopting a welfare philosophy within a framework ultimately derived from the ordinary courts of criminal law escaped official notice. The incompatibility of a conceptual framework underlying notions of welfare and treatment on the one hand with the conceptual framework underlying notions of crime and punishment on the other received explicit comment later in the United Kingdom in the Ingleby and the Kilbrandon Reports, which examined the law in its application to children in England and Scotland respectively.

Ingleby, in a much-quoted passage, commented:

> The court remains a criminal court in the sense that it is a magistrates court, that it is principally concerned with trying offences, that its procedure is a modified form of ordinary criminal procedure and that, with a few special provisions, it is governed by the law of evidence in criminal cases. Yet the requirement to have regard to the welfare of the child, and the various ways in which the court may deal with an offender suggest a jurisdiction that is not criminal. It is not easy to see how these two principles may be reconciled. (Ingleby report, para.60)

And in similar vein, though referring to the practical difficulty of implementing a preventive philosophy within the framework of the court, the Kilbrandon report argued that

> In drawing a contrast between a system resting primarily on ideas of crime, responsibility and punishment and one proceeding primarily on the principle of prevention, we are not, of course, suggesting that the methods of dealing with adult crime are entirely governed by the first concept or that a working compromise between them is not possible. In practice, the present arrangements represent such a compromise, and at any given time and certainly in relation to any individual offender, a balance has to be sought on an empirical basis between the conflicting claims of the two principles. (Kilbrandon Report, para.54)

The recommendations of the respective committees as to the

future development of juvenile justice were seen as providing viable and, perhaps more importantly, acceptable solutions to the particular problem associated with the juvenile court. The recommendations themselves, as we shall later see, though derived from a common concern, were fundamentally different and are indicative of the two opposing standpoints which can be identified in the relevant literature (see Cavenagh 1966). There are interesting parallels with the arguments made by the 'return to justice' movement.

One is based on the argument for the necessity of a judicial and legalistic mode of intervention in the lives of children, even where welfare is being considered, and hence the necessity of retaining the juvenile-court structure and form of proceedings. The principle of welfare, it is important to note, is not itself questioned by the advocates of the juvenile court (Morris et al. 1980). Rather, the source of the controversy was the implementation of welfare measures in particular and a welfare philosophy in general within an institution bound by the legal, judicial concepts associated with a criminal jurisdiction (see Elkin 1938; Cavenagh and Sparks 1965; Watson 1965; Pound 1946).

The other, in complete contrast, is based on the notion that an administrative tribunal or agency, without the trappings of the court of criminal jurisdiction, was more appropriate for dealing with children in terms of welfare (see Wootton 1968; Midgley 1975; Napley 1968; Harno 1951). The form of proceedings within a court setting itself was considered an obstacle to the provision of appropriate welfare measures for children, whether they were offenders or not (Wootton 1968). The form of proceedings associated with a criminal court required the establishment of guilt before sentence could be passed. The problem of the juvenile court, although it is not without significance for sentencing adult offenders (see Duster 1970; Kilbrandon 1966, p.118), is seen to be that there were two more or less distinct stages in the sentencing process. The first, the adjudication of the allegation, was dictated by judicial or legal concepts and was subject to rules of evidence. The other was the disposition or disposal of the case at the sentencing stage where consideration of the appropriate welfare measures was founded theoretically at least, upon a conceptual framework which far from assuming, in criminal cases, rationality and personal responsibility, presupposed a conception of human nature as essentially determined. This has been presented as the dilemma of western penal systems (Duster 1970).

Nor are the differences in the conceptual frameworks simply of philosophical interest; they are of considerable sociological significance in terms of the ideological orientations of the different agencies which comprise particular social-control networks. The changes introduced by the 1969 and 1968 Acts in England and Scotland, for example, were made in the context of the reorganisation of the social services in the light of their expanding role in the field of delinquency as well as the redefinition of delinquency in terms of a different ideological orientation.

Though the procedure of trial for children had been modified in a number of ways from the proceedings in summary court, the juvenile court was nevertheless, and still is, a court of law. In this respect, the juvenile court in England in the early days of its history did not experience the conflict between a 'welfare' and a 'court' or 'judicial' philosophy to the same extent as did the early American courts. The modifications made to summary court procedure never quite allowed for the same degree of 'socialisation' (see Waite 1921; Midgley 1975) as its American counterpart. Despite the attempts to simplify procedure, commentators, some of whom were advocates of the juvenile courts, recognised that proceedings in the English juvenile court may still be confusing for a child. The degree of informality in the juvenile court moreover in its early development did not involve the loss of protection afforded by the principles of due process and though perhaps true of American juvenile justice before constitutionalist revision (Waite 1921; Tappan 1946; Allen 1973; Van Waters 1922), it would not have been accurate to suggest of the English juvenile court that

> Emphasis upon legal rights of the accused, protection of the innocent, proof of guilt and sentence of punishment commensurate with offence was supplanted with a concern for determining the child's condition and prescribing and implementing a course of action aimed at relieving that condition and preventing its recurrence. (Faust and Brantingham 1974, p.145)

From the outset, where a child's welfare was in question, the decision as to measures appropriate to promoting welfare were made *only* after specific issues had been settled in accordance with the rules of evidence (Tappan 1946; Faust and Brantingham 1974; Fox 1974).

Since the juvenile court is basically a court of criminal law, the hearing of cases is governed by the standards of legal procedure and only when guilt has been established, in offence cases, can the child be dealt with, whether by measures of treatment or punishment. And even in its civil jurisdiction, such standards of legal procedure are also applicable where state intervention depended upon the establishment of matters of fact pertaining to the child's social, personal and environmental background. The establishment of specific allegations prior to state intervention has been seen as basic to a philosophy of juvenile justice implemented within a court setting:

> The so-called 'problem' is basic to the judicial procedure, whether civil or criminal. It is that specific allegations must be made and proved before a person can be subjected to compulsion on account of them, and the weight of the order is traditionally likely to be apportioned by the court to the gravity of the acts or situations established. (Cavenagh 1966, p.127)

The concentration on specific allegations offers a means whereby protection can be afforded to the defendant from undue intervention and interference with his liberty. Even where welfare measures are being considered, this does not preclude the need for children to be afforded protection (Elkin 1921; Cavenagh 1966; Midgley 1975). Again, it is not the principle of welfare as much as undue interference with individual, in this case children's, rights and liberty which underpins the argument for the retention of the juvenile court.

Such arguments have also recently been voiced in a number of countries (see Black Report 1979, Solicitor General, Canada, 1981) and in Britain the demands for a 'return to justice' are based on the belief that only within judicial proceedings in which the offence is itself of considerable importance can justice for children be accomplished. The main point is that proceedings derived from courts of criminal law offer children protection from undue intervention through the requirement to meet established standards of judicial procedure.

The reluctance to introduce changes in juvenile justice in favour of more incremental modifications to the proceedings and jurisdiction of the juvenile court has been a characteristic feature of developments in this field in many countries. As we shall now see, though the developments in England were based on an incrementalist approach, the changes in juvenile justice in Scotland were of a more radical nature.

England: The Ingleby Report

The Ingleby committee had also been unable to recommend the abolition of the juvenile court though it did recognise the weaknesses, thereby creating a dilemma as to the nature of any proposals it may have made (Boss 1967). One of the arguments given in the report for the retention of the juvenile courts had been that the courts 'were generally of good standing and worked well on the whole' (para.70). The changes recommended were again essentially of a procedural nature and recognised the unsuitability of dealing with children, especially younger children, by means of criminal jurisdiction. Though the juvenile courts were to be retained, it was recommended that efforts should be made to get away from the conceptions of criminal jurisdiction (1960, para.77), a proposal not dissimilar to that made by Clarke Hall and later by Wootton (1959). Nevertheless, the Report could not support the total abolition of the juvenile court which had objectives and considerations other than welfare alone to bear in mind.

> Although it may be right for the court's action to be determined primarily by the needs of the particular child before it, the court cannot entirely disregard other considerations such as the need to deter potential offenders. An element of general deterrence must enter into many of the court's decisions and this must make the distinction between treatment and punishment even more difficult to draw. (1960, para.7)

The solutions proposed were again indicative of the fact that it was not the principle of welfare *per se* which was objectionable so much as the proceedings which surrounded welfare considerations in decision-making. Decisions about children were still to be welfare-oriented but the proceedings were to be further modified so as to allow younger children to be dealt with by the court in its *civil* jurisdiction.

All children who appeared before the court and who were under 12 were to be dealt with as in need of care, protection and control (para.84). Because the court was to inquire into all circumstances surrounding court appearance, the mother and father of the child were to be required to appear. But even before proceedings were instituted, police and local authority personnel were to consult as to the necessity of court appearance (para.84). Ingleby had accepted the comments of those who opposed the retention of the courts on the grounds that the child would thereby be stigmatised (para.68). The notion of stigma and 'stigma theory' were to occupy a central role in the later, post-Ingleby, proposals for juvenile justice.

Children between 12 and 17 were to continue to appear before courts under the then-existing procedure; they were to be dealt with as offenders responsible in law for their own actions, or as in need of protection or discipline, subject in all cases to section 44 of the 1933 Act (para.105). Perhaps a development of a more fundamental nature was the recommendation (para.94) that the *doli incapax* rule should be abolished. The difficulty of establishing guilty intention generally, but particularly in children, it was agreed, meant that the criminal law was thereby administered inconsistently. More importantly, the *doli incapax* principle could in fact prevent children from getting help they needed where it had been proven that they had not known what they were doing (para.94). The 'knowledge of wrong' test, particularly since the implementation of section 44 of the 1933 Act was considered as inhibiting the application not of punitive measures, but of welfare measures (Williams 1954). Wootton also felt that 'in short, if the welfare, not the punishment of the child is the governing consideration, the safeguards of the criminal trial became irrelevant' and 'as I have tried to point out, these safeguards are inextricably related to a *punitive* judicial process. It is only because the approved school, the probation or supervision order and the attendance centre are inherently penal institutions, because they are places of punishment the road to which lies through the courts, that a specially elaborate procedure is necessary. Substitute an educational for a penal role and the need for that procedure will disappear' (1961, p.675).

Baroness Wootton's arguments are very similar to those made by the Kilbrandon comittee where more radical changes were made. The Ingleby committee had not recommended the fundamental substitution of philosophies for dealing with children, especially those who commit offences. Rather, the changes which it recommended concentrated on the issue of responsibility and its implication for the suitability of different types of proceedings. The inflexibility of the common law had meant that where criminal capacity had not been established, a child could not receive any necessary help or treatment. What makes the principle particularly difficult to apply is that children who are between the ages of 8 and 14 (following the 1933 Act the age of criminal responsibility was set at eight) are 'morally responsible not as a class but as individuals when they know their act to be wrong. Only then do they morally deserve punishment' (Williams 1954, p.497).

Court proceedings at the stage of adjudication in offence cases were determined by judicial and legal notions such as *doli incapax* and responsibility, whereas the sentencing stage where welfare was considered operated in terms of a different conceptual framework. The Ingleby solution to the dilemma was further to alter the proceedings but not abandon the welfare ethic, so that decisions as to welfare in cases involving younger children would logically follow from a form of court procedure whose guiding precepts were not antithetical to those governing welfare. Welfare measures, it was hoped, would not then be imposed on children in whom had been created expectations of 'just deserts' by means of the court proceedings. What are particularly interesting are the assumptions about the cause of delinquency underlying the main recommendations of the report.

The responsibility for crime by juveniles was considered to be shared by the child and 'those responsible for his upbringing'. Amongst 'those responsible' were parents, family, school and the community and the child could therefore himself only be held partly responsible for his behaviour. (Ingleby viewed the family particularly as a potent source of delinquency.)

Nevertheless, in later years children had to accept greater responsibility for their behaviour, presumably until they had attained the status of normal, fully responsible, law-abiding citizens. The influence of such assumptions in the recommendations of the committee has been remarked upon by Bottoms.

> In other words, the model was, in crude terms, one of social pathology for the younger child, but more classical assumptions about choice of evil for the older child; and these models were to be reflected in the differing procedures – civil proceedings for the younger child and criminal for the older. (Bottoms 1974, p.324)

The resolution of the dilemma of the juvenile court was in effect

> to inject the pathological model in to the *whole* of court proceedings for younger children, and for older children to reduce the force of the conflict by stressing moral responsibility for crime and thus minimise the pathological model at the sentencing stage. (Bottoms 1974, p.342)

Despite the apparent neatness of such a proposal, the ideological conflict between a welfare and a punitive orientation could not be completely resolved where considerations of welfare are, theoretically at least, to be given to all cases. Indeed, the imposition of a rehabilitative ideal on a court-based approach to dealing with adult offenders has presented just such problems.

Though the report was considered by some to have been ineffectual and unimaginative (Midgley 1975), the committee's recommendations themselves did not receive complete legislative expression. With the 1963 Children and Young Persons Act, the age of criminal responsibility was certainly raised but only to ten; the jurisdiction of the court over care and protection cases was modified to care, protection and control. Other than these changes, the only condition of major importance in the 1963 Act was the provision for *preventive* powers to be exercised by local authorities.

Whereas the Ingleby report may well have been rather conservative in its recommendations, more radical proposals that were to be made in England in the 1960s aroused considerable hostile reaction, with the result that the incremental and evolutionary, rather than revolutionary, character of the development of juvenile justice south of the border was continued.

Post-Ingleby Developments

The rather conservative approach to change in juvenile justice proposed in the Ingleby report did little to stem the demands for more radical reform. Wootton, a prominent commentator throughout this period, summed up the reaction of many to the report when she said:

> We had been hoping for a bold and imaginative reconstruction of the whole system for dealing with unfortunate children in this day and age. What we got was a number of useful technical minor reforms on a system which in the judgment of many of us is already outmoded. (*Hansard* H.L. 1962 CCXLIV, 815)

The report also received criticism in a Fabian pamphlet devoted to commentary on the Ingleby proposals (Donnison et al. 1962). There were two criticisms. Though Ingleby had identified the family as a major source of delinquency, as had other reports previously (see Kahan 1966), it was felt that little had actually been done to provide a service which would truly be designed to alleviate family need (Jay 1962). Moreover, though the report had also recognised inherent weaknesses in the juvenile court system and the problem of the stigma associated with court appearance, the report had in fact not taken sufficient steps to keep children out of the court. These were issues that were to be firmly taken up in the Longford Report (1964).

Though the Longford Committee had been established to consider the prevention of crime and the improvement and modernisation of penal practice as a whole, a substantial part of the report was in fact devoted to problems associated with juvenile delinquency. In response to thinking which had expressed concern at the absence of any effective 'family' service (see Jay 1962) and at the stigmatisation of children who appeared before court, the committee recommended

> the establishment of a family service with the aim of helping every family to provide for its children the careful nurture and attention to individual social needs that the fortunate majority already enjoy, and, secondly, changes in judicial procedure which will take children of school age out of the range of the criminal courts and the penal system and treat their problems in a family setting.

Once again we find that not only is there a shift in orientation to the problem of dealing with children but that the implications of changing philosophies are reflected in the recommendation for the reorganisation of the services hitherto responsible for the presentation of information about children to the courts and for the execution of court orders. Now, under the notion of a family service, which in terms of the report would be responsible for the diagnosis of problems experienced by children as well as for decisions as to appropriate measures of treatment, this meant that both functions would be carried out mainly by social workers. This would have necessitated a considerable expansion in the role of such services and the Report anticipated further developments in this direction.

The Longford Committee represented the integration of fragmented local authority services as desirable in that there would be overall planning with a more efficient use of skilled manpower. The concept of a 'family'-orientated service itself also provided the foundation for change in dealing with delinquents with the proposal for a non-judicial agency to determine appropriate welfare measures. The proposal to remove all children of compulsory school age from the ambit of the criminal law was not new, though the Longford report gave it official backing. But the proposals involving the creation of a family service by each local authority did not completely do away with the court. A 'family' court, which was to be a judicial agency, was to deal with cases where the family service could reach no agreement.

It also would have responsibility for other than simply children's cases. Cases of 'serious' delinquency could also be referred to the 'family' court directly by the family service or the police and this exemplifies the difficulty of accommodating children who commit offences within a system based completely on a welfare ethic, with its underlying assumptions of pathology (Kilbrandon 1964; Morris 1974).

The logic behind the proposals was that of the unsuitability of the juvenile court for dealing with children, none of whom in early adolescence ought to be subjected to criminal proceedings. The measures applicable to children of compulsory school age who had not been involved in offending were considered appropriate for those who had been so involved; consequently, the form of proceedings for such children, who were in no essential respects different from other children, should similarly be of a non-judicial nature. The Longford proposals were incorporated within the abortive white paper, *The Child, The Family and The Young Offender* (1965) which contained the government's 'provisional proposals for practical reforms to support the family, to forestall and reduce delinquency and to revise the law and practice relating to offenders up to 21' (p.3).

An addition made within the recommendations of the white paper was that a 'family council' should be appointed whose function would be to hear cases and, through the family service, to be responsible also for the execution of measures decided upon. It was to deal with all cases of delinquency, care, protection and control and was to work as far as possible in consultation with, and with the agreement of, the parents. And though the family council was to be a non-judicial body, as with Kilbrandon, the white paper did not propose to dispense completely with the court since the child's right to protest his innocence was preserved (see Jacobs 1971; Elkin 1938; Cavenagh 1967 on this point) as indeed it is in the Scottish system.

The arguments that had been mentioned in the Longford report, pertaining to stigma and a family service, were supplemented by others. First, the task of the courts had become one mainly of making decisions about appropriate measures, as the majority of children who appeared before the court did not dispute the facts of the allegation. Again, this was similar to an argument made by Kilbrandon and it is difficult to believe that the Scottish report was of no significance in influencing developments in England. Secondly, and related to all this, treatment measures were to be imposed in the form of court orders and were thereby not flexible enough for the implementation of a welfare philosophy. The purposes behind the white paper were to remove children from the jurisdiction of the criminal law and to separate as far as possible arrangements for the trial from the process of making decisions as to appropriate measures for children. Perhaps not unexpectedly in view of the radical nature of the proposals, the magistracy, lawyers and probation service were hostile to such developments.

In reference to the argument that facts were not disputed in the majority of cases, Cavenagh argued that both the white paper and the Kilbrandon report were mistaken in their assessment of judicial procedure in this respect.

> Both wrongly assume that therefore the criminal court has no real function to perform in such cases. But the criminal jurisdiction protects the liberties of the offender not only by requiring proof of offence before liability to compulsion but by limiting the exercise of compulsory powers over a convicted offender. (1966, p.128)

The delegation of responsibility for investigation of cases involving young offenders to non-judicial bodies was considered fraught with problems, and was an unwarranted shift from the concepts of crime, responsibility and punishment to a concept of treatment based wholly on the needs of the offender. Yet such a shift necessarily rendered the judicial protection of children inappropriate, given that the framework of intervention was to be based on welfare or need. The shift in the philosophical basis would also have involved, it was argued, an unnecessary revolution in English juvenile justice.

> Juvenile delinquency is not a new problem. The criminal law has been dealing with it just as long as it has been dealing with adult crime. A system of such antiquity is unlikely to be fundamentally unsound. (1966, p.133)

Again the principle of welfare itself may well have been acceptable but what was not acceptable was the complete abolition of the juvenile courts whose functions were not solely restricted to dealing with considerations of welfare. The danger of too radical a shift in philosophy was to concentrate too much on the welfare of children at the cost of other objectives.

> Dealing with breaches of the criminal law appears to be the proper responsibility for the judiciary. After all the child and his parents are not solely involved; the public also has an interest in the administration of the law. (1966, p.133)

Though approval had been voiced by some at the attempt to

remove children from the courts (Scott 1966), others were
doubtful as to the 'efficacy' of such proposals in dealing with
juvenile crime (Cavenagh 1966; Cavenagh and Sparks 1965)
and also as to the ability of the family councils to be any more
successful at producing a consistent policy of decision-making
than had been the magistracy (Patchett and McLean 1965,
p.699ff.).

That the family councils were to have been composed of
local-authority social workers was an obvious focus of criticism
by members of the probation service. Though probation work
was based on the same ideological orientation as that of other
branches of social work, the probation service was an integral
element in the court network. Whereas social work was based
on the local authority, probation work was conducted within
the framework of the courts and the service was independent of
the local authorities. Probation officers, in view of the apparent
success of probation work (see Jarvis 1966), were unable to
accept the merits of the proposal that a new body of social
workers should be given responsibility for a field in which they
had been traditionally involved and in whose development they
had been influential. Members of the service too emphasised
that judicial intervention as opposed to decision-making by
non-judicial bodies was necessary as a means of protecting the
defendant.

Conversely, at a time when there were increased demands for
the professionalisation and unification of social work, the proposals contained in the Longford report and in the white paper
were not unacceptable to the members of the various local
authority and other social services (Kahan 1966).

But the dominant criticism of the proposals was against the
removal of the child from the jurisdiction of the criminal law
and the abolition of the juvenile courts in favour of a more
administrative approach to delinquency control. What must
have undoubtedly offered support to such criticism were the
developments at that time in America, where the trend in the
1960s was to a more formal process of intervention. By the
beginnings of the 1960s the problems associated with the scope
of discretionary decision-making in the juvenile court in the
United States had been recognised with the result that there
followed a number of changes in juvenile justice which introduced a more formalistic approach to decision-making based on
the principles of due process (see Faust and Brantingham 1974).

The proposals in the English White Paper were then defeated

and the government were forced to think again. Though the recommendations in *The Child, The Family and The Young Offender* met with widespread disapproval, a White Paper produced only three years later was incorporated into the 1969 Children and Young Persons Bill with only minor modification. The proposals in the 1968 White Paper, *Children in Trouble,* were made within the context of the juvenile court framework and it is the retention of the juvenile courts that has been seen as giving respectability and acceptability to the recommendations. The later proposals in this way did not pose such a threat to 'the ancient principle that no subject of the Crown, however young or undistinguished, may be deprived of his liberty except by order of a properly constituted court of law' (Watson 1970, p.ix).

Whereas the two White Papers differed in their intentions towards the juvenile courts, the less radical *Children in Trouble* nevertheless made recommendations which were influenced by the recommendations of the earlier paper. In particular, the move to keep children out of court as far as possible was still predominant, though the 1968 recommendations sought to achieve this without the abolition of the juvenile courts. Similarly, both papers recognised the need for the reorganisation of the social services as a prerequisite to the provision of adequate measures for children, whether offenders or not. Such a trend was welcomed by Wootton who stated 'I submit that up to compulsory school-leaving age every child should be treated in an educational and not a penal atmosphere and should not be liable to any penal proceedings whatsoever' (1965, p.29ff.).

The nature of the 1968 proposals was to allocate to informal consultation between the different agencies within the social-control network the functions that would have been carried out by the 'family councils'. The nature of intervention was therefore either to be through court proceedings or informal, voluntary contact with the social-services department.

The White Paper had proposed new legal procedures in relation to juvenile offenders over the age of ten which was to remain as the age of criminal responsibility, below which children, as before, would not be subject to criminal proceedings. In relation to offenders aged ten and under fourteen, however, an offence was no longer to be a sufficient ground in itself for bringing children before the court. Where proceedings were to be necessary, they were to be brought under care, protection or control procedure, and where a child had been involved in an offence, it had to be established that he had committed the offence and that he was 'not receiving such care, protection and guidance as a good parent may reasonably be expected to give'. There was then a double-tier requirement whereby it had to be shown that a child was in need of care and that one of the other conditions, one of which was the commission of an offence, was satisfied. But even before proceedings were instituted, the local authority and the police had to consult as to the necessity of such a step.

The prosecution of children between fourteen and seventeen was also restricted and, except on a charge of homicide, would only be possible on the authority of a summons or warrant issued by a magistrate, a proposal that did not meet with universal approval.

In terms of the measures for offenders, the 1968 White Paper was no less committed to treatment and welfare than the earlier paper had been, and it made a number of modifications that had important implications for the increased role of the social services. First, the approved-school order was to be abolished and replaced by an order committing children to the care of the local authority. Secondly, provision was to be made for a new form of treatment, intermediate treatment, which was to be developed as neither a community nor a residentially-based programme, but which was to fall somewhere between the two. Thirdly, all supervision of children under fourteen was to be by the local-authority social services. This last proposal did not meet with the approval of a departmental committee which reported in the same year.

The 1965 White Paper, we have noted, urged examination of the local-authority social services, as the reform of the law in relation to children highlighted the need for organisationally improved services to offer help to the family and to prevent delinquency. Accordingly, in the same year, the Seebohm Committee was set up to 'review the organisation and responsibilities of the local authority personal social services and to consider what changes are desirable to ensure an effective family service'.

Whereas, perhaps not unexpectedly, the Seebohm Committee welcomed the main recommendations of *Children in Trouble*, it nevertheless differed in a number of ways from the White Paper. The Seebohm report dealt with the shortcomings of the then existing social services, namely the inadequacy in the level, range and quality of provision, and (as a consequence of the fragmented nature of the local-authority social services) the lack of co-ordination which contributed to the difficulty of access to the appropriate services. The major recommendation of the committee was that a new local-authority department be set up which would include the various services that had hitherto existed: the children's department, welfare departments, mental health services and educational services. What in effect was proposed was an organisational restructuring of different local authority services which complemented the drive towards the unification of social work as a profession and the acceptance of the concept of generic social work (see Sinfield 1970). The influence of the social-work profession on the 1968 White Paper is displayed by the shift in orientation away from the assumption about social pathology, made in the Ingleby Report and the 1965 White Paper. *Children in Trouble* had also recognised the importance of the family as a potential source of delinquency but it placed greater emphasis on individual pathology. 'A child's behaviour is influenced by genetic, emotional and intellectual factors, his maturity, and his family, school, neighbourhood and wider social setting' (para.6).

Whereas factors other than those of an individual nature were cited, the proposals for treatment measures concentrated on the child. This was also apparent in the Seebohm report where it was suggested that the diagnosis, assessment and treatment of delinquency could only be improved with the restructuring of the social services. Even though the juvenile courts were to be retained the social services were to play a central role in the diagnosing and treatment of delinquency which was construed in terms rather of pathology and its social ramifications than in terms of legal definitions and implications. Indeed, the retention of the juvenile court may have deflected the attention of the magistracy and the legal profession from the fact that the involvement of the social services was only minimally less than that proposed under the 1965 White Paper. The fact that the approved-school order was abolished meant that, as with the care order, the decisions as to appropriate measures were to be made by the local authority. The decision by the magistrates, as was well appreciated later, was to commit children to the care of the local authority, not to determine what the particular measures of care would be. That was for social work judgment and 'magistrates had failed to realise how far the traditional functions of the juvenile court were being eroded' (Bottoms 1974, p.335).

Whereas the 1968 White Paper had envisaged a divided responsibility between the social services and the probation service, Seebohm disagreed and recommended that all children and young persons under seventeen be supervised by the social-services department alone. Once again a government document was proposing to diminish the responsibility of the probation service in the field of delinquency.

Three principles then had been stated in the 1968 White Paper which with minor modifications became the basis for the 1969 Children and Young Persons Act. First, children were to be offered treatment rather than punishment with the distinction between delinquents and non-delinquents being further eroded. Secondly, treatment was to be flexible with the introduction of intermediate treatment and the integration of all residential institutions into a system of community homes, a proposal that had been made earlier. Finally, there was to be participation of all concerned with the welfare of children, which was also to include the parents of children involved, and which would allow more children to be kept out of court by being dealt with informally. In this respect the interdependence of the proposals made in the 1968 White Paper and the Seebohm report with the necessary reorganisation of social service provision both in practice and in concept had been anticipated in Scotland within the Kilbrandon Report itself.

Scotland: The Kilbrandon Report

Prior to the 1968 Social Work (Scotland) Act, there had in effect been no uniform system of juvenile justice in Scotland. Though the 1908 Children Act establishing juvenile courts had applied to both England and Scotland, the evolution of juvenile justice thereafter took a very different form.

The 1908 Act had made legislative provision for juvenile courts to meet at different times and in places dissociated from the system of criminal justice as it applied to adults. But when the Morton committee (1928) – appointed to examine the treatment of young offenders and young people requiring care or protection – reported, it emphasised the fact that juvenile cases were at that time still being heard in Sheriff courts or the Burgh courts. Only in Lanarkshire were the juvenile courts, attached to the Justice of the Peace courts, operating as intended. The committee also referred critically to the lack of personnel qualified in dealing with children as neither lay magistrates nor legally qualified sheriffs were considered appropriate for the task. Consequently, the report had recommended that cases involving children and young offenders should be referred to specially constituted Justice of the Peace courts. The members of such courts were to be drawn from a panel of justices selected by virtue of their knowledge and experience in dealing with juveniles. The committee further recommended that the age of criminal responsibility be raised from seven to eight.

The recommendations of the Morton committee were embodied in the 1932 Children and Young Persons (Scotland) Act, later consolidated by the 1937 Children and Young Persons (Scotland) Act, and as with the 1933 Act in England, the magistracy were enjoined to have regard to the welfare of the child.

Nevertheless when the Kilbrandon committee was appointed in 1961 to 'consider the provisions of the law of Scotland relating to the treatment of juvenile delinquents and juveniles in need of care and protection or beyond parental control, and, in particular, the constitution, powers and procedure of the courts dealing with such juveniles', only in four areas were the specially constituted justice-of-the-peace juvenile courts established. (These were Ayrshire, Fife, Renfrewshire and the City of Aberdeen.) Before the 1968 Act there were then four different types of courts dealing with juvenile offenders. These were the Sheriff court, the Burgh or Police court, the Justice of the Peace courts and the specially constituted courts (see the Kilbrandon Report, paras 43–6).

Whereas the Sheriff court was presided over by a single, legally qualified judge, the Burgh or Police courts were presided over by a single baillie who held the office as an elected town councillor and was appointed by election by his colleagues. Lay judges sat in the Justice of the Peace courts; in the specially constituted courts, the panel of justices were appointed from their own number. Moreover, the three different Police courts in Glasgow which sat as courts of summary jurisdiction for adult cases also sat as juvenile courts. Of these, the Central court was presided over by a legally qualified stipendiary magistrate with a full-time appointment whereas the other two, the Marine and Govan Police courts were presided over by baillies.

The object in presenting such a catalogue is not simply to give a description of the provisions for children in Scotland but to highlight the lack of uniformity in the courts which had jurisdiction over juvenile cases in different parts of Scotland. In addition, as Kilbrandon points out, the choice of court for the hearing of a case could be affected by various considerations (see paras 43–6).

What had evolved in Scotland was a system of juvenile justice which unlike that of England and Wales, lacked any coherence or uniformity, a factor which must surely have contributed to the acceptance of the radical recommendations made by the Kilbrandon Committee (see Bottoms 1974; Morris 1974). It was against such a background that the Committee reported and recommended that the existing means of dealing with children were unsuitable and should be replaced by a new system of Children's Hearings. However, it was not simply the organisational and administrative incoherence in Scottish juvenile justice which prompted such proposals – rather, the Kilbrandon Committee had found an inconsistency in the principle of dealing with children in terms of welfare within a framework of criminal jurisdiction.

Increasing delinquency rates, though treated with caution by the Kilbrandon Committee, were attributed in part to the inadequacy of the available means of dealing with delinquents. The particular form of social control in Scotland was treated as a contributory factor in delinquency causation.

The solution to the problem of juvenile delinquency was not simply to modify the existing court arrangements which had fostered such general dissatisfaction, but to make wholesale changes in the very organisational and administrative structure of juvenile justice. Fundamental, not incremental, change was proposed.

What was to follow in the report was a more concise appreciation of issues essentially similar to those tackled in the Ingleby Report, the disjunction between the two stages of adjudication and sentencing being given particular examination and analysis. It is also possible in the report to recognise issues and arguments that were to appear later in the major reports and White Papers in England. Kilbrandon, in particular, had argued that the ineffectiveness of the existing arrangements for combating delinquency could be attributed in part to the lack of co-ordination amongst the welfare services as well as to the inappropriateness of the attempt to implement a welfare philosophy within a court-based agency. Neither was equipped realistically to implement welfare principles. It was the proposed solution to the 'dilemma of the juvenile court' that was to lead to a fundamentally different model of juvenile justice in Scotland from that in England. This was despite the fact that the underlying philosophies were essentially the same (May 1971).

In reference to criminal procedure, though modifications had been made for children, the report stated that

> Criminal procedure . . . is clearly well adapted to determination of questions of fact, from which the accused's guilt or innocence may be inferred . . . In relation to juvenile offenders, however, statute law introduces a further set of considerations. A court in dealing with a juvenile is required to have regard to the welfare of the person before it. 'Welfare' is of course, irrelevant to the question of determination of innocence or guilt and relates to the second stage of the proceedings, namely, the form of treatment appropriate to the case once the facts have been established. (para.50)

These two functions rested on a framework of concepts that were fundamentlly different from each other. Whereas the adjudication assumes a high degree of personal responsibility and focus on a specific act, an offence, welfare considerations were not based on an assumption of responsibility and welfare measures are determined by rather broader factors. Where the measures available to a court had been determined by a retributive or deterrent philosophy, then punitive measures following on adjudication could well be influenced by the questions relating to the degree of responsibility. The conceptual frameworks underlying adjudication and punishment are essentially similar.

The committee were not solely concerned at the incompatibility of a crime-and-responsibility-and-punishment philosophy with a treatment philosophy that was 'curative' in nature. Rather, the crime–responsibility–punishment approach militated against the principle of *prevention* (paras 52–3), by the necessity of establishing a specific offence or act, a point considered by Cavenagh to be crucial to justice. The report identified four ways in which it felt the two approaches to be incompatible.

First, where no proof of involvement in an offence could be established, or where the offender was not criminally liable, no action could be taken even where preventive measures appeared necessary (para.54 (1)). An important difference between Scotland and England in this respect, as we have seen, is that children in Scotland were not offered the protection of the rebuttable presumption of being *doli incapax*, which was available to children in England until their fourteenth birthday.

Secondly, punishment was too restrictive in its application to offenders only; other children could and should be included in a programme designed on preventive or welfare principles (para. 54(2)).

Thirdly, the meeting of the needs of the child could be inhibited by the crime-and-responsibility approach where punishments would mainly be related to the nature of the child's involvement or the nature of the offence (para.54(3)). Indeed, the intention of the report, which was not accepted fully, had been that the concept of criminal responsibility should be completely abandoned.

Lastly, punishment is once and for all whereas treatment or welfare measures may require to be altered in the light of changing needs (para.54(4)). Flexibility of approach was therefore necessary in dealing with children in terms of need and not simply in relation to specific offences. Given the emphasis in the report also on parental involvement, some of the proposals and the principles underlying them do seem to have been influential in determining the character of later English proposals.

However, in view of the difficulty in reconciling the principles underlying crime and its punishment on the one hand and those underlying welfare or, as Kilbrandon referred to it, educative ones on the other hand, the Committee did not accept that further modification to the existing system of juvenile justice would have made any real impact on the problem (see para.57). Whereas both Ingleby and *Children in Trouble* attempted to resolve the dilemma of the juvenile court by making a number of procedural modifications, Kilbrandon argued that the two functions, adjudication and disposal, should be separated. The argument was given extra strength by the further claim that the skills required for adjudication of questions of fact were mainly legal or judicial and the question of sentencing was 'an entirely separate one and calls for quite different skills and qualities from these to be applied in deciding on the action to be taken in relation to delinquent children once the fact is established' (para.70).

Though the 1968 White Paper in England had proposed alterations to procedure, the retention of the juvenile courts meant that magistrates could still be involved in questions of fact and questions of welfare, though welfare decisions were also to be made by the social services. The Kilbrandon solution was 'to devise a procedure whereby juvenile offenders would in all cases be brought before a *specialised* agency whose *sole* concern would be the measures to be applied on what amounts to an agreed referral' (para.73).

Such a specialised agency would also benefit parents in allowing them a more realistic opportunity of becoming involved in the process of making decisions about their own children, thereby fostering parental responsibility (para.76). The courts had not been able to give sufficient attention to the role that might be played by parents in formal proceedings (para.36).

By analogy with the office of public prosecutor, the committee recommended that the initial referring agencies (police or social services) should not have the responsibility of forwarding cases to the juvenile panels. This was to be the function of a new type of official, to be known as the Reporter, who would make initial assessment of cases and decide as to the necessity for referral to the panels. And though he would be required to make preliminary assessment of cases in terms of need for treatment (para.97) he would also be required to be competent at handling both the legal issues and wider questions of public interest (para.98). Though he was obviously to be involved as a 'filter' through which only appropriate cases would be referred to the panels, the lack of a definitive statement as to his qualifications (see para.102) has meant that, with the wide discretion involved, different policies have evolved in different geographical and administrative areas. His role is a crucial determinant of the numbers of children dealt with by formal means of intervention as well as of those alternative measures available which he can employ.

Even where the sole function of the 'specialised' agency was to be the consideration and application of appropriate measures, offence behaviour was not completely without significance. For

> The offence, while the essential basis of judicial action, has significance only as a pointer to the need for intervention. Its true significance will not necessarily be found on the basis of any preconceived standard i.e. by viewing the offence simply as an act in isolation and judging its potential seriousness simply by the ready-made standards offered by the range of sanctions which the law (and thus society at large) attaches to the particular class of offence which it exemplifies. (para.71)

Definitions of delinquency in legalistic and judicial terms were considered inappropriate in their inability to express the nature of children's needs of which delinquency was merely symptomatic. Delinquency was no longer to be conceived of simply as a legal label or category but was a behavioural condition requiring diagnosis, assessment and treatment. Accord-

ingly, it was not appropriate to deal with it through the medium
of the criminal law as it was essentially similar to other forms of
behavioural conditions or circumstances, such as truancy. Delinquency in concept was theoretically removed from the jurisdiction of criminal law and in practice was to be the responsibility of the new 'public agency', which was in itself an extension of the social services concerned with children's needs
(para.234). It is perhaps worth noting that not all commentators
on the English and Scottish systems have been convinced on the
theoretical and pragmatic merits of such a 'treatment' approach
(Morris and McIsaac 1978; Fox 1974).

So far the arguments against the juvenile courts were that the
procedure inhibited the implementation of a treatment philosophy; that parents could not be wholly involved in the decisions about and application of measures in respect of their
children; and that chidren's needs were in general being met
only inadequately. Delinquency was not really a problem for the
courts and was not simply a legal or judicial status conferred on
children but was symptomatic of some underlying condition or
circumstances which fell within the domain of a welfare institution whose primary objective would be that of meeting need.

Lord Kilbrandon himself was later to assert more explicitly
that the treatment of children was no longer to be a small part of
the system of criminal jurisdiction but was instead to become a
small though important part of the system of the social services.

The very fragmented nature of the social services themselves
was another focus of critical attention for the committee, who
considered that any attempt to deal with delinquency necessarily required the supporting framework of a single agency
charged with the responsibility for the prevention and reduction
of juvenile delinquency (para.39). And though the terms of
reference of the committee were restricted to provisions for
children, the committee anticipated that their proposals would
have benefits for young and old alike, consonant with the con-
ceptualisation of delinquency as one form of social need. Consequently, Kilbrandon proposed a new department, the social
education department, which would have overall responsibility
for dealing with children and would represent a merging of all
the existing services whose primary concern was with the problems of children in need. Such a department would not only
provide diagnostic and assessment functions but would also be
responsible for executing the decisions of the new panels. The
proposal that decisions about need and measures of care should

be made both by the new panels and by the new social work departments, left it unclear as to who was supposed to be the correct assessor of need.

An interesting feature of the report was that whereas the committee had a treatment or welfare philosophy, and had recommended the extension of supervisory provisions, there was still a role to be played by the courts. Children could still be required to appear in court for a number of reasons. Despite the promise of the legislation, there remains an intricate network of relationships between the courts and the Hearing system in Scotland. At a time when England retained the court structure, it is perhaps not surprising that in Scotland the Children's Hearings were not given the monopoly for dealing with children who may be 'in need of compulsory measures of care'.

Despite the creation of a specialised tribunal to make decisions in terms of the need for compulsory measures of care, and the rejection of the judiciary as being ill-equipped for making decisions about the welfare of children, there is nevertheless considerable contact between the courts and the Hearing system. With the retention by the Lord Advocate of the right to prosecute, children in Scotland may still be dealt with in court for a number of reasons. Conceptions of the Children's Hearing system as a radical form of juvenile justice have to be qualified by the reminder that children in Scotland over the age of criminal responsibility may still be prosecuted.

What has to be remembered is that though the conceptual framework underlying the system of Children's Hearings is based on a philosophy of welfare and determinism, the age of criminal responsibility in Scotland remains at eight. A sharp reminder of this was presented in the unfortunate case of nine-year-old Mary Cairns (see Bruce and Spencer 1973), the Glasgow child involved in a stabbing incident with one of her friends. Thus, though the Scottish system accepts the philosophy of welfare for dealing with certain children it does not for those others who may be prosecuted. It could be argued that whereas the conceptual ambiguity of care and control was resolved in England by the distinction of 'care' and 'criminal' proceedings within the juvenile court structure, the Scottish solution was to separate the two realms of operation. There was, however, no exclusive commitment to welfare. This is also reflected in the fact that, of those children who are indeed prosecuted, some may well be sent to exactly the same residential institutions as those who were dealt with by the Children's Hearing.

Further, where a child or his parents do not admit the ground of referral at a Hearing, the case, as is by now well known, must be referred to the Sheriff who must decide whether the facts of the case have been proven or not. Where they are, the child will again appear before a Hearing for appropriate disposal. What appears as an apparently cumbersome procedure is derived from Kilbrandon's recommendation to separate the adjudication process from the decision as to the appropriate measures of care.

These areas of contact in fact recognise the different spheres of operation of the courts and the Hearings in that adjudication and prosecution are legitimate judicial enterprises, whereas the function of the Hearings is to reach the most appropriate decision.

The solution of the committee to the problems associated with delinquency then involved taking children under the age of sixteen outside the scope of the criminal law, with notable exceptions; to replace the juvenile courts by a system of juvenile panels; to appoint an intermediate official who alone would refer cases to the panels and to establish a matching fieldwork support which would be charged with the assessment and diagnosis of children's needs as well as the execution of the necessary measures of care.

Post-Kilbrandon Developments: Social Work and the Community

The White Paper, *Social Work and the Community*, which followed the report, accepted the main proposal of the committee in respect of the abolition of the juvenile courts in favour of a system of juvenile or children's panels. There had however been criticism as to the applicability of a 'social education department' as the main supporting fieldwork agency and the government in fact suggested that a social work department would be more appropriate. Morris (1974) sees the change from social education to social work department as one of 'status gains' and 'moral victory' with no fundamental difference in the functions of the two proposed agencies. What had been conceived of by Kilbrandon as the functions of a social education department were indistinguishable from what is usually considered to be family casework. The appointment of a joint working party to advise the government had also been composed of three prominent individuals closely associated with social work, a fact that may well have contributed to the changes included in the White Paper. Moreover, the Child Care Association, which had welcomed the welfare orientation of the report, expressed doubts about the responsibilities of the new agencies being given to a social education department (*Scotsman* 1964). The Association argued that, as the McBoyle Committee had proposed an extension of the responsibilities of local-authority child welfare services, it would be more appropriate if the new fieldwork agency were composed of the members of such departments. The civil service had in fact been criticised for having established two separate committees with terms of reference to examine issues and questions which had broadly similar underlying circumstances (see Morris 1974).

The bulk of the criticism of the White Paper was to come not from the magistracy, even with proposed abolition of the juvenile courts, but from the probation service. The general criticism of any proposal which would establish an administrative agency for dealing with problems of delinquency had been that there would be insufficient safeguards. In fact, though the Kilbrandon Report had urged the abolition of the juvenile courts, children could still have resort to the courts. Where a child denied the facts on which a referral was based, his case could be heard by the Sheriff, as the committee had only separated the functions of adjudication and disposal and had not done away completely with the court. Moreover, the right of appeal was to rest with the Sheriff in the first instance, a proposal that was to create difficulty in its implementation (see Grant 1976; Asquith 1979). But children could also under the Kilbrandon proposals be prosecuted: the Lord Advocate was to retain the right of prosecution but was to exercise his power 'only exceptionally and on the gravest crimes, in which major issues of public interest must necessarily arise, and in which, equally as a safeguard for the interests of the accused, trial under criminal procedure is essential' (para. 127). Such a proposal may then have satisfied the judiciary, some of whom later commented favourably on the recommendations (Aikman Smith 1974), in that they were theoretically still charged with safeguarding the liberty of children, though not of all children who were caught up in the formal means of intervention.

However, the probation service made similar representations to those their southern colleagues were later to make in reference to the 1965 White Paper in England. The Scottish Branch of the National Association of Probation Officers maintained that the requirements of a judicial system would not be met satisfactorily under the new proposals (1965). But as Morris argues

(1974) even the criticism by the probation service of the proposals for the abolition of the courts' representatives diminished by the time of the 1968 Social Work (Scotland) Bill. By that time, the Scottish probation service, which lacked the co-ordination of the English service, was devoting its energies to fighting inclusion in the new generic social work department, a battle which in Scotland they were to lose (Morris 1974).

The solutions to the basic conflict of the juvenile court, introduced by the 1968 Act in Scotland and the 1969 Act in England, were very different in terms of organisational and administrative structure. Both however are the outcome of ideological debates which have occupied so much official attention since the turn of the century. Both appeal to a common set of principles. Amongst these are greater commitment to non-punishment forms of delinquency control; the need for proceedings appropriate to the age of the children involved; the blurring of the distinction between the child who offends and the child who is in need for other reasons; the promotion of *preventive* measures; and the need to keep children out of court as far as possible. What is particularly interesting about current demands in a number of countries for further change in juvenile justice is that they are in fact based on philosophical principles diametrically opposed to the trends which culminated in the 1968 and 1969 Acts. In terms of 'return to justice', children who offend are to be held responsible, liable to retributive sanctions and to be conceived of, and indeed treated, differently from children that are in need.

Chapter Two

IDEOLOGY, RELEVANCE
AND SOCIAL POLICY

Any comparison between forms of juvenile justice, the Scottish and English for example, is meaningless without some awareness of the deeper conceptual considerations involved in the historical development of the respective systems. For that reason the significance of a historical review lies not merely in terms of its descriptive content but in the contribution it may make to our understanding of the reasons for the organisational and administrative structure, and all the ambiguities they may contain, adopted at present within a particular system of justice. Moreover any comparative analysis must involve not simply statutory and legal comparisons but must include empirical data about the processes involved in the practical accomplishment of juvenile justice.

The main focus of the research to be discussed in this book is, for that very reason, the practical implementation of the policy statements governing juvenile justice within two very different administrative frameworks – the children's hearing and the juvenile court. The main empirical focus of this work is *how* decisions about children who commit offences are made by individuals operating within formally different institutional frameworks. The objective then will be to articulate the relationship between the ideologies of delinquency control maintained by key personnel and the structural arrangements which provide the context of decision-making. Earlier writers have argued (Morris and McIsaac 1978) that though the ideology of the decision-makers is crucial the type of tribunal is unimportant. In this work, no such *a priori* assumption is made. The significance of the form of hearing within which cases are heard and the role played by the different agencies which constitute the social-control network is a matter for empirical inquiry. There are theoretical reasons for such an approach which derive from recent developments in the field of criminology itself and have particular merit in the area of policy analysis.

A presupposition common to both the 1968 and 1969 Acts in Scotland and England respectively is that delinquency is a behavioural condition – rather than a simple legal or judicial category – which requires diagnosis and assessment prior to the application of appropriate welfare measures. The semantics of delinquency control are based upon medical analogies and metaphors as if delinquency were an illness and were pathological. As Rock points out, a danger associated with such usage of metaphor is that the metaphor becomes reality and that delinquency becomes sickness, disease, or illness (Rock 1973, p.16). Nosological analogy becomes nosological reality and, by this very means, delinquency control has increasingly come to be the responsibility of the 'experts' (Bean 1976). Moreover, the true nature of the actual functioning of juvenile justice systems may well be obscured by a process of mystification (Matza 1964), whereby the logic of euphemism (May 1977) deflects attention from the true nature of juvenile-justice administration. The concentration of attention upon the offender and the tendency to construe 'needs' as if they were objective properties of individuals serve to obscure the problematic nature of the conceptual framework on which particular systems of juvenile justice are based.

The rhetoric of therapy and the quasi-medical terminology in which the government reports and white papers leading up to both the 1968 and the 1969 Acts are phrased endow the problem of delinquency control with an air of straightforwardness. Since, in accordance with the principle of individualised justice, the main criterion of intervention is considered to be 'need', the appropriate measures of care for dealing with delinquency are to be determined by reference to individual children's needs. But the identification of need is not such a straightforward process despite the recurrent use of medical metaphor and the involvement of agencies such as the social services which allegedly have the expertise necessary for the diagnosis and treatment of children's problems.

As we have seen, the official pronouncements contained in both the Seebohm and the Kilbrandon Reports recommended the reorganisation of social service agencies in accordance with the redefined role of social work in the meeting and prevention of social need. The relevance of this for juvenile delinquency was that delinquency was reconceptualised as being symptomatic of 'need' and therefore an appropriate area of social work concern. But the decisions as to the necessity of measures of care as envisaged in the two major reports were to be the responsibility of agencies which were not part of the social services. Thus, in England, children were still to be dealt with by the courts though welfare was to be a prime consideration; and in Scotland, though children could still be prosecuted and appear in court for other reasons, decisions in the main were to be made by a non-judicial body. Though the administration of juvenile justice is officially determined in both countries by a formal philosophy of welfare and need contained in the respective government documents, this does not preclude the possibility that in practice official objectives are supplemented or even supplanted by other objectives. The existence of a formal philosophy of delinquency control does not imply that there is consensus as to how best to deal with delinquency as there may be competing philosophies in evidence in society at any one time (Stoll 1968). Part of the purpose of this study was to examine the extent to which those involved in the operation and administration of juvenile justice share similar philosophies of delinquency control. In particular, the selective and interpretative activity of social control agents, in this case panel members and juvenile magistrates – governed as such activities will be by their systems of belief – are seen as important determinants in the practical accomplishment of juvenile justice.

Social Control and Ideology

Research which attempts to relate the background characteristics of children to the decisions made in respect of these children depends entirely on inference when attempting to draw conclusions about how such decisions were reached. Thus, whereas different authors acknowledge the importance of the interpretative activity of control agents, they have not always adopted a methodological strategy appropriate for the analysis of how individuals within control networks assess information and make decisions. And whereas this approach, which typifies much of traditional delinquency and criminological research, treats the nature of the social control process as non-problematic, other approaches acknowledge that

> the issues of defining and enforcing the (criminal) law are now regarded themselves as problematic and not objectively given. (Downes and Rock 1971, p.351)
>
> Deviance is not a quality of the act the person commits, but rather a consequence of the application by others of rules and sanctions to an 'offence'. The deviant is one to whom

that label has been applied successfully; deviant behaviour is behaviour that people so label. (Becker 1963, p.9)

Influenced by the development of a sociology of deviance, emphasis in criminological research has increasingly been directed away from the causes of delinquent and criminal behaviour. A major focus with the more recent development has become the nature and mode of operation of the institutions of social control, not only in the maintenance but also the generation of definitions of deviance. Deviance has come to be seen as a quality that is ascribed rather than as a property inherent in a person and thus subject to rigorous scientific examination. The relocation of the focus of criminological studies on the institutions of control and on the process whereby deviance or criminality is ascribed does not in itself logically imply that aetiological studies are thereby theoretically futile. That needs careful argument. However, the significance of a sociology of deviance is the very fact that it does treat the social control process as problematic.

Identifying this process of ascription as a major determinant of deviance also relocates deviance or criminality in its complex relationship with legal institutions (Matza 1964). The invocation of the criminal law as a process of social control has now become a more important focus for sociological studies of crime and the law than are criminality and offenders.

Moreover, such a process may well be determined by factors other than the officially stated objectives of social control. The importance of the previous chapter in tracing the conceptual and historical evolution of juvenile justice in England and Scotland is that it presents a statement as to official and formal objectives in delinquency control. And 'such an examination will benefit by heuristically distinguishing the official goals of the court from its functions, particularly those which sociologists call unintended or unanticipated consequences of purposeful action' (Lemert 1970, p.136).

The historical endowment of juvenile justice – for the purpose of the present argument, a commitment to a welfare-oriented philosophy – may well be fundamentally modified in its implementation since there is no easy translation of policy into practice (Matza 1964). Comment has been made on the euphemistic nature of the language associated with therapy and individualised justice and their distortion of the true nature of the administration and organisation of crime control (Allen 1964; Tappan 1949). Nor has displacement of officially-stated goals or objectives (Rock 1973) passed unnoticed in the context of other welfare institutions. Kogan, for example, reviews the traditional approach to studying organisational structures in which they were viewed as if they pursued objectively-defined goals and as if the organisation operated monolithically (Kogan 1971). He criticises the failure of such an approach to attach significance to the subjective ideas held by members of such organisations for the actual implementation of formal policy statements. That is, the ideological orientations of members of relevant organisations affect whether or not, or to what extent, the objectives contained in the formal or official ideology are actually realised (see also Platt 1975).

For similar reasons, the object of inquiry in this book is how the informal working ideologies of those responsible for implementing a treatment or welfare-oriented philosophy in the respective systems of juvenile justice in Scotland and England will affect the way in which, or the extent to which, the policies stated in the relevant official pronouncements have actually been put into effect. Therefore, by identifying the ideologies of delinquency and deviance maintained by the various agents of social control, possible sources of strain in the social control network can be identified (Stoll 1968). Further consideration must therefore be given to the notion of ideology, and its implications for the administration of juvenile justice in Scotland and England.

Smith's definition of ideology as 'a configuration of relatively abstract ideas and attitudes in which the elements are bound together by a relatively high degree of inter-relatedness or functional interdependence' (Smith 1976, p.50) is particularly useful.

Moreover, he adds that an ideology may be (a) *formal* as an abstract system of ideas or (b) *informal* as an operational philosophy that organisational members employ in determining action and decision-making. The philosophy ('formal ideology') underlying the two Acts in question, based on a re-conceptualisation of delinquency as symptomatic of need, may well be mediated in practice by the operational philosophies (informal ideologies) of those responsible for implementation of the legislation. This is particularly important for a number of reasons.

First, official statistics relating to the number of different disposals reached by panel members and by magistrates, such as those contained in the Annual Social Work (Scotland) Statistics and the Criminal Statistics for England and Wales, can tell us relatively little about the process by which decisions in terms of

need are made about children. Official statistics are not necessarily accurate indicators of the level of need or the extent of
criminal behaviour in the community. Indeed, it has been
argued that such statistics may reveal more about the circumstances in which they were produced (Kitsuse and Cicourel
1963; Hindess 1973). Official statistics are construed as the
outcome of successive stages of selection and identification, by
different agents within the social-control network, of those
children deemed to be 'in need' or 'delinquent'. With particular
reference to juvenile court practices, Tappan has indicated the
influence on the administration of juvenile justice of the different interpretations by personnel working within an organisational structure with wide terms of reference consonant with
discretionary decision-making. Cicourel criticises traditional
sociological theories of deviance: 'nor is there attempt to show
how the "man-on-the-street" and law-enforcement officials,
through the former's conceptions of "wrong doing" and the
latter's policies and day to day decision-making, are key elements in how juveniles come to be known as delinquent'
(Cicourel 1968, p.31).

The significance of the ideological orientations or operational
ideologies of law enforcement personnel has also been recognised in the context of police work (Skolnick 1966; Bordua
1967) and prosecution (Blumberg 1967) where the notion of
police and prosecutors operating within the strict parameters of
legally prescribed procedures and relevances (Box 1971) is
shown to be a misrepresentation of policing and prosecution.

Though, within the formal ideology espoused by government
reports and underlying the particular forms of delinquency control introduced by the two Acts, the main criteria of intervention are based on 'need' and the need for compulsory measures
of care, neither of the reports provides an adequate conceptual
framework by which need can be defined. That is, though the
logic of delinquency control is the meeting of need there is a
failure to provide definitive statements as to what actually
constitutes social need and how it can best be assessed and met.
Had only 'professional' social agencies been involved in the
social-control network then such an omission would not have
been quite so significant in that the operational definitions of
need would have been provided by the ideological orientation of
the profession concerned. (Though even 'professional' conceptions of need are subject to diffuse interpretations.) But the
development of delinquency control in the context of both the

1969 and the 1968 Acts allowed lay persons, panel members in Scotland and magistrates in England, to have the ultimate responsibility for decision-making about children in need, at least in the first instance. The absence of a definitive statement as to 'social need' means that prime notions such as 'need' and 'delinquency' obtain their very meaning only in the process of ascription by the various personnel operating within the social-control network. Conceiving of delinquency or need as social constructions rather than simply as properties intrinsic to individuals necessitates a closer examination of how decisions and compulsory measures of care are reached by agents within that network.

An equally important reason for considering the significance of the operational ideologies of those personnel responsible for the administration of juvenile justice is that there is an essential difference between a notion of justice in theory and the notion of justice as an operational concept. Blumberg (1967), for example, suggests that the criminal justice system in the U.S.A., though theoretically guided by a due-process ideology, is primarily oriented to the depersonalised goals of 'production'. The modification of the formal ideological prescriptions are a consequence of the fact that

> The rule of law is not self-executing. It is translated into reality by men in institutions. Traditional constitutional elements of criminal law, when placed in the institutional setting of a modern criminal court, are reshaped by a bureaucratic organisation to serve its requirements and goals. (Blumberg 1967, p.5)

In considering the status of key individuals in the administration of juvenile justice, conceptual niceties give way to practical difficulties. It is the very possibility of disagreement with the rationale behind juvenile justice systems that differentiates between a notion of justice in practice and in theory.

Social policy in general and penal policy in particular (Rock 1973) is only realised through its implementation within an administrative framework. In the process of implementation, policy objectives and the means of achieving these may be redefined by the individuals operating within that framework since there is no easy translation of policy into practice. A degree of strain (Stoll 1968) may then appear between the objectives of the formal ideology on which the policy is based and the objectives set by the informal working ideologies of those responsible for its implementation. This is particularly so in a

system of justice where the lack of definitive statement, theoretical or legislative, as to children's needs is accompanied by
wide discretionary powers. Against such a background, despite
the promise of the legislation, concern has been expressed about
the extent of such discretionary powers available to the members of the systems of social control with particular responsibility for children (Matza 1964; Fox 1976; Grant 1976). The
movement towards an ideology of welfare or treatment has
meant that the criteria on which decisions about children are
based will necessarily be more diffuse than those established by
an ideology of punishment. Not unexpectedly, juvenile justice
may then become riddled with 'rampant discretion' (Matza
1964). And since the principle of individualised justice according to needs requires examination of these diffuse social, personal or environmental characteristics, the relation between
the disposition and the criteria of judgment is not easily ascer-
tained. This is the danger of examining the process of decision-
making only by inferring the operation of organisational
or administrative structures from official statistics without
assigning significance to the role of operational ideologies in
determining and generating information summarised in such
statistics.

As an aid to reaching decisions under the principle of individualised justice a wealth of material is collated in respect of
children. But information to be used in decision-making has to
be interpreted and in the process of interpretation the individual
has to be able to identify what is for him information relevant to
the purpose of decision-making. The relevance ascribed to information for this purpose will differ from individual to individual, from agency to agency, since, though all may be oriented
to the same system of juvenile justice, 'the articulation of that
orientation with actual events and discussions is an empirical
issue basic to sociological interests in social organisation'
(Cicourel 1968, p.45).

The emphasis on organisational members' operational ideologies has hitherto mainly been concerned with 'professional'
ideologies (Strauss et al. 1964; Silverman 1971; Smith 1977;
Hardiker 1977). But what is particularly interesting about
juvenile justice as realised in the Hearing and Court systems of
Scotland and England respectively is that, despite the medical
and technical rhetoric associated with a welfare ideology that
pervades official literature, responsibility for decision-making
about children in need rests finally with 'lay' persons. That is,

the lay panel members in Scotland and the lay magistrates in England are charged with the responsibility of making decisions about children, though professional agencies are involved in the important functions of the assessment of need and the execution of welfare measures. Indeed the differences in the Scottish and English legislation suggest that even decisions as to welfare have become the responsibility of the English social services department with a consequent loss of power for the magistracy (see below).

There is a difference of approach to decisions about children between 'professionals' and 'lay' people. An examination of this difference shows how important is the fact of the lay status of the decision-makers. And by focusing on the issue of what constitutes relevant information as a basis for decisions about children in need, sources of ideological conflict can be identified in a system where sociological and philosophical interests converge. In particular, the move at a formal level from a punitive, judicially oriented philosophy of juvenile justice to a more welfare-oriented philosophy does not preclude the possibility that the operational ideologies of those responsible for the disposal of cases do not completely agree with official pronouncements and intentions.

Professional Ideologies and Relevance

In an attempt to minimise the injustices that can arise from discretionary decision-making, there have been a number of demands that welfare decisions be subject to judicial review and the rule of law. In reference to juvenile justice, the most recent advocates of such a move have been Morris et al. (1980). The dangers associated with discretionary decision-making in the context of social policy in general have initiated a concern to establish appropriate parameters to restrict the scope of discretion, and in juvenile justice in particular have promoted a constitutionalist revision of the mode of state intervention in juvenile delinquency, especially in the United States (Faust and Brantingham 1974, Part IV). But even in this country, there has been concern that the gradual move towards an approach to delinquency control based on a welfare philosophy has been at the cost of adequate legal protection. The status of children's rights (MacCormick 1976; Watson 1976) makes the imposition of measures in terms of need a particularly complex issue.

In the development of juvenile justice in Britain, the initial assumption of jurisdiction by the courts over cases of neglect and deprivation was the beginning of a process in which delinquency was redefined as being an appropriate area for social-work intervention. Accordingly, both in terms of size and responsibility, the social services have expanded considerably and their contribution to delinquency control has been emphasised by the fact that two government reports urged the reorganisation of the social services in an attempt to deal better with delinquency. But even where 'professionals' such as social workers, psychiatrists and psychologists are involved in a system of juvenile justice, this does not necessarily imply that all share the same approach to the assessment and treatment of behavioural conditions. Because any system which operates in terms of individualised justice necessarily entails wide discretionary powers, the lack of definitive objective criteria of need suggests that the ideologies characteristic of different professions may be important determinants of the approach to delinquency control adopted. Though members of different professions may be able to justify particular decisions and measures in terms of professional judgment within the ideological orientation of the profession this does not imply that there will be agreement between different professional groups. The clearest example is perhaps the basic disagreement between the social workers and the police in their definition of and approach to delinquency and crime control – something that is reflected in the interpretation of annual crime statistics.

Though it is by no means easy to stipulate clearly what a profession is, the attraction for particular occupational groupings of being considered 'professional' has been noted by Johnson, who states 'professionalism is a successful ideology and as such has entered the political vocabulary of a wide range of occupational groups who compete for status and income' (Johnson 1972, p.32).

Though 'socialisation' into particular forms of knowledge and the acquisition of specific skills and expertise, mainly through training, provides suitable qualifications, there is more to professionalism than that. Prestige and status are indeed important elements. Thus what Etzioni (1961) and Pearson (1975, p.16) can refer to as the semi-professions may well adopt the quasi-medical, technical terminology of more established professions such as psychiatry or even law, but have not yet attained an equivalent position of status. Social work is a classic example of this.

It would be naive, however, to assert that within professional groups it would be possible to identify a single dominant ideology expressed in the practical accomplishment of their task. Even within groups there is the opportunity for ideological conflict, the best example perhaps being of social work (Smith 1977; Hardiker 1977), though even in other contexts, particularly the medical and psychiatric fields, there is empirical evidence for this (Strauss et al. 1964). Recent debate and controversy about the methods adopted by the headmaster of Wellington School (one of the Scottish List D schools) resulting in his dismissal is as much indicative of ideological conflict about how to deal with children as it is about the relationships between the personalities involved.

A distinction can be made in relation to the types of checks which may operate on discretionary decision-making by considering administrative (Adler 1976) and 'professional' decision-making. Under a model of administrative decision-making, decisions are made with reference to a body of rules and regulations and the ultimate justification of the decision is that it has been made in accordance with those rules and regulations. Decisions made by a children's hearing or a juvenile court can then be judged in terms of whether they meet the statutory requirements governing procedure. But under a model of professional decision-making the ultimate justification for a decision is that the decision was made through the correct exercise of professional judgment. The criteria on which a decision is made are drawn from a stock of professional knowledge and though the professional may exercise discretion, some check can be made on his decision by reference to that stock of professional knowledge which creates for him a *frame of relevance*. Information has to be subjected to a process of interpretation by which only that which is relevant is retained. The relevance of information about children's needs depends not so much on the existence of identifiable objective criteria as on the conceptual framework underpinning the selective or interpretive activity of individuals which for the professional rests on four main assumptions (see Berger and Luckmann 1966, p.130ff.).

First, there must be a body of knowledge that accounts for delinquency and need. Secondly, there must be a corpus of diagnostic concepts indicative of clearly defined symptoms. Only by appropriate diagnosis can a condition be identified. Thirdly, there must also be accepted measures for treating identified conditions. Finally, there must be some statement as to the objectives sought. Interpretation of information about children suspected of being in need will be made by reference to that frame of relevance provided by the knowledge, diagnostic tools, accepted measures and objectives from which the individual derives his professional identity.

A frame of relevance provides the professional with a set of generalisations or typifications about delinquency that allows him to identify particular cases as coming under a more general category. Definitions of need and assumptions about causation then relate to a variety of factors such as broken home, deprived areas and so on, depending on the particular professional stance. Thus, the process of interpretation of need against a particular frame of relevance allows the professional to make sense of a wealth of potentially ambiguous information. But he is also able thereby to construct an explanation of delinquency in particular cases and though the assumed causal theory may be unsound or contestable the causes it identifies will at least have heuristic value. That is, whether they truly are the causes of delinquency or not has less significance than the value they have for the individual by allowing him to make sense of and impose explanations and order on information in his role as professional. In this way, a degree of clarity and routine is imposed on the decision-making process. Moreover, a frame of relevance allows for discretion to be exercised in accordance with particular professional knowledge and though there may be room for disagreement as to professional decisions and their appropriateness, a common frame of relevance provides the basis for shared understanding of a problem. Decisions can then be checked by reference to the professional standards and knowledge of the profession, though, as in the case of social work, some professional bodies are characterised by a lack of consensus as to knowledge base and practice.

But the very lack of objectively relevant criteria as to the causes of delinquency and the needs of delinquent children has implications for the relationship between different professions within the social control network, e.g. between the police, social worker, psychiatrist, psychologists and so on. The lack of a consistently defined frame of relevance means that they do not share a common understanding of behavioural problems. Because relevance is a quality that is ascribed to information and not an intrinsic property of information, the operation of juvenile justice based on welfare is circumscribed by competing frames of relevance. Because of the existence of a number of different professions within the organisational network for ad-

ministering juvenile justice, and because of the lack of a consistent conceptual framework underlying the legislation, each
profession operates in terms of its own background knowledge,
diagnostic concepts and objectives. An important medium
through which members of occupational groups are introduced
to the ideological orientation of their profession is through the
training and recruitment programme. The new recruit or novi-
tiate (Bankowski and Mungham 1977, ch.4) is 'socialised' and it
is this process of professional socialisation which lends solid-
arity to occupational structure since 'with . . . a generally homo-
geneous group there tend to be fewer divergent points of view
which would clash over the meaning of facts and thus give rise
to interpretations on a more theoretical level' (Mills 1963,
p.527). Matza has also referred to the importance of training and
professional background of these people operating within a system of juvenile justice characterised by 'rampant discretion'
(Matza 1964).

However, the interpretation of children's behaviour and the
decision as to the appropriate measures for dealing with behavioural problems made by the police, social workers, psychiatrists and so on may differ more fundamentally in their acceptance of different frames of relevance.

Discretion is a contextually defined concept – it cannot be
exercised *in vacuo*, but must always be in reference to a particular frame of relevance. In this way, limits can be placed on
the exercise of discretionary judgment by reference to the body
of professional knowledge from which different agencies derive
their professional identity. Thus, although the policeman and
the social worker both have considerable discretionary power, it
is exercised within different professional contexts and checks
on decision-making can be made in terms of the principles of
police and social work respectively.

However, since no frame of relevance, whether it be that of
the social worker, psychiatrist, policeman, or psychologist, has
necessarily any prior claim to validity: 'contradictions in the
ideologies of deviance held by various agents will create strains
in the social control network' (Schur 1971, p.166).

The difficulty confronting the panel member and the magistrate is that not only are they not professionals, claiming allegiance to a particular frame of relevance (though as we shall see,
the distinction between 'professional' and 'lay' status is not an
easy one to sustain), they are nevertheless required to make
decisions on the basis of information provided by the various

professions. How then does the 'lay' panel member ascribe relevance to information provided by the main agencies in the social control network and what implications does this have for the practical accomplishment of juvenile justice?

Relevance and 'Lay' Ideologies

A professional frame of relevance not only provides a means of interpreting and explaining behavioural characteristics of children but also provides a means whereby professional expertise can be acquired through a process of learning and training. The social worker and psychiatrist are both seen as professionals in their own right in as much as they have sufficiently acquainted themselves with the body of knowledge, diagnostic concepts and accepted treatment-measures of their respective professions. In other words, a frame of relevance determines not only who is to be treated but also who is to be responsible for deciding on and administering treatment. However, despite the rhetoric of therapy that pervades delinquency control, those responsible for decision-making, panel members and magistrates, are in fact 'lay' persons. For the purpose of this book, the use of 'lay' is slightly different from that commonly employed in the literature. 'Lay' is here taken to refer to the status of organisational members of the respective systems of juvenile justice who are not 'professional' members of the social-control network. In this respect such usage differs from that in which the term 'lay' is used to refer to the operational ideologies of those in the social-control network, whether they are professional or not. Thus Cicourel can refer to the lay theories of delinquency sustained by the police, social workers etc. (Cicourel 1968). For expediency, 'lay' ideologies here refers to the operational philosophies of those involved in the system of juvenile justice for whom professional status is not claimed.

As we shall argue, the lay status of panel members and magistrates is of particular importance for a number of reasons. First, panel members and magistrates are responsible for making the decision as to whether or not a child is in need of compulsory measures of care. Secondly, though panel members and magistrates are not themselves professionals, they nevertheless have to assess information presented by different professional agencies and individuals, none of whom may necessarily share the same orientation to the assessment of children, particularly children who commit offences. Thirdly, and related to the last point, panel members and magistrates have the opportunity of assessing information contained in the different reports and of supplementing this with information gleaned from discussions with the child and his parents or with certain of the professionals in the course of hearing a case. For these tasks, panel members' and magistrates' 'lay' ideologies of delinquency control are significant in their impact on discretionary decision-making. But unlike the professional, the lay person has no professional stock of knowledge which provides a frame of relevance and for the purpose of examining the nature of lay ideologies and frames of relevance, we shall employ the notion of available ideologies.

Available Ideologies

As a 'lay' person, the panel member and magistrate has access to what has been referred to as 'a socially approved system of typifications and relevances' (Schutz 1970, p.121) on which depends everyday social interaction. That is, for the purpose of ordinary social intercourse, he shares in a stock of public knowledge which allows the individual to select those elements in a social situation which are relevant for adopting particular courses of action. Much in the same way as a body of knowledge provides for the 'professional' a frame of relevance, so does this stock of public knowledge provide a means of interpreting and explaining events in the world. Indeed, through typifications certain events in the world can be anticipated, allowing responses to such events or patterns of events to be constructed. Similarly, it provides a means of shared communication and understanding. But whereas the professional frames of relevance can be acquired through learning and training, the frame of relevance providing an interpretative scheme for the 'lay person in everyday life originates in the biographical situation of the individual' (Schutz 1970). The formation and use of commonsense concepts also allows for a variety of 'lay' frames of relevance as a consequence of the varieties of individual experience.

This is particularly important since several studies have revealed the social-class bias of membership of the Children's Hearings and Juvenile Court (Smith and May 1971; Hood 1962). The implication of this is that the administration of juvenile justice is mediated by assumptions of a group broadly similar in their values about delinquency control. However, though for the purposes of communication and understanding in the wider social context, 'lay' frames of relevance are fundamentally similar because of their origin in the stock of publicly available knowledge, the individual's own experiences create for him a frame of relevance which is not totally public.

But in relation to his role as panel member or magistrate, through his own private frame of relevance, the individual brings to the hearing public and lay conceptions of delinquency, its causation, and how to deal with it. The suggestion that delinquency control operates in practice in terms of a treatment philosophy is fallacious since this ignores the social context of the decision-making process. The actual implementation of a treatment philosophy in the form of a court or hearing system is in particular mediated by values and assumptions about delinquency employed in the broader social context.

Such values and assumptions though not the same as more 'scientific' or 'professionally' respectable statements may nevertheless be the source of lay theories which are 'reflections and refractions of professional theories past and present, which have been transmitted like rumours, from the writing of "experts"' (Box 1971, p.180).

In this way, 'scientific' or professionally respectable theories of criminality or delinquency, its identification and its treatment provide what may be referred to as 'available ideologies' from which lay versions may be derived. 'Available ideologies' mediated and reinterpreted by agents of social control then, either implicitly or explicitly, provide the basis of the ideological orientation for such persons and a means for the identification of those deemed to be delinquent or criminal. The epistemological respectability commonly associated with scientific or professional theoretical statements about human behaviour is diminished when the actor is himself considered as a social theorist (see Giddens 1976; Schutz 1970; Cicourel 1968). For

> the relation between technical vocabularies of social science and lay concepts, however, is a shifting one; just as social scientists adopt everyday terms – 'meaning', 'motive', 'power', etc. – and use them in specialised senses, so lay actors tend to take over the concepts and theories of the social sciences and embody them as constitutive elements in the rationalisation of their own conduct. (Giddens 1976, p.159)

Giddens·then goes on to suggest that though causal generalisations in the social sciences are similar to natural scientific laws, a crucial difference is that they 'depend upon reproduced alignments of unintended consequences' (1976, p.159). This has several implications for a system of juvenile justice in which the main criterion for intervention is the need for compulsory measures of care.

Decisions about the need for compulsory measures of care are made within the context of moral discourse. Pearson (1975, p.15) has pointed out that the 'medicalisation' of delinquency was assumed to have placed the problem of delinquency control outside the realms of moral and political discourse, since decisions as to treatment measures were seen to be the responsibility of the technically competent. A similar comment has been made in relation to 'mental illness' where the conceptual problems posed by a logic of treatment are not unlike those raised by the notion of treating 'delinquents'. Questions are asked as to whether 'the only relevant criterion for evaluating the success of therapy is in terms of its *efficiency* in achieving this "objectively defined" goal, and therefore that moral considerations do not play any part' (Sayers 1973, p.2). Such a position ignores two things. First, a decision always has to be made at some point as to which behaviour is to be treated. No amount of research evidence can itself sustain an argument that particular forms of behaviour are indicative of a need for treatment since, in relation to delinquency at least, some decision has to be made first of all about which forms of behaviour are to be called 'delinquent' (see, for example, Bean 1976). The decision is essentially a moral one and conflicting arguments are essentially indicative of conflicting moral viewpoints, the outcome of which may be a social policy with a strong moral basis (see Duster 1970). Secondly, and more importantly in this context, at the level of implementation, actual decisions about particular cases may reflect different moral stances.

Because decisions about 'need' are not made in vacuo, the meaning attributed to delinquent behaviour is influenced by the lay and commonsense notions of justice and theories of delinquency employed by the panel members. But though there may be agreement that 'need' is the main criterion of intervention, the relativity of the notion of need means that there may be disagreement as to what actually constitutes 'need'. This may be reflected in the fundamental disagreement between the different agencies within the control network as between individuals whether they be 'lay' or 'professional'. Because professionals are themselves members of a community, the adoption of a professional frame of relevance does not preclude the possibility that this too is also influenced by 'lay' conceptions of delinquency. But though delinquency control has apparently become the realm of the 'expert' (Gillis 1974; Bean 1976), both panel members and magistrates were nevertheless still to be 'lay' persons.

As we saw earlier in the first chapter, a problem for juvenile justice has always been that of attempting to deal with children who offend by means of a process ultimately derived from criminal justice in its application to adults. It is subject therefore to the rules of evidence and criminal procedure. In reference to Western criminal policy, Duster (1970) identifies the conflict in a criminal justice system where the individual is treated as a rational, responsible being up until the point of conviction. But from the point of sentencing onwards, he is subject to measures and professions whose conceptual base reflects a philosophy of pathology, or more broadly, determinism. There is then an ideological clash between the more judicially or legally oriented ideology of the initial stages of proceedings and the welfare ideology underpinning the later ones. The separation of adjudication and disposal in the Scottish system where the need for compulsory measures of care is decided upon by panel members was an attempt to resolve this. Similarly, the introduction of a mixed system of care and criminal proceedings in the 1969 Children and Young Persons Act, though not so radical as the Scottish developments, was also made in recognition of this ideological clash. As to the nature of the balance struck in England: 'the model was, in crude terms, one of social pathology for the younger child, but more classical assumptions about the choice of evil for the older child . . .' (Bottoms 1974, p.324). The criminal law, even in its application to children where youth was recognised as a mitigating factor, assumed a high degree of personal responsibility, a fact which had received considerable criticism in the 1960s (Kilbrandon Report, especially paras 60, 71, 72).

But also in the course of everyday social interaction, for the purpose of ascribing praise, blame or punishment, it makes a difference whether an act had to occur or not and the designation of responsibility, conformity and deviance depends on this commonsense assumption (McHugh 1970). Some concept of agency is necessary for the judgment of behaviour and it is in this respect that questions about the justice or otherwise of the way in which we deal with those who do wrong are inextricably linked to particular notions of human action.

Though the rhetoric of therapy theoretically removes the issue of delinquency control from the realms of moral discourse, lay theories of justice and delinquency derived from that stock of knowledge about delinquency causation may introduce an element of moral judgment to the juvenile-justice process. In the chapter which follows different conceptions of human action and the way in which these are accommodated within different philosophies of delinquency or crime control will be considered. This is for a number of reasons.

First, it is commonly assumed that treatment or welfare and punishment are diametrically opposed. Such an assumption is unwarranted because of the conceptual complexity surrounding the relationship between treatment and punishment.

Secondly, the history of the development of juvenile justice has not been one of a simple trend away from punishment to treatment.

Finally, the different notions of action, punishment and treatment provide what we have referred to as 'available ideologies' from which lay notions of delinquency control are derived. Whereas the juvenile-justice systems in this country have developed in accordance with a more welfare-oriented philosophy, paralleled by the expansion of the role played by 'experts' or professionals, 'lay' persons occupy crucial positions. It is an objective of this work to examine empirically the extent to which lay persons operating within two organisationally and structurally different contexts employ notions of delinquency control derived from such 'available ideologies'.

Chapter Three

ACTION, EXPLANATION
AND CRIME CONTROL

Because there is no definitive statement on the 'causes' of delinquency or how to deal with it, the assumptions and beliefs about
delinquency and its control maintained by control agents are
crucial factors in the practical accomplishment of juvenile justice. And though such individuals may not themselves be professionals or experts they may well draw upon more 'scientific'
or 'professionally' respectable theories which provide 'available
ideologies'. These publicly 'available ideologies', mediated and
reinterpreted by those responsible, in this case, for dealing with
children, then constitute the basis for the accomplishment of
justice through the provision of a means whereby information
can be identified as relevant for the purpose of decision-making.
That much informed the argument in the last chapter.

In this chapter, the main aim is to identify major perspectives
on the explanation of action and their association with different
philosophies of crime control and to present these in the form of
what appear to be logically and reasonably tenable positions.
This will not amount to a full-blown philosophical account of
the concept of action or of the morality of the different means of
dealing with those who perform untoward or what is conventionally taken to be deviant behaviour. Rather, the account
presented will be mainly descriptive, aimed at dovetailing with
the argument that 'available ideologies' provide the origins of
the working frames of relevance manifested by those who are in
the position of having to make decisions about children who
commit offences.

The chapter will be presented in two sections. In the first,
three broad perspectives on action will be considered:
    i) Indeterminism and Responsibility
   ii) Determinism and Responsibility: the Incompatibility
       Thesis
  iii) Determinism and Responsibility: the Compatibility
       Thesis

In the second, the justification for punishment of those who commit crime will be analysed in relation to the different conceptions of human action. These are:

iv) Indeterminism and Punishment
v) Non-punitive Treatment
vi) Punitive Treatment

In broad terms, discussion of (iv) will relate mainly to retributive accounts of punishment whereas (v) and (vi) will be more concerned with accounts of crime control which have their roots in utilitarian philosophy. In (v) the focus will be on approaches to the control of crime which is based on determinist assumptions and which is described as non-punitive treatment. The main thrust of this approach is that offenders ought only to receive some form of treatment and cannot justly be punished. This of course is based upon the belief that no one, and not only offenders, is ever responsible for their actions. However, it is wrong to assume that individuals are either responsible or not responsible for their actions or that an easy distinction can be drawn between punishment and treatment. This is developed in (vi) in which will be described a stance on punishment which includes treatment (loosely defined) as a consideration. In contrast with the non-punitive treatment philosophy of hard determinists this is often referred to as punitive treatment, a term adopted in this book.

In terms of criminal behaviour and ordinary moral discourse, whether or not the individual is seen as responsible for his actions is crucial to questions about the legitimacy of punishment or blame, its social analogue. The relevance of this for present purposes is that the difficulty of stipulating the age from which children can be held criminally responsible and therefore liable to punishment crystallises the more general problem of deciding when anyone can be held morally responsible. The practical problem for systems of justice is that whereas theories of delinquency and crime causation have generally been couched in terms of causal antecedents, systems of delinquency control have historically all been characterised by the retention of some concept of responsibility. Moreover, and just as importantly, moral language by its very nature necessarily requires some notion of responsibility whereby action may be subject to moral judgment.

The concept of action is significant for the argument in this book in several ways. In our ordinary employment of language, moral discourse focuses on actions and more especially actions that in some way have deviated from accepted norms and stand-ards. Questions of moral responsibility arise when we feel that an action has not been performed which ought to have been. As Austin (1961, p.128) says: 'the situation is one where someone is accused of having done something, or (if that will keep it any clearer) where someone is *said* to have done something which is bad, wrong, inept, unwelcome, or in some other way untoward'.

Somebody against whom such an accusation is made may defend himself in a variety of ways: 'X is wrong, but I didn't do it' – *denial*; 'although X is normally wrong, there were special circumstances which made it the right thing to do in this case' – *justification*; 'although X is wrong, I am not to blame for doing it, because of these special circumstances . . .' – an *excuse*. An understanding of the last category, excuses, is of special import-ance for understanding the idea of responsibility: excusing con-ditions exclude responsibility. Moreover, the material criteria considered as appropriate to excuse an individual from being held responsible for his behaviour are determined in part by the knowledge and information available and conventionally em-ployed at any point in time. As Pitkin (1972, p.150) argues, 'a further implication of taking "excuses" as central to moral discourse is that morality emerges as both conventionally trad-itional and pragmatically mundane, and consequently as having very definite limitations'.

Both the formal and the material nature of excusing con-ditions are topics for moral discourse. It is obvious that ordinary everyday language does not display consensus over the material nature of excuses, that is, what counts as a good excuse (though we may all agree as to their logic or form). Similarly, moral philosophers themselves display no little disagreement about the relevance of the factors which they are prepared to accept as absolving an individual from responsibility for his actions. The lack of consensus does not merely reflect different moral pos-itions as such. It is more basic than that. A fundamental prob-lem for discussions about judgments of behaviour is that of understanding exactly what is meant by 'action'. In this respect, as we shall see below, the so-called Free-will/Determinism debate finds its parallel in the sociological literature where epistemological questions about the relevance of natural science as a model for the social sciences presuppose disagree-ments about the similarity, or otherwise, of human phenomena to natural phenomena. In moral discourse, the issues are similar. How we identify 'action' for which an individual is or is not responsible depends on the conception of human nature to which we adhere. And depending on the conception of human action maintained, the moral justifications offered for punishment or blame will vary.

Indeterminism, Determinism and Responsibility

What the libertarian or indeterminist thesis asserts, in brief, is that a necessary condition of moral action is that the agent or actor acted of his own free will in the sense that he could have done otherwise. It is on this that depends both the ascription of responsibility and agency and the very use of the language of moral discourse. 'Agency', in its literal sense, means acting and doing, which is very different from events happening or being caused. The libertarian or indeterminist then insists that an individual is responsible and free if he could have chosen to do otherwise than he did do. He adheres to a model of human action as being purposive and intentional, and in this way clearly distinct from other events and processes in the natural order.

In contrast, by determinism, we refer to that general philosophical thesis which states that for everything that happens, human action included, there are conditions such that, given their existence, nothing else could have happened. All phenomena, human and natural, are the product of preceding causes. Whereas libertarians argue that moral discourse is dependent on a libertarian world view and that determinism negates moral discourse, this very point is one element in the controversy. Philosophical debate has not been limited to the relative merits of libertarianism or determinism but has also considered the extent to which determinism is in fact compatible with or even presupposed by the existence of moral discourse as a meaningful and intelligible type of discourse. The relevance of such debate for our purposes rests in the fact that with the development of criminological positivism, explanations of delinquency and crime in general have moved away from the conceptions of offenders as responsible and therefore punishable to a form of explanation which demands the identification of the causes of delinquent behaviour. The problem this presents for ordinary language is that causal explanations of behaviour do not rest easily with moral discourse (Asquith 1979); for formal systems of control, this is reflected in the questioning of the validity of the concept of criminal responsibility (Wootton 1959) and in the attempts to reconcile judicial and welfare ideologies.

Indeterminism and Responsibility. Libertarians claim that it is a necessary presupposition of our use of moral language that human beings are capable of choice and can be responsible for what they do since they possess free will. Nevertheless, though human beings have this capacity to initiate actions, and it is this capacity for action that distinguishes man from other phenomena, human beings are also the subject of events in the world that are beyond their control. As well as being agents in the sense of acting in and on the world, they are also affected by what 'happens' in it. This not only refers to external events, but may also refer to the very constitution of human nature. Kant argued that man is both a rational being who operates in the world and a sensory being in his physical and physiological constitution.

Explanations for action cannot always be, though they may be on occasion, given in causal terms since man is on occasion free to choose how to act and therefore responsible for what he does. Arendt would question (1958, p.157) whether behaviour which could be explained in causal terms could in fact be called 'action' at all. But in Kantian terms, man may be the cause of his own behaviour and is therefore self-determining and a non-causal explanation of action as self-determined behaviour is required. 'Indeed Kant's suggestions that men live in two worlds, and is subject to two different sorts of causation, is a metaphysical way of bringing out the logical distinction between those two sorts of explanation' (Benn and Peters, 1959, p.203).

Thus, the libertarian thesis has to accommodate means for recognising when people may be held responsible for their actions and when their actions are the result of events beyond their control thereby negating responsibility and agency. This much is embodied in the spirit of the Kantian maxim that 'ought' implies 'can'. To assert that someone ought to have done something or ought not to have done something and to hold him morally responsible is to imply that he in fact could have behaved otherwise than he did.

Libertarianism, adopting a purposive, intentional model of action must allow for those events in the world which are *prima facie* actions but which on closer investigation are in fact beyond the control of the subject. It is in this dimension of moral discourse that excusing conditions are crucial since it is important for our moral concepts of responsibility and of action to know when we withdraw our assumption that a person is responsible for what he does. When we assert that a person is responsible we do more than simply describe a sequence of events ultimately traceable to the action of an individual (see Hart 1968). The essence of moral judgment, as of action, is not discernible by observation alone. It is for this very reason that the method of the natural sciences with its emphasis on observation and experiment is seen as an inadequate model for the social sciences. Responsibility like action cannot *per se* be observed and described. Moral judgment and interpretation of action depend on the conventional and mundane standards drawn from the social milieu. Nor are these static since conceptions of responsibility and who is to be held responsible do and have changed in line with development in knowledge of the behavioural sciences (Clarke 1975). But the advances made both in philosophy and sociology reflect the contention that adequate or sufficient explanation of human action can never be given in causal terms alone (Peters 1958). The indeterminist then holds that a person can only be responsible for an action when he could have acted otherwise and further that he could have chosen to have acted otherwise. Moral responsibility on this view is incompatible with determinism since choice is itself not the product of antecendents.

What defences then would the indeterminist allow that would serve to excuse someone from responsibility? There are two broad categories of excusing conditions – those in which it can be shown that the agent was in some sense compelled to act as he did and those in which he did not really know what he did. Both point to purpose or intentionality as the condition of responsibility. Moreover, excusing conditions are no less important in the law than they are for morality. They may be more important, for as Hart argues excusing conditions 'maximise within a framework of coercive criminal law the efficacy of the individual's informed and considered choice in determining the future and also his power to predict that future' (1968, p.46).

Where there are features of a situation unknown to or mistakenly believed by a person accused of having done something wrong and these factors are relevant to the ascription of responsibility then he may be held non-responsible. It is obvious however that though ignorance may on occasion be used as a defence, it is not applied without qualification as the phrase 'ignorance of the law is no excuse' testifies. What we are concerned with are these states of affairs which we maintain as accepted impediments to purposive or intentional action. Important requisites for moral responsibility are therefore awareness of circumstances, awareness of the wrongfulness and awareness of the possible consequences.

There are of course exceptions in criminal law, especially Anglo-American, where the requirement of *mens rea* is not absolute. Offences of strict liability, vicarious liability and negligence are examples where ignorance of certain states of affairs is no excuse. This in itself is testimony to the fact that though there are major overlaps between the criminal law and morality, the two are not completely co-extensive (Hart 1968; Devlin 1965; McNeilly 1966).

But in moral discourse, it is in some cases an accepted defence to claim ignorance of some features of the situation which if known would have been another set of variables in the choice of action.

Where ignorance or lack of knowledge may be sufficient to absolve a person from responsibility in particular situations, compulsion, on the other hand, though it does refer to particular instances of action, may also inhibit the capacity for intentional and voluntary behaviour generally. This does of course depend on what definition of 'compulsion' is accepted and the debate about the compatibility of a determinist thesis with moral discourse rests on subtle distinctions. Compulsion may take a variety of forms and may be either internal or external (Downie 1971). Examples of external compulsion are where

   i) the action was the result of an accident;
   ii) an individual is forced to behave or act in a certain way
      under duress or threat.

Since one of the objectives in ascribing responsibility for behaviour is to place limits on the causal nexus leading up to the commission of an act, then where a person accidentally commits an act or commits it under duress, he is not the last link in the chain as it were. His behaviour was not 'purposive', 'intentional', 'voluntarily done' or done through choice.

Determinism and Responsibility: the Incompatibility thesis. What the determinist thesis does, in a sense, is to expand the applicability of the causal framework in analysing human action to the point of claiming that all behaviour is in fact the product of antecedent conditions. This ontological shift, with its ramifications for the epistemological basis of social science, implies that the language of moral responsibility is in fact invalid and irrelevant to human action. Since, on this perspective, there is essentially no difference between human and other phenomena, 'responsibility is an illusion and a linguistic convenience' (Downie 1971).

For those who adopt a purposive and intentional model of human action, there is a necessary distinction between action and other phenomena such as bodily movement. The general philosophical thesis of determinism maintains that for everything that ever happens, there are conditions such that given them, it would be impossible for anything else to have happened. The modern theses of determinism have their origins (Ruska 1974) in the developments made in the natural sciences in the seventeenth and eighteenth centuries, particularly with the shift to observation, experiment and the search for descriptive laws. The ontological and epistemological implications of this empiricist conception of scientific endeavour is not without significance for contemporary debate on the inadequacy of positivism as a model for the social sciences (Ryan 1970; Philipson 1971; Schutz 1970). But the real significance of the trend was that explanations of events in the world including actions and states of affairs were grounded in scientific and rational accounts in opposition to the metaphysical and theological tenets of earlier philosophies (Ruska 1974). Only the facts empirically verified by methods akin to those employed in the natural sciences could attain the status of knowledge.

In terms of relevance for moral discourse, 'determinism may without logical fault be the thesis that physical events and states cause such things as decisions and actions' (Honderich 1969, p.115). If action is caused, what are we to make of the concept of freedom? Can the freedom available to individuals ever be categorical in Kant's use of the term? If we are not free, then how can we be held responsible for actions that in fact we could not help doing? Moreover, the concept of responsibility is problematic not only in that it is difficult to establish when people are responsible for their actions but also because the language of determinism is *prima facie* incompatible with the language of morals (Wootton 1959). If actions are made to happen, then the purposive and intentional types of explanation are without application. The logic and language of excuse is without application since all events and actions are the outcome of events which could not be otherwise (Downie 1971).

The idea that all events are the consequence of causal antecedents means that the incompatibility thesis does not allow for 'self-determinism' since human choices, decisions and actions are themselves caused. All are necessary consequences of some antecedent circumstances. Human actions as a subcategory of natural events are necessary effects of such antecedent states of affairs. The implication for morality is then that if we are not free to act other than we did, if we could not act other than we did, we are therefore not free to act in such a way as to be responsible agents. Given similar states of affairs similar events cannot but occur. The determinist can therefore argue that his thesis implies that events are predictable and that accordingly events are particular instances of the effect of universal invariable laws governing the universe (Willer and Willer 1973; Ryan 1970; Glover 1970). It is this philosophy which underpins prediction studies in criminology.

Whether true or not, this ontological commitment to the existence of typical patterns of causal sequences both in natural and human phenomena – there is no real distinction – requires a causal account of human behaviour, action and motivation. Thus far, we have been speaking about the *logic* (the formal component) of determinism but what different theoretical accounts of human action have to be able to do is to fill in the *details* (the material component) of the sequences between cause and effect (Ryan 1970). In the next chapter, a number of the more important accounts of delinquency causation that have been developed within a determinist framework will be examined.

Determinism and Responsibility: the Compatibility thesis. For the libertarian, to have what was referred to as free will entails having a will that is categorically free and exempt from the causal laws that the determinists posit as governing human action. To be morally responsible requires that individuals *qua* agents *can* act according to choice and can choose as they will. Moral responsibility, in terms of the libertarian conception, is therefore incompatible with compulsion, if by compulsion we mean 'subject to the influence of causal laws'. It is precisely in rejecting this notion of compulsion that Schlick (1939) is able to argue that human action can be free and at the same time the product of antecedent circumstances. He therefore claims that he has resolved the apparent antinomy between free will and determinism claiming that it was 'really one of the greatest scandals of philosophy that again and again so much paper and printers ink is devoted to this matter' (1939, p.143). Schlick was concerned to provide an account of responsibility that would allow people to be held responsible for their actions without committing us to the view that the determinist thesis is false. Some philosophers have also argued that it is impossible anyway to claim, as the indeterminists do, that choices and actions are not determined but are freely willed and categorically so. The indeterminist thesis is in this respect unsound since it would make it theoretically impossible to link the making of choices or the doing of actions with antecedents such as background, nature, desire and so on. Hobbes and Hume in particular both maintained that a satisfactory account could not be given of decisions unless they were seen as necessary consequences of such antecedents as desire or disposition. To view decisions as freely made while totally rejecting the deterministic thesis is in their opinion illogical.

Following the formula proposed by Schlick the *prima facie* antinomy between moral responsibility and determinism can be resolved thus. Whereas decisions may be caused, we can and often do act freely. As we shall see the conception of responsibility maintained by the compatibility theorists, and by implication its significance for questions about the morality of blame or punishment, is in a number of respects different from the libertarian conception.

The solution to the problem rests on clarification of what we mean when we refer to human action as 'free'. 'Freedom' for those who adhere to the compatibility theory is taken to mean the lack of constraint and the lack of compulsion. It is further claimed that there is no incompatibility between conceiving of decisions as the necessary consequences of preceding causes and believing that we are not constrained or compelled to decide as we do. But compulsion, on this perspective, does not mean the same as causation, since it is misleading to assume that causes compel (Downie 1971). Purposive language, and the purposive-intentional model of human action can be reduced to causal language since the freedom required is not, as Campbell maintained, of a contra-causal kind (Campbell 1951).

Hobbes conceived of the lack of constraint or freedom as the absence of physical force thereby allowing a man to do as he pleased. Similarly, Schlick suggests that 'Freedom means the opposite of compulsion; a man is *free* if he does not act under *compulsion*, and he is compelled or unfree when he is hindered from without in the realisation of his desires' (1939, p.150). To say a man decided freely means that he decided as he wanted, unhindered by external forces. But Schlick, developing Hobbes' position, accepts that there are also internal forces which may possibly impede freedom of decision thereby absolving an individual from responsibility. As examples, he cites action performed under the influence of drugs, and mental illness in which case not the individual 'but his disease is responsible' (Schlick 1939, p.151).

People who act in accordance with their desires and are not hindered in their decision by forces referred to above therefore act freely. In this way, the strength of the claim that responsibility demands acceptance of the determinist position rather than its rejection can best be appreciated (1939, pp.222–51). Questions about the capacity to act in a morally responsible manner are negative in the sense that they refer to the absence of factors whose presence would otherwise negate responsibility and freedom of choice. Hart makes the same point: 'Yet, nonetheless, what is meant by the mental element in criminal liability (*mens rea*) is only to be understood by considering certain defences or exceptions . . . most of which have come to be admitted in most crimes, and in some cases exclude liability altogether, and in others merely reduce it' (1968, p.152). Hart is not here giving a full-blown argument in support of the compatibility thesis. But elsewhere, in what appears to be the only formal statement of his position with regard to this, he suggests that his concern with the defeasibility of concepts such as responsibility is not incompatible with the determinist thesis. He satisfied himself with the claim that 'the defence I make in this paper of the rationality, morality and justice of qualifying criminal responsibility by excusing conditions will be compatible with any form of determinism which satisfies certain . . . requirements' (1968, p.28). That is, for Hart at least, the concept of responsibility is defeasible in that responsibility can be established not so much by indication of the presence of a necessary mental or subjective element but the absence of the generally or formally accepted excusing conditions. Determinism is compatible with such a standpoint.

In ascribing responsibility, the compatibility theorists are not so much concerned with identifying remote causes – for example when a man has inherited his behaviour from his great-grandfather (see Schlick 1939). Rather they are only really concerned with the question of who can effectively be rewarded or punished. Punishment for Schlick is an educative measure. Such a line of thinking is apparent in the psychological hedonism of utilitarians such as Mill, who argued that the human will was governed by motives and that the threat of punishment provided an additional motive for refraining from criminal behaviour.

A man is only morally responsible if those motives which

brought about the act can be affected 'in respect of his future behaviour by the educative influence of reward and pain'. The conception of human nature is one in which man is seen as conducting his life in terms of a hedonistic and moral calculus.

The incompatibilist position espoused by the determinists could not accommodate the logic of excuse within its explanatory framework. The libertarian position posited excusing conditions, or at least their absence as a prerequisite for the ascription of responsibility. The compatibility theorists, in reconciling determinism with moral discourse, accept the necessity of excusing conditions but for very different reasons from those of the libertarians. There are those categories of individuals for whom the prospect of reward or pain would be completely ineffective; these are children and the mentally and physically ill. Similarly, to hold as responsible those who acted in ignorance or through compulsion (in the compatibilist sense of the term) would be unjust for the same reasons. It is however by no means easy to separate the question of efficiency and justice since 'Questions of reconciliation of determinism and moral responsibility have stressed that determinism does not make all blame ineffective, but have largely ignored the question of whether or not determinism makes all blame unjust' (Ayer 1954). It is considering what to do about those who behave in an untoward manner that the distinctions that characterise the three positions identified in this section are further drawn. It is also particularly in relation to delinquency control that the decision as to the appropriate forms of measures is by no means easy.

Punishment and Justification

As we have seen, the discussion of moral responsibility and action has usually been in the context of the free-will/determinist debate. The significance of this for the present thesis is that the historical and theoretical development of criminology, underpinning many of the modifications in the legal and penal system, reflects the move away from a perspective on crime based on an assumption of rationality and free will (classicism) to one based on a deterministic framework. In no case more so than that of children has the criminal law been more subject to continued modification (Bean 1976), paralleled by an increasing emphasis on children as appropriate objects of inquiry for positivist social science. As Gillis points out (1974), though 'delinquency' and 'adolescence' were only 'discovered' or 'invented' comparatively recently, moves which were to culminate in the reconceptualisation of delinquency as a behavioural problem had their origins in the 'scientisation' of youth criminality.

Questions of the justification of punishment arise at two important levels (though as Hart says they are not necessarily mutually exclusive). These are in reference to the very idea or institution of punishment and the moral validity of particular acts of punishment. Such concerns are paralleled by the two main traditions in the justification of punishment since retributivism mainly answers questions about the justification of punishment in particular instances; utilitarianism on the other hand considers mainly questions pertinent to the morality of punishment as an institution. Since the argument in this book is that the main justifications of punishment (like the main scientific theories about delinquency) provide 'available ideologies' from which ordinary commonsense approaches to delinquency control are derived, it is important that at least the main salient features of retributivism and utilitarianism respectively are identified. The history of the juvenile court has been one in which retributive justifications for the punishment of children have been gradually eroded and replaced with more utilitarian concerns, though juvenile-justice systems continue to be riddled with conflation of the two perspectives. And 'in any case it should at least be clear that part of the juvenile court system dealing with offenders was an amalgam of features reflecting and justified by two distinct moral points of view' (Watson 1976, p.198).

Indeterminism and Punishment. A problem with punishment is that, *prima facie*, those behaviours or actions which we call punishment are in many respects similar to the rule-breaking behaviour, whether it be in a legal or other context, which provoked its infliction. As punishment involves the deliberate, intentional infliction of some form of unpleasantness, the legitimacy of such a practice is *prima facie* doubtful and calls for moral arguments.

In moral philosophy, there is disagreement between those who consider that the moral worth of an action is determined by reference to the motive of the agent and those who consider that the moral worth of an action is determined by reference to the consequences of that action. Retributive theories of punishment offer as justification a past act, the offence, which is considered a wrong requiring punishment. Perhaps the essential differences between retributivism and utilitarianism are most concisely summed up by Kant: 'Punishment can never be administered merely as a means for promoting another good, either with regard to the Criminal himself or to Civil society, but must in all cases be imposed only because the individual has committed a crime' and later, 'For one man ought never to be dealt with merely as a means subservient to the purpose of another' (Hastie 1887). The obligation or imperative to punish is categorical inasmuch as it would be morally wrong to allow an offence to go unpunished. In this respect, the retributive justification of punishment has been seen as self-validating (Quinton 1954) requiring no further moral validation outside itself. To follow Kant in asserting that punishment of offenders for offences is good in itself is to reject the need for further justification. But to assert that a man be punished because he has committed an offence is to assume a relationship between offence and sanction. It is in this respect that retributive justifications of punishment rest on the indeterminist thesis and consequently seek to promote non-treatment punishment. For the retributivist, a man is punished because he deserves punishment, or he may even be said to have a right to be punished.

The justification for punishment then rests on what the offender has done and not in any consequences that may accrue from punishing him. To seek justification in the consequences of his punishment is on this view to use individuals as mere means to ends and not in Kantian terms as ends in themselves. Furthermore, to assert that only those who have committed an offence can justly be punished is supplemented in retributivism by the contention that only those who are 'responsible' for their offences can be punished (Watson 1976; Honderich 1969). The offender is punished justly if, and only if, he behaved culpably. The indeterminist thesis therefore supports a conception of man as having the capacity for rationality, choice and intention, that is free will; it also supports a justification for punishment in which punishment is deserved and just where the offender behaved culpably or responsibly. Punishment is not and ought not to be associated with any attempt to promote other ends such as the reformation or rehabilitation of the offender.

However, the indeterminist thesis also accommodates excusing conditions which serve to absolve individuals from responsibility and the possibility of punishment. Similarly, it is recognised that there are categories of offenders who are not and cannot be morally responsible, such as young children or the mentally ill and who cannot therefore be justly punished. Because of their incapacity to form choice or intent such persons are not responsible. Rather than be the subjects of non-treatment punishment they ought to be offered non-punishment treatment. But these are residual categories, and though conceptions of responsibility have been increasingly subjected to modification as the result of advances in the behavioural sciences, resulting in the expansion of such categories (Clarke 1975), the indeterminist thesis is central to retributivist justifications of punishment.

A number of consequences follow from the postulated relationship between culpability, desert and punishment. Since there are varying degrees of culpability, punishment deserved by the offender must be proportional to his wrongdoing or 'the depravity of the act' (Rawls 1955). Or as Honderich (1969) claims, 'the penalty will give satisfactions equivalent to the grievance caused by his actions'. A corollary of this for retributive philosophy is that like offences ought to be treated in a like manner so that the principle of proportionality is supplemented by the principle of consistency (see Morris et al. 1980). That is, not only must a punishment be proportional to the culpability of the offender or to the nature of his act, but in like cases the same punishments will be inflicted. The similarity between retributivist arguments and the formal requirements of justice such as 'treat like cases alike' which underpins considerations of due process and natural justice is apparent (see McCloskey 1965). But as with justice, the formal criteria have to be supplemented by material or substantive criteria (Lloyd 1964; Perelman 1963) by which the logic of likeness can be given context. For the retributivist, 'likeness' is determined in terms of desert or merit. What is commonly referred to as the tariff system (see Thomas 1970) embodies the principles of proportionality and consistency in the form of a penal calculus (see Morris et al. 1980). Thus, a prime element in the retributivist position is that the severity of the sanction should in some way be related to the culpability of the offender and the amount of harm done by the offence. Some retributivists however would say that 'the amount of blame and therefore the severity of the penalty should be governed by the offender's intentions and not by the actual result' (Walker 1969). What this does is to introduce the particularly difficult task of establishing the state of mind of the offender at the time of the offence.

Whereas for the retributivist a person is punished because he had done something to deserve punishment, a distinction has to be drawn between 'desert' as justification and 'desert' in Hart's terms, as a limiting factor. Thus punishment ought not to be decided upon simply with atonement in mind since a limit, a retributively appropriate limit, should be imposed on the severity of the sanction. In terms of 'retribution in distribution' the importance of the moral culpability of the offender is further signified by Walker (19669, p.31) in the principle that 'society has no right to apply an unpleasant measure to someone against his will unless he has intentionally done something prohibited'. Those who behaved responsibly can justly be punished and the justice of the sanction can be further enhanced by its correspondence with the desert of the offender. It is because retributivism emphasises the questions of who can justly be punished and what form punishment can take that retributivism has been seen as being not a moral but a logical doctrine (Mundle 1954). But in general where retributivists in the main agree is that punishment must in some senses fit the crime, that the punishment must be deserved and that offenders in fact have a right to punishment by virtue of their moral agency (Quinton 1954; MacCormick 1974). Penal sanctions moreover take the form of non-treatment punishment except in the case of certain categories whose capacity for moral responsibility is in doubt. Whereas the indeterminist thesis supports retributivists' justifications of punishment, both the determinist and compatibility thesis espoused different approaches to responsibility and therefore also different perspectives on how to deal with offenders.

Non-punitive treatment. As was noted above, the question prompted by the determinist thesis on action is not that of who may be held morally responsible and therefore punishable but whether anyone can ever be deemed so. Modifications in the criminal law and in penal sanctions have paralleled, and in part been attributable to, the increasing recognition that there are categories of offenders who may not be justly punished. Rather, treatment and help are considered more appropriate forms of intervention. In this section, the argument that criminality is analogous to illness and disease requiring help or treatment will be considered as will be the implications that such a position has for the concept of responsibility.

The notion of 'treatment' can have a wide or a narrow application (Watson 1976). In its wider application, which is more fully developed in the following section, treatment may also entail the notion of punishment since certain theories of punishment seek to obtain ends and objectives such as the reformation of the offender. The vagueness of the concept of treatment has, in this wider use of the term, been compounded by the fact that many authors and government reports use treatment or training, reformation or rehabilitation interchangeably (Bean 1976). However in its narrow application treatment is non-punitive and excludes punishment as a suitable means for preventing or reducing crime, referring mainly to the application of non-punitive measures. Similarly, the offender, rather than being conceived as a responsible individual, is seen as being non-responsible in that his behaviour is the result of predisposing factors (Wootton 1959; Flew 1973). Thus the crime, or more correctly, criminality, is conceived of as analogous to disease (Flew 1973). As we noted earlier, the medicalisation of delinquency, or the application of the medical analogy to criminality culminated in the dissolution of the metaphor of 'as if'. That is, where formerly criminality may have been conceived of *as if* it were disease, it came to be construed *as* disease. The 'as if' drops out and criminality is disease.

From such a viewpoint, there is little reason to seek to establish the moral responsibility of the offender whose behaviour is seen as pathological, or symptomatic of need. There are two arguments here. First, because the treatment or medical approach to crime is built upon a deterministic framework, it is *theoretically* futile to attempt to establish moral responsibility. This argument associates the treatment model with positivist criminology (Radzinowicz 1965). However, it is also seen to be *practically* difficult for courts to inquire into the question of whether or not a person could have done other than what he did do (Wootton 1959). Since Wootton argues that this is impossible, she is logically committed to the position that the very question of responsibility should be bypassed. Thus, her position rests on a blend of theoretical and practical implications. In the literal sense of the word, criminals are patients in that they suffer from or experience conditions such that their criminal behaviour is a necessary outcome. From this viewpoint then, crime is disease and should be dealt with in a manner similar to that employed in the prevention or curing of medical ailments. What such a perspective ignores, however, is the social and cultural context not only of criminality and also of the definitions of the behaviours which constitute 'crimes' (Phillipson 1971), but also of the paradigm of medicine (Flew 1973). Nevertheless, a number of others adopt a treatment or social-hygiene approach to criminality, rejecting the need to establish and ascribe responsibility. Eysenck, for example, argues

> We would regard behaviour from a completely determin-
> istic point of view . . . Therefore to attribute to individuals
> greater or lesser degrees of responsibility seems, from this
> point of view, a rather meaningless procedure.

Glueck, quoted by Wootton, stated earlier

> The question of responsibility would not have to be raised,
> if the concept of the management of the anti-social indi-
> vidual were changed from that of punishment as the main
> instrument of control, to a concept of the anti-social indi-
> vidual as a sick person, in need of treatment rather than of
> punishment. (Wootton 1959, p.248)

And in favour of the abandonment of the concept of responsibility, Wootton herself recommended

> a shift in emphasis on the treatment of offenders away from
> considerations of guilt towards choice of whatever course
> of action appeared most likely to be effective as a cure in
> any particular case. (1959, p.251)

The semantics of crime control as Tappan appreciated some
time ago has thus undergone considerable change with the
differing theoretical frameworks. The language of crime, responsibility and punishment with the advent of the medical
model has given way to the technical jargon of pathology, diagnosis and treatment.

One argument advanced in favour of an approach based on
curative or preventive measures and seeking to promote social
hygiene is that it would be a scientific and rational mode of
crime control rather than a system of punishment (see Haksar
1963, 1965). The reasoning is that less value-judgments would
be made since the decisions to treat and deal with offenders in
particular ways would be purely technical questions based on
the diagnosis and prognosis of the professionally competent (see
Pearson 1975). But this would be to ignore that even a system of
prevention, whether it be punitive or treatment-oriented, is
required to stipulate which behaviours ought to be treated or
dealt with and that is a matter for moral judgment (Bean 1976;
Haksar 1963, 1965). The medicalisation of delinquency does
not thereby remove it from the context of moral discourse
(Pearson 1975).

Under the treatment approach, offenders are however seen as
being in need of treatment which is dictated by the 'nature' of
the condition and its supposed causes, not by reference to the
offence. The conception of human nature employed is essential-

ly deterministic with important implications for the means accepted as appropriate for dealing with offenders. The treatment model, for example, is often associated with the evolution of individualisation whereby measures are designed to meet the needs of the offender; it is also associated with the growth of discretionary powers available to those responsible for sentencing. Consequently, the treatment model in practice requires considerable information on the offender for the purpose of diagnosis and treatment and in this respect the link between such a philosophy and positivist criminology is obvious for a number of reasons (Hart 1968; Bean 1976). First, the positivist conception of the unity of scientific method has meant that offenders became the object of inquiry in an attempt to locate the 'causes' of criminality. Only by discovering such causes can crime ever be dealt with in a scientific and rational manner. What has been referred to as the deterministic position on crime (Radzinowicz 1965) and 'scientific ideology' has fostered the idea that the control and prevention of crime is better suited to a form of intervention based on scientific principles. The elimination of responsibility is therefore a logical consequence of a treatment philosophy in which criminality is considered to be the necessary outcome of predisposing conditions. That these conditions are subject to scientific inquiry, at least according to positivist criminology, further enhances the theoretical framework of positivism as a basis for crime control.

Moreover, positivist criminology sought to estabish general laws or generalities about the causes of criminal behaviour, thereby laying the basis for an argument that *preventive* action rather than simply curative action could be taken. Given that general statements could be made about what causes crime, then crime, as could illness or disease, could be predicted and anticipated. Wootton's work, as does that of others, conceives of criminality as a treatable condition not only similar to, but in actuality being, mental abnormality. But as we shall see later, the theoretical prescriptions about criminality or delinquency and their causes are not restricted to purely pathological formulations. What they all share however is the principle that offenders may not be justly punished since their actions are the result of causal antecedents beyond the realm of their control. That is, they are not punishable because they are not morally responsible.

Non-punitive Treatment. In terms of retributivist justifications of punishment, only those who are morally responsible can justifiably be punished for criminal behaviour. The conception of the offender as deserving his punishment and as having a right to punishment (MacCormick 1974) ultimately derived from the libertarian thesis that to have free will entailed having a will that is categorically free. Retributivism is by these criteria essentially backward-looking in that if focuses on the offence and the offender's capacity at the time of the offence for rational action.

But as we have seen, there are those who argue that the truth of determinism does not *ipso facto* preclude the possibility that individuals may still be held responsible for their actions. The justifications for punishment then which derive from this philosophy are radically different from the retributivist position though, again, this is not to imply that they are mutually exclusive either theoretically or practically. What may be broadly termed utilitarian justifications of punishment differ from the retributivist ones by being mainly goal- or end-oriented. That is, in opposition to the backward-looking character of retributivism, utilitarianism promotes a justificatory framework for punishment which is essentially forward-looking. The types of justification offered are mainly those of deterrence or reformation. And as we shall see, the utilitarian argument for bringing about some change in the offender through punishment was also developed into an argument that offenders could not be justifiably punished but were in need of help or treatment.

Utilitarian justifications of punishment can therefore be said to be forward-looking in that punishment can only be justified in terms of its beneficial consequences. The justification for punishment therefore rests in the value of its consequences, and the only valid reason for punishing is to prevent crime, not to seek to avenge it. Whereas the retributivist approach, founded in indeterminism, supported non-treatment punishment, the utilitarian perspective promotes treatment-punishment since punishment is end-oriented and forward rather than backward-looking. And though prevention may be the overall objective, the attainment of such an end can be achieved in a number of ways. Bentham argued that there were three major means of preventing crime: incapacitation, deterrence and reformation.

Earlier we saw that, according to Schlick and others, a man can be held responsible if his motives can be influenced favourably by reward or punishment. Schlick further argued that the question of a man's responsibility is the question of whether punishing him will have good effects. With reference to deterrence theory in particular, there does not appear to be the same controversy about free will and responsibility as with retributivist justifications (Honderich 1969, pp.127–31). Far from its being the case that deterrence is incompatible with causal accounts of human action, a number of philosophies have associated deterrence with some form of determinism. Since punishment in utilitarian terms is wholly a matter of preventing crime and attaining certain stated ends, it is quite reconcilable with the compatibility thesis on human action. Mill (1962), for example, argued that the human will was governed by motives and that the threat of punishment provided an additional motive for abstention from criminal behaviour. Both actual offenders and potential offenders could then be deterred by the prospect of certain punishment. More recently, the relationship between punishment and responsibility, echoing the arguments of advocates of the compatibility thesis, has been stated thus 'a man is not punishable because he is guilty; he is guilty because he is punishable' (Nowell-Smith 1954, p.51). It is by such an argument that utilitarianism has been defended against the commonplace retributivist claim that it allows for the punishment of the innocent, theoretically justifiable because of the beneficial consequences that may accrue. The possible consequences, claim the retributivists, could be used to nullify any injustices perpetrated in particular instances. But utilitarian justifications do impose limits on the scope and the extent of punishment in accordance with a principle of economy of threats (see Sprigge 1965). Punishment, if it does not and cannot serve to deter an offender cannot be justified, and it is in this respect that, for utilitarians, the question of how severely to punish is determined by the same criterion as the question of whether to punish at all (Moberley 1968). And since it is not the severity but the certainty of punishment that has a deterrent effect, only as much punishment is necessary or justified as will be sufficient to deter either actual or potential offenders (Beccaria 1963). Severity as a preventive of crime by itself may actually defeat its own ends, an argument which applies as much to punishment as an institution as it does for specific acts of punishment.

But there are also categories of offenders who cannot justly be the subject of punishment at all and who are not guilty because they 'are not punishable'. This is because in these instances, punishment can only be ineffective. Children, the mentally ill and the physically ill cannot be punished on utilitarian principles since they and their like are generally not susceptible to deterrence by threat. However, where children are considered punishable, such as those about the age of criminal responsibility, it could be argued that in certain cases, punishment is appropriate, though this may be as much for reasons of reformation as of deterrence. Likewise, the significance of excusing conditions is that, in this perspective, it would be meaningless and ineffective to punish anyone who acted under duress, mistake or who could claim any of the generally acceptable means of defence. The threat of penalties or sanctions could not deter anyone who found himself in such circumstances (Benn 1973). But in general such arguments serve to differentiate between those who could and those who could not be justly punished, not so much in terms of responsibility, though this is one factor (Watson 1976), as in terms of susceptibility to threats of punishment.

An important feature in utilitarian justifications of punishment, especially in regard to its deterrent function, is that punishment must serve as a warning and must therefore be as public as possible (see Moberley 1968). It would appear to follow logically that if a justification of punishment entails consideration of beneficial consequences such as deterring potential offenders, then punishment ought to be publicly displayed to have the maximum effect. The public denunciation of offences and offenders has been advocated by a number of authors (Beccaria 1963; Fitzjames Stephen 1883) and has undoubtedly influenced the development of most western systems of criminal law. As we saw earlier, the development of therapeutic or treatment philosophies for dealing with offenders has been paralleled by increasing attempts to eliminate the symbolic dimension of social control. This is nowhere more so than in the case of children, and provides an appropriate area of contrast between systems of juvenile justice that are court-based and more recent developments in favour of administrative tribunals.

Moreover, it need not necessarily be the case that deterrence theory is irreconcilable with other utilitarian justifications such as reformation, especially where the reformative influence can be said to apply to those other than the offender as well as the offender himself. Punishment may in fact reform through deterrence though this argument is aided by the difficulty of establishing what reform actually is.

In their concentration on the past act, retributive justifications for punishment tell us very little about the nature of punishment. And as we discussed earlier, the constituent elements of retribution echo the main principles of justice in their emphasis on proportionality and consistency (see Hart 1968). The maxim 'treat like cases alike' resembles retributive prescriptions as much as it does the basic tenets of the concept of justice. Theoretically, with reference to utilitarian justifications of punishment, the principles of consistency, proportionality and equality of treatment give way to the application of measures related to the personal characteristics of the offender with some end in mind. (See Watson 1976 for a concise statement of the areas of conflict between retributivism and utilitarianism.)

But to return to our earlier argument, deterrence can be construed as having a reformative effect. Ewing (1929), for example, suggests that whereas punishment as deterrence does not in itself 'reform', it does provide a means by which the criminal law will eventually be obeyed from moral motives and not just through habit. This applies both to actual and potential offenders, though in the case of the latter, Ewing's argument sounds more akin to psychological speculation than to philosophical theorising. (The opposing stance is taken by Benn (1958) who maintains that the reform of offenders cannot be attained through deterrence.) Conversely, reformation could be attained by means other than punishment such as education, vocational guidance or social work, none of which necessarily entail, though they may, the experience of distress or suffering which Flew considered one of the prime characteristics of the institution of punishment (Flew 1954; Honderich 1969).

We have seen that retributive justifications were essentially backward-looking, concentrating on the offence and the state of mind of the offender at the time of the offence. In contrast, utilitarian justifications, though they do not ignore the offence and rationality of the offender, were essentially forward-looking in that the consequences of punishment were employed in its justification. Thus, the protection of society, deterrence and the reformation of the offender are amongst the objectives propounded. However, inasmuch as even in retributivist philosophy some benefit does accrue, such as the annulment of wrong and the restoration of right, it could be, and has been, argued that retribution is merely disguised utilitarianism. Hart's argument that at different points in a legal system, different types of justification may be required, finds its parallel in a compromise theory of punishment. Gordon also argues that though the law is mainly utilitarian, because of its concern with the ordering of society, nevertheless because 'it is closely bound up with ordinary morality . . . it contains many deontological features' (Gordon 1978, p.48).

The historical significance of utilitarianism for both penal philosophy and criminological thought is that it laid the foundations, through the classical and neo-classical school, for the more therapeutic and treatment oriented developments that were to follow.

> The move toward a therapeutic response to crime can be seen as, at least in theory, an outgrowth of the utilitarian outlook. If one is going to evaluate punishment solely in terms of its social consequences – e.g. its capacity to reduce crime – one might reasonably reach the conclusion that therapy would do a better job of bringing those consequences about. (Murphy 1973, p.8)

Chapter Four

DETERMINISM AND
THE CAUSES OF CRIME

Formally, as we have seen, determinist accounts of action rely on concepts such as cause, predictability and the existence of invariable laws and are committed to an empiricist epistemology. Materially, however, there exists considerable divergence over what are the mechanisms through which causal sequences operate, i.e. what the causes of behaviour actually are. Different theoretical accounts of delinquency which assume determinism, in some form, postulate different mechanisms. This

> brings out a certain flexibility in the determinist position as outlined here. The determinist is not committed to the view that the causal laws governing human behaviour *must* be psychological, *must* be physiological, *must* be chemical or *must* be physical. All he claims is that there is some set of causal laws, at whatever level or levels of explanation, that entail tight-fitting predictions of human behaviour, and that there is no human behaviour that is in principle unpredictable on the basis of a knowledge of these laws and of the initial conditions in which they operate. (Glover 1970, p.45)

Thus, though the logic of determinism has had considerable influence, particularly through the development of positivist criminology (see Matza 1964; Taylor, Walton and Young 1973) a variety of perspectives have been adopted in the attempt to explain how delinquency and crime comes about. And again though there may be no consensus as to the appropriate measures, an approach to delinquency control through non-punitive treatment has been of particular significance in the development of a less punitive and less judicially oriented system of juvenile justice.

Indeed, the inability to locate objectively determined factors to account for delinquency has meant that formal systems of delinquency control have taken various forms and are continually under review. Because the difficulty in 'identifying' the causes of delinquency is more theoretical than practical, changes in the administrative and institutional structure of juvenile justice are usually dependent on emerging theoretical prescriptions on the causes of delinquency and how best to deal with it. Within a utilitarian framework, as in the neo-classical penology (Taylor, Walton and Young 1973), which has dominated courtroom and penal practice, the introduction of experts such as psychiatrists and social workers reflected the acceptance of information which could be used in mitigation without challenging the concept of responsibility fundamentally. But whereas penal practice has been dominated by such an approach, criminological and sociological research has been conducted within a more rigorous positivistic framework with all the assumptions about determinism and the rejection of responsibility implied therein. As Taylor, Walton and Young state (1973, p. 10) 'Periodically, the two models clash, and indeed, the debates about responsibility in penal philosophy bear testimony to the attempt of the classicists (Hart 1968) to resist the positivist incursions' (Wootton 1959; Eysenck 1970).

One of the implications of the treatment approach is that there exist those who know how to identify and how to treat the conditions or causes of criminality and delinquency. As in medicine there must be a diagnostic framework and conceptual apparatus which determines not only who is to be treated but also, just as importantly, who is to treat (Berger and Luckman 1971). With the medicalisation of delinquency, treatment can only be legitimately carried out by people qualified and familiar with particular bodies of knowledge and techniques. Thus, the ideological clash referred to by Taylor, Walton and Young finds expression in the lack of consensus about delinquency control displayed by the different agencies that compose and participate in social control networks (Asquith 1977). Treatment and meeting the needs of offenders are explicitly accepted within a theoretical framework which derives from a deterministic formulation of criminality. The conflict between justice and therapy is thus epitomised in the developments which have given responsibility for decision-making to experts who are more concerned with assessing, diagnosing and classifying deviants than with considerations of justice (Bean 1976). The paradox is that in many systems of justice resting on the treatment philosophy such responsibility is not given to experts but ultimately to lay people.

Though discussions of treatment often refer specifically to

the treatment of individuals by 'psycho-social' experts (Bean 1976), theories of delinquency do not always account for the phenomenon in terms of characteristics or properties intrinsic to the individual. It could be argued for instance that more recent developments in the sociology of crime and deviance, which are less concerned with factors in an individual's background, are for this very reason difficult to reconcile with a correctionalist approach to delinquency or crime control. Presented in the next section are brief statements of what are taken to be important orientations in theories of crime. These are

    i) Biological determinism
    ii) Behaviourism
    iii) Psychoanalytic determinism
    iv) Sociological determinism
    v) Processual determinism

Once again our concern is to identify possible available ideologies from which the working frames of relevance of lay members of the community may be derived. May (1971), Box (1971) and Giddens (1976) have all suggested the importance of formal theoretical prescriptions in informing the layman and in providing him with stereotypes of delinquency, as well as assumptions about causation. The significance of the five perspectives which will be discussed in rather crude simplistic terms is that they are all couched in the language of determinism (though they differ in substantive focus) in which conceptions of responsibility and considerations of punishment may not be easily accommodated. Again we are not suggesting that each logically tenable position is in fact held exclusively by individuals nor that the different orientations can be articulated by people such as panel members or magistrates. Rather, we wish to suggest that lay ideologies of delinquency causation and control may be informed to some extent by more formal theoretical considerations. In ordinary commonsense moral discourse, it may in fact be possible to identify elements of a number of the different orientations offered since logically tenable positions are not always maintained in practice.

Biological Determinism

Biological or physiological explanations of crime, associated with the development of positivist criminology, particularly the early work of Lombroso, have their roots in the wider implications of biologism for social theory. In reference to behaviour in general '. . . all biological explanations rest on the basic logic that structure determines function. Individuals behave differently owing to the fundamental fact that they are structurally different' (Vold 1958, p.43). There are basic 'constancies' (Pearson 1975) which can be identified in biological determinism.

A recurrent theme in the theories of the early biological determinists was the notion of biological inferiority or difference, notions which had both substantive and methodological implications. Thus in the work of Lombroso (1913) and Garofalo (1915), biological inferiority is an important principle. Lombroso, for example, attributes criminality to the 'atavistic' characteristics of offenders. That is, criminals were evolutionary throwbacks and criminality could be identified by the presence of physical 'stigmata' such as supernumerary nipples or unusual skull size. The nature of the biological differences are as varied as the theories but they all have in common the assumption that the criminal is biologically abnormal – different from or inferior to the law-abiding citizen.

With the emphasis on constitutional inferiority, it is not surprising to find that criminals were also conceived of as in some ways mentally as well as physically inferior. There has been a long tradition in criminology in which criminality has been associated with low intelligence or mental feebleness (Vold 1958). The implications of defects of reason or the will for the capacity of individuals to realise the nature and quality of their behaviour is obvious.

Derived as their theories were from Darwinism, the biological determinists placed great importance on heredity as a crucial factor in criminal aetiology (see Vold 1958). The more recent proponents of biological determinism have postulated specific factors as in the case of the XYY theory in which criminality is attributed to abnormal chromosal composition. And whereas Lombroso had sought evidence in the atavistic features of man, genetic and physiological studies have been a recurrent feature of biological explanations of crime (Healey 1915; Burt 1944; and see Sarbin and Miller 1970; Taylor, Walton and Young 1973).

Though the theories differ sustantively in the factors adduced as contributing to criminality, the importance of heredity is reflected in commonsense assumptions about crime causation. As Vold suggests 'Explanations . . . in terms of heredity go back to commonsense observations that children tend to resemble their parents in appearance, mannerisms and disposition. The popular adage "as father, so son" is a much older description of everyday folk knowledge than any scientific study of family influence' (1958, p.90). A criticism made by contemporary, new criminologists of biological determinism is that the search for characteristic differences between criminals and non-criminals rests upon what they consider to be a false assumption.

The 'earlier criminal type myths' categorised criminals in terms of their membership of different categories usually derived from the assumptions of the different theoretical frameworks employed. The very notion of the criminal type itself is derived from the logic of difference between offenders and non-offenders and depends as much on the notions of biological inferiority as on heredity. Perhaps the best example of 'typing' is in the relationship drawn by Kretschmer (1921 and later Sheldon (1940)) between criminality and body shape.

The development of biological determinism, associated as it was with the emergence of positivistic criminology had a number of implications. With the emphasis on difference or abnormality, heredity and types, the biological approach further emphasised the need to study the offender. Whereas the 'classical school had exhorted man to study justice, the positivist school had exhorted justice to study man'. Thus as well as providing theoretical accounts of the causes of crime, the biological determinists at the same time challenged the validity of legal concepts such as responsibility (see Ferri 1917) and, as Bean points out (1976), provided the entrée for a body of experts into the criminal justice system. The need to understand the offender became a constituent stage in the process of deciding to deal with him.

Behaviourism

The most important advance made by Eysenck (1970) and one which makes his theories more sophisticated than those of the early biological positivists is that he does not only set out to explain why people offend. Rather, he also seeks to establish how it is that people do not offend. His theory of human behaviour tells us as much about the process of socialisation as it does about the disposition to commit offences.

The early criminologists, but Lombroso less than others (Radzinowicz 1965), had largely ignored the influence of environmental factors (Morris 1957). But Eysenck's theory of criminality presupposes an interplay between genetic or biological constitution and more social or sociological factors. His conception of human nature is in that respect additive, the cumulative product of the influence of certain social forces such as the family on biological givens. It was on this element of Eysenck's work that Trasler (1962) was to construct his analysis of the apparent class bias in the distribution of criminality.

Behaviourist psychology assumes that aberrations in behaviour, such as neurosis or criminality, are not merely indications of some endopsychic conflict but are maladaptive responses acquired by a process of faulty learning. Criminal behaviour is but one maladaptive response.

Eysenck suggests that behaviour can be acquired by learning or by conditioning, susceptibility to which is related to the degree of extraversion displayed by an individual. It is by conditioning, or as Trasler (1962) calls it 'social learning' that values and attitudes of the social mores are acquired and which serve to check asocial or hedonic impulses. Criminality can then be explained as a phenomenon which occurs when there is a lack of social conditioning as a result of which the individual has no means of restraining himself from the pursuit of primary atavistic impulses.

Following Pavlov (1927), Eysenck attributes susceptibility to conditioning to physiological processes underlying behaviour (especially the mechanism of excitement and inhibition) and conceives of personality as linked to this biological endowment. Criminals or delinquents are characterised by high levels of neurosis and extraversion, which makes them biologically poor subjects for conditioning.

However, we would expect a random distribution of criminality amongst the population if conditionability were truly associated with endowment. As Trasler himself noticed, this does not appear to be the case and it is in his attempt to account for the apparent class bias in the distribution of criminality that he develops Eysenck's earlier position.

Socialisation, if it is adequate, should provide the child with the accepted behavioural repertoire and basic values of his social milieu. Trasler (1962) comments that a significant number of convicted offenders come from families of unskilled workers but that this is not to be taken to suggest that the values of this group are at variance with the rest of society. Techniques employed during socialisation must follow certain stipulations if it is to be adequate, and since this does not appear to be the case amongst those in lower socio-economic positions, their children will be more disposed to criminal and delinquent behaviour.

Trasler's argument is based on the notion that there is a marked difference between the child-training techniques employed by the middle classes and the lower classes. Because the distribution of extraversion is assumed to be fairly even, the higher incidence of criminality in certain sections of the community can be explained by reference to the way in which they rear their children. In particular, child-rearing techniques as practised by middle-class parents inculcate moral principles; working-class children are not however offered the same opportunity for acquiring general principles but are brought up in such a way as to relate punishment and reward to particular actions. The social avoidance responses which should occur on the contemplation of an idea or an intention to perform asocial actions can only be activated by a degree of autonomic response which the working-class child has not necessarily been induced to associate with such behaviour.

Since there is a higher incidence of broken homes in working-class areas, the child from such a background is more likely to be subjected to a very inconsistent programme of socialisation. On this argument it is not so much that coming from a broken home or a home in which there are considerable problems *ipso facto* determines that an individual will become delinquent or criminal. Rather, it is by living in circumstances in which there is an absence of proper parental care or in which such care is inconsistently administered that determines susceptibility to delinquency or criminality. Moreover, even where conditioning is technically effective, children in the process of socialisation may also quite simply learn anti-social values where these form an important element of the social and cultural milieu. The very social values offered to children may be antisocial in nature and in this way contribute to the class distribution of criminal and delinquent behaviour.

Derived as it is from Humean empiricism, behaviourism regards behaviour from a completely deterministic stance. 'The individual's behaviour is determined completely by his heredity and by the environmental influences which have been brought to bear upon him' (Eysenck 1970). In this respect, this theory can be associated with behaviourist philosophy in general (see Skinner 1973; Beach 1969).

Psychoanalytic Determinism

Despite their many differences, there are a number of points of fundamental similarity between psychoanalytic and behaviourist theories of crime or more correctly criminality. The psycho-analytic framework for example suggests the means by which the accomplishment of normal social behaviour is achieved and does not simply concentrate on delinquency or criminality. There is little analytical difference between 'normal' and 'abnormal' or deviant behaviour since psychoanalytic explanations of aberrant behaviour rest on the assumption that the very antisocial impulses which motivate a person to criminal behaviour are not absent in the law-abiding citizen (Vold 1958; Friedlander 1947; Glover 1960). As with behaviourism, explanations given of deviant or delinquent behaviour are derived from more general statements central to psychoanalytic theory about the process of socialisation. Delinquent behaviour can therefore be explained by the same rationale employed to account for apparent abnormal features or 'parapraxes' (Horney 1947) such as slips of the tongue. As we shall see, one importance of psychoanalytic theory has been that it helped underpin, especially through the work of people like Bowlby (1969), the notion of the family as a significant force in the growth and development of children. The growth of social work as a profession and the role it has played in attempts to control or meet the problems of delinquency can in part be attributed to its origins in a knowledge base that itself prompted ideologically attractive explanations of criminality (Bean 1976; Pearson 1975).

Despite the many varieties of psychoanalytic explanations of crime, what they have in common is the assumption that crime is the result of psychic conflict (Vold 1958; Friedlander 1947; Glover 1960). Most psychoanalytic theories of delinquency refer to the potential for conflict between the innate instinctual drives of the individual and the demands of a truly social life. Glover (1960) for example, attributes delinquency to the failure of 'domestication' of a naturally wild animal. Friedlander (1947) posits the imbalance of the psychic elements as the condition of which delinquency is but a manifestation. More prosaically, Aichorn (1936) sees antisocial behaviour as representing the 'coefficient of friction' between parental influences and the instincts of the child. An added factor in Aichorn's work is that his 'wayward' concepts refer to all children who display behavioural problems, not just delinquents.

A number of generalisations can be made about the way in which psychoanalytic theories characterise crime and account for the different mechanisms of failure in the socialisation process.

Rickman (1957) suggests that the instinctual drives can erupt and express themselves either directly or indirectly. Indirect expression involves a turning in of hostile attitudes on oneself with subsequent feelings of guilt and shame. Such feelings, he argues, can only be dissipated by infliction of some form of punishment, hence the drive towards asocial behaviour in general and delinquency in particular (see Vold 1958). More direct expression is associated with the inability of the individual to control his instinctual urges and prevent their expression in overt behaviour. Thus as well as the guilt-ridden and neurotic delinquent, Friedlander (1947) is also able to identify the un-socialised delinquent whose basic urges are allowed to run wild through faulty socialisation: 'Psychologically, their behaviour is due to the fact that they are still dominated by the pleasure principle instead of the reality principle' (p.110). Criminals then ought not to be viewed with respect to their position in society but as individuals with a particular way of dealing with their instinctual urges (Rickman 1932). Certainly, the picture that is often drawn in the literature of the delinquent is that of a person who is selfish, aggressive, hedonistic and emotionally infantile (see Glover 1960; Aichorn 1936; Friedlander 1947; Rickman 1957; Bowlby 1969).

What is important for psychoanalytic thought is that explanations of delinquency are historically and biographically rooted. The significance of this position is best epitomised by one of the more famous writers in this tradition – John Bowlby. His general thesis rests on the importance of the family and especially of the mother in the laying of foundations in the first year of life. Thus in 1951 he stated: 'It is submitted that the evidence is now such that it leaves no room for doubt regarding the general proposition – that the prolonged deprivation of the young child of maternal care may have grave and far reaching effects on his character and so on the whole of his future life' (1951, p.46). It was on this basis that he posited the notion of 'maternal deprivation' as the crucial factor in the disposition to delinquency and to other forms of psychological disturbance (see Bowlby 1969). Children who do not experience the bond of normal relationships with a mother or mother substitute are therefore more likely to develop a delinquent or disturbed personality. In particular, Bowlby and others (Bender 1947) had noted the fact that delinquents who were affectionless and could not sustain stable relationships with others, especially adults, had experienced traumatic separations from their mothers. They may also have experienced institutional care. It is perhaps at this point that the similarities between behaviourist and psychoanalytic theories of delinquency, particularly in reference to parental care and guidance, are most pronounced. Certainly, Bowlby and others (Glueck and Glueck 1950; Wootton 1959) had noticed the relationship between delinquency and the broken home. Friedlander (1947) had also perceptively argued that the significance of such factors as coming from a broken home were not so important in delinquent aetiology as the effect they had on character formation (see West and Farrington 1969).

Bowlby's work had highlighted the importance of the family, and especially the mother, in its effect on the growth and development of children. This had a number of implications. Since the mother-child relationship was considered important in delinquency causation, his theories not only presented an explanation of why people became delinquent but at the same time were employed to criticise the existing institutional arrangements for children in care. It is no surprise to find alternative suggestions in his work, especially in the direction of breaking children's homes up into smaller units, and the greater use of foster care (1969). Concern with the degree and quality of discipline afforded to children meant that the family increasingly became the focus for social work intervention. This was obvious in both the Kilbrandon and Seebohm reports alluded to earlier.

Just as important, however, was the fact that the psychoanalytic framework was used to promote preventive measures in an attempt to forestall delinquency. Again, this was a recurrent theme in the debates relating to the development of juvenile justice in this country. The organisational restructuring of social work both in Scotland and England was not simply in the interest of greater efficiency – it was also based on changing conceptions of social work and welfare provision and the role that could be played by early social-work intervention in preventing delinquency and other behavioural problems. The recent history of juvenile justice, as we have seen, reflects increasing acceptance of a conception of delinquency as symptomatic of some underlying disturbance and of the expansion of the role played by a profession whose ideological roots (Bean 1976) lay in psychoanalysis.

Sociological Determinism

There has been a long history of association between the causes of delinquency and such factors as broken homes and deprived areas which are commonplace in the public imagery of delinquent causation (May 1971). A number of authors have argued that the first real theoretical advances in constructing a 'scientific criminology' were made, not by the biological positivists but by early sociologists such as Mayhew (Taylor, Walton and Young 1973; Voss and Peterson 1971; Carson and Wiles 1971). In this section, we intend to discuss the core assumptions of the early sociologists of crime, especially the ecological perspective and briefly to trace some of the later sociological developments which were either derived from or emerged in opposition to the main tenets of human ecology.

There are a number of reasons for tackling this section in this way. First, it is by analysing the influence of positivism on the ecological perspective that we can more readily appreciate the conception of human nature as determined by environment. Secondly, the attempts of later sociologists to escape such environmental determinism can be seen as a response to the theoretical bankruptcy of ecology. Lastly, there have been more recent attempts to revive ecology, particularly for the purposes of urban sociology, under various guises, the most recent British effort being 'areal epidemiology' (Baldwin and Bottoms 1973).

Whereas the biological positivists had argued that the personality, and more specifically criminality, could only be studied in relation to genetic or constitutional make-up, the ecologists argued in turn that the social structure or cultural tradition of an area could only be analysed in reference to the local environment (Morris 1951; Voss and Petersen 1971; Taylor, Walton and Young 1973; Baldwin and Bottoms 1976). The cultural or social structure is imposed upon or epiphenomenal to the biotic substructure (Park 1936).

But by employing concepts drawn from plant ecology, the early Chicagoans (Park 1936) sought to articulate the relationship between the social organisation and distinctive physical characteristics of what they termed 'natural areas', by which they usually meant urban neighbourhoods. The healthy community was one characterised by homogeneity and social organisation with little disruption of social life; the pathological community was characterised by social disorganisation, evidenced by such factors as high rates of poverty, high rates of delinquency, and physical and moral deterioration. For Burgess, social disorganisation was the 'basic general fact'.

Though these pathological areas were seen as being isolated from the integrative values of the larger organism, the city, they were nevertheless themselves conceived of as communities in their own right with both structure and character: '. . . it is assumed that people living in natural areas of the same general type and subject to the same social conditions will display on the whole, the same characteristics' (Park 1936, p.36). It was the irreconcilability of 'pathology' and 'cultural diversity' within the ecological tradition that provided much of the impetus for later developments. Likewise, the explanation of social problems such as poverty and delinquency employed a conception of man as determined by environment (Alihan 1938; Morris 1957), a deterministic assumption which later sociology sought to dispel (Wrong 1971).

The more specific links between delinquency and criminality, and environment were made by Shaw and McKay (1942). Though the ecologists placed great emphasis on physical deterioration of areas and neighbourhoods, and though such areas were characterised by constant delinquency rates despite frequent changes of population, Shaw and McKay argued that it was not their belief that delinquency is caused simply by the external fact of location (Shaw and McKay 1942). A significant feature of their work is that their discussion of differences between communities related as much to attitudes, values and traditions as it did to physical attributes of natural areas (Voss and Petersen 1971). Similarly, their concern with the situational contingencies of life in these areas improved on the cruder determinism of Park. The emphasis of Shaw and McKay was on the social disorganisation of areas which displayed features such as continually changing population and physical deterioration. It was social disorganisation and the cultural transmission of values at odds with other communities which accounted for the ecological distribution of delinquency.

> The common element (among social factors highly correlated with juvenile delinquency) is social disorganisation or the lack of community effort to deal with these conditions . . . Juvenile delinquency, as shown in this study, follows the pattern of the physical and social structure of the city being concentrated in areas of physical deterioration and neighbourhood disorganisation. (Shaw and McKay 1942, p.xxvi)

Shaw and McKay then do not only attribute delinquency to physical environment but see it along with other factors as providing the context in which boys residing in areas with a high rate of delinquency are exposed to delinquency values (Voss and Petersen 1971). In areas of low delinquency rates, children are thereby exposed to conventional and anti-delinquent values; in high rate areas, children are presented with a variety of contradicting standards and forms of behaviour (1942, p.172) and 'powerful competing values' (1942, p.317). It has been argued that in this respect Shaw and McKay recognising the cultural diversity of areas were admitting not social disorganisation but differential social organisation (Voss and Petersen 1971). The inherent conflict between the concepts of 'pathology' and 'diversity' were never really resolved by them, a source of criticism of internal inconsistency made by Cloward and Ohlin later (1960). But the theoretical implication of this tension provided a baseline for later developments which recognised the inappropriateness of a consensus of values. Even Shaw and McKay cite Sutherland (1949) because of the similarity of their work with his theory of differential association (Carson and Wiles 1971; Voss and Petersen 1971).

What Sutherland had argued was that the cause of crime or deviance was an excess of definitions favourable to the violation of law over those definitions unfavourable to it. The notion of crime or deviance as learned behaviour recognised the theoretical bankruptcy of crime as individually (biological determinists) or socially (ecologists) pathological. At the same time, the emphasis attached to learning meant that differential association and differential organisation were to be readily accommodated within what Taylor, Walton and Young refer to as behaviourist revisionism.

Carson and Wiles also argue that the ecologists had prepared the way for Merton's theory of anomie, or at least had anticipated it because they 'speculated about the possible association of unconventional conduct with a discrepancy, particularly economic, between idealised status and practical prospects of its attainment' (1971, p.51). Thus what had originally been a source of internal inconsistency in the work of the ecological school did in fact result in a number of developments which concentrated on the transmission of culture in a framework of 'ecological pluralism'. The works of Sutherland (1949), Cloward and Ohlin (1960) are all seen as being related to the ecological school either through direct heritage or in reaction to some of the major principles contained in their theories (Voss and Petersen 1971; Carson and Wiles 1971; Morris 1957; Taylor, Walton and Young 1973).

Equally importantly, the growth of interest in the cultural transmission of deviant values gave rise to the important tradition in delinquency theory which concentrated on the origin of delinquent subcultures. Particularly prominent in this is Cohen (1955; 1966). Whether children came to learn delinquent values which competed and conflicted with more conventional values was the source of debate to be found not only in Cohen's work but also in that of Matza, Sykes and Matza (1957), Miller (1958), Cloward and Ohlin (1960) and Downes (1966) amongst many others.

What writers such as Shaw and McKay had appreciated, and what was taken up in these other developments in sociology, was that the emergence of crime and delinquency required some theoretical conception of the cultural transmission of a criminal tradition: 'The ecologists were not just painting elaborate backgrounds against which deviants could strut. They were trying to provide links between dilapidated houses and gang life, between population density and delinquency, between physical deterioration and moral deterioration' (Taylor 1971, p.128).

Biological and personality theories of crime had in the main posited internal forces as the determinants of delinquency and criminality and as the means by which delinquents could be differentiated from non-delinquents. Though more sociologically oriented theories do attempt to relate the individual to his environment, whether symbolic or physical, they are themselves generally no less deterministic or positivist but have merely relocated the search for causes. One of the more significant contemporary problems in sociological theory is the attempt to evolve a theory of society and man which reconciles the competing concepts of voluntarism and determinism (Giddens 1976). It was just this failure of the ecological school and of later sociologies to articulate the relationship between man and his environment that makes them subject to the criticism of determinism (Alihan 1938; Taylor, Walton and Young 1973; Matza 1964). Even in subcultural theory, the nature of constraint is only different in content, not in form, from biological or personality theories. Matza states: 'It is ironic that the sociological view which began as a protest against the conviction that the delinquent was something apart has managed again to thrust the delinquent outside the pale of normal life. Such is the force of the positivist determination to find and accentuate differences' (1964, p.18).

Processual Determinism

In this section we shall consider what has variously been called labelling theory, interactionism, social reaction theory and social control theory. Though there are subtle differences between the statements presented by the main theorists it is what is common to their work that is our concern here: the relativity of the concept of deviance and the importance of the notion of process. Just as importantly, it is argued that attempts to confront the problem of delinquency or deviance, far from alleviating it may well aggravate or perpetuate the phenomenon since social control either leads to or creates deviance. Any adequate analysis of deviance must then focus on the nature of social control in the processing of deviance which is conceived of as 'some sort of transaction between the rule breaker and the rest of society' (Cohen 1966).

Deviance is not only objectively but also subjectively problematic since as we shall see, a major area of concern for labelling theory was the influence of societal reaction or social control in the commitment to deviance. The importance of such a position is concisely stated by Kitsuse: 'I intend to shift the focus of theory and research from the forms of deviant behaviour to the processes by which persons come to be defined as deviant by others' (1963, p.247). Lemert likewise argues: 'The task of sociology is to study not the theoretical "stuff" of delinquency but the process by which a variety of behaviours in context are given the unofficial and official meaning that is the basis for assigning a special status in society' (1967, p.24). The focus of the labelling theorists, and the orienting bias of the sociology of deviance is to the forms of social reaction and the processing of deviance. Becker again argues that 'Social groups create deviance by making the rules whose infraction constitutes deviance . . . From this point of view, deviance is not a quality of the act the person commits, but rather a consequence of the application by others of rules or sanctions to an offender' (1963, p.9). For that reason alone Becker and others are less concerned with the social or personal characteristics of offenders than with the process by which they came to be labelled outsiders. Thus the very notion of deviance itself is based on the presupposition of norms or social rules whose infraction evokes reactions that are in themselves influential in the development of a deviant character. Nor is this in theory a one-sided determinism (Gibbs 1966; Taylor, Walton and Young 1973) since the relationship between the rule violator and the agents of social control whether they be teachers, policemen or social workers is one of interaction. It is the dialectic of social control and self that provide the basis for commitment to deviance since the concept of self maintained by the individual and his long-term behaviour may be modified as a result of contact with the agents of social control (Schur 1971). Whereas more traditional criminologists had conceived of delinquency or criminality as something that could be *de*scribed and observed, in true empiricist fashion, the labelling theorists identified deviance as an *a*scribed status.

The relevance of this for the study of deviance is that since the self is socially located, contact with systems of social control can in fact have a negative effect on the rule-breaker's self image. The alleged deviant may come to conceive of himself, and thereby alter his behaviour accordingly, in terms of the very reactions presented to him by the agents of social control. Farrington (1977) provides empirical evidence to the effect that the labelling process can itself lead to the likelihood of further delinquency. Even where the alleged delinquent has not committed the acts which have evoked a hostile reaction, such is the potency of social redefinition that it may still be powerful in promoting a negative self image (Becker 1963; Taylor, Walton and Young 1973). The transformation of self or the re-negotiating of identity is more readily accommodated within a framework which espouses a model of deviance as sequential or processual. The analysis of deviance in this respect has benefited from concepts employed in other sociological fields, especially those of career, career contingencies, and master and auxiliary traits (see Hughes 1944; Lemert 1967).

Above we suggested that labelling theory does not focus exclusively on the societal reaction or definition. This was for the following reason. The labelling approach emphasises the importance of the social reaction in the development of a self image (Erikson 1962). However, it does not entirely ignore the precipitating factors (Schur 1973), those factors which contributed to the commission of a deviant act in the first place. In this way rather paradoxically, Schur (1973) and others (Lemert 1967) do not deny the relevance of the types of factors postulated by the earlier criminologists but suggest that their importance has been rather overstated. We then have the anomalous position whereby deviant commitment can be, and theoretically has to be, explained in terms of the social reaction approach. The commission of initial acts of deviance, however, on which the social reaction is based is to be explained in a different way. This parallels Lemert's distinction between (i) primary deviation, the original causes of the deviant attributes which he suggests are polygenetic, i.e. they arise out of a variety of social, cultural, psychological and physiological factors. These have little influence on the transformation of self; and (ii) secondary deviation, by which he means 'a special class of socially defined responses which people make to problems created by the societal reaction to their deviance' (1967). Importantly, secondary deviance refers to the person and his commitment to further deviance whereas primary deviance refers only to his acts and not to the reorganising of psychic structure. The influence of the social psychological assumptions of Mead is obvious.

Critical as were others of what he termed the 'crude sociologistic determinism of Becker and Erikson', the distinction made by Lemert was devised to confront two different research problems: how deviant behaviour originates and how deviant acts are symbolically attached to persons and the consequences that these have for future acts of deviance. The polygenetic factors, the subject of a very different methodological strategy are less important than adverse social reaction which as secondary deviance evokes deviance commitment. The potential that such an analysis has for research into deviance, or more correctly deviation, is in fact that deviance is a consequence of social control (Schur 1973). Social control becomes the independent variable and though primary deviation cannot be explained in this way, secondary deviation can. And, in referring to the psychic structure of the deviant, Lemert is thereby explaining the nature of deviant commitment, a process attained by the realignment of self. In reference to the operation of the juvenile court, Lemert adds that 'we assume that deviation qualitatively changes in relation to the processing and to the impact of the court and other agencies who take control over the child. Deviation becomes secondary in nature and in a real sense deviation begets deviation' (1970, p.59). One of the implications of all this is that attempts to control deviance by extending the scope of social control may well have quite the opposite effect, either on individuals or on areas. In consequence, a more appropriate policy would be to restrict the sphere of social control in an attempt to reduce the potential for secondary deviation. It is such a proposal that Schur makes in suggesting radical non-intervention (1973) and Lemert in advocating judicious non-intervention (1970). The theoretical significance of the perspective as a whole, despite the misgivings that have been voiced (Gibbs 1966), was its relocation of the focus of criminology on the very nature of social control itself. Though often referred to as 'transactionalism' or 'interactionist perspective' most of the discussions focus on social control and social reaction as determinants of deviance. Akers epitomises the one-sidedness of the approach: 'One sometimes gets the impression from reading this literature that people go about minding their own business and then 'wham' – bad society comes along and slaps them with a stigmatised label. Forced into the role of deviant, the delinquent has little choice but to be deviant' (Akers 1967, p.46, quoted in Taylor, Walton and Young 1973, p.149). Now this is a criticism that can also be made of other determinist perspectives but for present purposes it serves to identify the inability of the social reaction approach to transcend the simplistic mechanistic explanations we have already discussed above (see Mankoff 1971). The social-reaction theorists failed to achieve the dictates of what Matza termed the naturalist perspective in that despite statements to the contrary, they fail theoretically to offer deviants a choice in a framework that can be characterised as processual determinism.

PART TWO

EMPIRICAL STUDY

Chapter Five

FRAMES OF RELEVANCE:
METHODOLOGICAL IMPLICATIONS

So far we have examined 'available ideologies' and the extent to which they find expression in formal systems of social control. We now consider the significance of the apparent ambiguity between welfare and more legalistic approaches to delinquency control, and begin by comparing the frames of relevance employed by panel members (in Scotland) and juvenile magistrates (in England) in the process of interpreting information and the making of decisions. In the early research literature on the operation of the Children's Hearings system in Scotland (May 1971; Smith and May 1971; Mapstone 1972) much was made of the fact that juvenile justice in that country would be subject to the stereotypes and typifications of lay people, i.e. the panel members. Yet, in many respects, though there are of course important differences between juvenile magistrates and panel members they share a number of similarities. Not least is the fact that juvenile magistrates are themselves 'lay persons', though the process of selection and training may differ from that experienced by panel members.

Panel Members

The Kilbrandon Committee in its rejection of the juvenile court (based in part on the inappropriateness of the skills of the judiciary for making decisions about the welfare of children) was thereby committed to establishing alternatives. The committee had recommended that the Sheriff in each area should be charged with the duty of appointing a sufficient number of persons who were in his opinion 'specially qualified either by knowledge or experience to consider children's problems' (para. 92(a). What makes the choice of the Sheriff as the person to bear this responsibility particularly surprising is that all along the report had claimed that the judiciary did not have the skills necessary for dealing with children. Yet, the proposal meant that reliance would be placed on the ability of the judiciary to select people who did have the appropriate skills. The fact that delinquency was conceived of as a behavioural condition and not a legal status makes this even more surprising. This was altered in the white paper *Social Work and the Community* (Cmnd 3065), which also emphasised the desirability of the involvement of the community in meeting the problems that arose within it. Panels were to be composed of people 'drawn from a wide variety of occupation, neighbourhood, age group and income group' (para.76) and acquainted with the neighbourhood from which the child came. Moreover, panel members were to be 'suitable people whose occupations or circumstances have hitherto prevented them from taking a formal part in helping and advising young people' (para.76).

The difficulty in selecting panel members who were both 'representative' of the community and were 'suitable' (which was never clearly defined) was an issue that was given considerable attention later (see Spencer 1973; Smith and May 1971; Asquith 1977). Analyses of the applications and membership were later all to reveal that neither initial applicants nor successful applicants were representative of the community (see Mapstone 1972; Moody 1976; Smith and May 1971).

What is particularly interesting is that though the language of therapy, pathology and the medical analogy pervade the Kilbrandon Report, the ultimate responsibility for decision-making was not to rest with 'experts' or 'professionals'.

The recommendation made in the Kilbrandon Report was specifically for 'lay' membership of the proposed panels and seems to have been made more in terms of the negative aspects of the judicial framework for dealing with children. What the arguments were for 'lay' membership are not particularly clear and this is reflected in a telling statement produced later:

> It is unnecessary for members of panels to be expert social workers. The expertise necessary in their work will be supplied by the local authority's social work department. Members will, however, need a good knowledge of treatment methods and of facilities available for applying them . . . Many people will lack some of this knowledge and experience. Panel members will therefore require a certain amount of training, and it is proposed that at the outset this training will be arranged for them by the local authority.
> (Social Work and the Community 1966, para.80)

There are two comments that can be made here. First, though the panels are to make decisions about the children's needs, it is the duty of the social work department to provide the appropriate measures of care. There does then seem to be an element of conflict in that if the provision of appropriate measures of care is a professional task, the identification of need and the decision about what measures are to be applied would also seem to call for professional social-work expertise. Indicative of the lack of a consistently stated conceptual framework is the fact that whereas the Kilbrandon Report envisaged that a Social *Education* Department was the appropriate agency to deal with delinquent children, it was only in the White Paper of 1966 that the Social *Work* Department was proposed as being appropriate (though Morris (1974) rightly points out that the notion of social education contained in the Kilbrandon Report may not differ fundamentally from what is usually implied by 'social work'). Secondly, the distinction between 'lay' and 'professional' becomes somewhat blurred. We suggested earlier that in the social control network no particular frame of relevance necessarily had any prior claim to validity.

Comment has already been made (Smith and May 1971) on the difficulty of selecting not only those who would be 'suitable' panel members but also those who would be 'representative' of the community since dealing with delinquency was conceived of as a process involving community participation. Though 'representativeness' has certainly not been achieved (Spencer 1973), the criterion of 'suitability' is not without its problems. There being no professional agency envisaged, there is theoretically no professional frame of relevance by which the selection of panel members can be determined. Nevertheless, they are expected to have some knowledge and experience of children's problems and in the absence of clearly stated criteria of 'suitability' the influence of the professions in the process of selection and training has turned out to be of particular significance. Since panel members 'require a certain amount of training' (see above), successful applicants will then go through a programme of instruction, visits to institutions, lectures from interested individuals who have either experience in behavioural problems of children or general social work experience or who have conducted research on the system, and workshop or seminar type discussions on the role of the panel member (see Martin and Murray 1976). What is obvious is that in the training of panel members several professional bodies are involved and not just the social work profession.

We have suggested earlier (Asquith 1977) that the distinction

between 'lay' and 'professional' status is perhaps best represented by points on a continuum and not in terms of mutually exclusive categories. The significance of this is that though not a
professional, the panel member has to assess and interpret information and material from a number of professional organisations. Moreover, the only measures for dealing with children
who commit offences, supervision at home or residential supervision, will involve such organisations, particularly social
work. The move away from a punitive non-treatment approach
has then in Scotland resulted in a system of juvenile justice in
which an administrative form of tribunal manned by lay persons is serviced and provided with information from a number
of ancillary services. (The Children's Hearings are in fact subject to the same statutory requirements and rules as are other
forms of tribunals, e.g. Supplementary Benefits Tribunal, Rents
Tribunal etc.)

Juvenile Magistrates

Cavenagh points out that the development of the juvenile
court, as we have seen, has been continual in the light of grow-
ing experience and of increased knowledge about children
(1966). The advances in knowledge and understanding of child
development and the social and emotional factors involved in
child delinquency has meant a greatly increased role for the
child care and social services. It was precisely because of the
inappropriateness of decisions about the welfare of children
being made by the judiciary that the Kilbrandon Report had
recommended the creation of a new body of individuals who by
virtue of their expertise or personal qualities were to be successful in their application for panel membership. In England, however, with the retention of the juvenile court it would have been
difficult to construct an argument for relieving magistrates of
their duties in the juvenile court. Yet since the 1969 Children
and Young Persons Act one of the concerns voiced by magistrates is that they are losing the power to make decisions about
the welfare of children. The social services department has in
fact been granted the right in a number of cases to determine the
nature of the measures to be adopted for particular children. In
relation to Care Orders for example the magistrates can only
decide whether to commit a child to the care of the local authority or not; their decision is not about the nature of the care
considered appropriate. The relationship between the social
services, the magistracy and the juvenile justice system in

general in England then is a very different one from that between the social work department, the panel members and the
Scottish system.

One of the areas in which the respective systems differ is that
whereas in Scotland the Hearings are held in buildings completely unassociated with and divorced from the courts *and* the
police, in England the police may actually conduct the prosecution in a case and play a considerable role in conducting the
affairs of the court. The police in England and Wales are then
more involved in the actual operation and administration of
juvenile justice as conceived within the framework of the 1969
Children and Young Persons Act. The broader implication of
this for the present study is that the organisational network in
the respective systems is characterised by a number of potentially competing ideologies to which different agencies (panel
members and magistrates, the police, social work profession
etc.) might adhere in varying degrees.

We saw that panel members are meant to be, as far as possible,
both 'suitable' and 'representative'. Though this has obviously
caused some concern north of the border (Spencer 1973; Smith
and May 1971), precisely the same issue has been important in
the selection of persons to the magistracy in England.

Magistrates are to be suitable in point of 'character, integrity
and understanding' (Magistrates Association 1975, para.2).
Moreover, the Advisory Committee, responsible for selection
and training in the different areas 'must not only recommend
suitable people but they must also make sure that each Bench is
broadly representative of all sections of the community it has to
serve' (para.10). What is implicit in this ideal is more than the
suggestion that the Bench should be representative; it also
brings into relief the way in which the selection process itself
can influence the profile of the Bench in a particular area. For
example, the Royal Commission on the Justices of the Peace
commented on the political nature of the selection made and
recommended that each committee should see to it that there
be no political bias in the composition of the Bench.

Similarly, the Royal Commission had also pointed out (para.
232) that 71 per cent of all magistrates were either non-employed,
professional men or employers and only a small proportion were
wage earners (see Hood 1962).

Magistrates may not be appointed to the Bench for the first
time if they are over 60 and indeed the Magistrates Association
(1975) urges the recruitment of younger magistrates. Lord

Hewart, Lord Chief Justice, as long ago as 1935 commented, with specific reference to the juvenile court: 'Is it not desirable that magistrates in these juvenile courts should be of parental age, varying from 40–60 rather than of the grandfatherly period which runs from 60 to a happily distant future'. What also has to be remembered in this respect is that only those who are magistrates in the adult court can be magistrates in the juvenile court. Magistrates are thus required to deal with diverse issues and are not, in the case of juvenile court, exclusively concerned with the deeds or needs of children.

Given that the development of the juvenile court has been in association with increasing commitment to the need for specialised expertise in dealing with the problems of children, training of successful nominees would appear at least *prima facie* to be of extreme importance. Indeed since January 1966 it has been obligatory for all magistrates to take basic training. Panel members as we have seen are also offered training but because of the different objectives related to their task, the training in general differs. Magistrates, whether in the adult or in the juvenile court, not only sentence but, rather obviously, also decide on what may be called the 'allegation issue'. That is, they must also determine responsibility or liability in offence cases. Basic training 'is designed to enable them to understand the nature of their duties, to obtain sufficient knowledge of the law to follow normal cases, to acquire a working knowledge of the rules of evidence and to understand the nature and purposes of sentences' (Magistrates Association 1975). Magistrates are required to familiarise themselves with the basics of legal and judicial procedure, as well as the issues relating to sentencing, though in the 1948 Royal Commission Report it was recognised that it would be difficult, if not impossible, to give the lay magistrate considerable knowledge of extensive and complex law. It is for that very reason that Hood (1962) highlights the importance of the Clerk of Court.

One important difference between the role of panel members and that of juvenile magistrates is that, as well as working within a more legal and judicial form of proceedings, magistrates can in fact do a lot more than commit juvenile delinquents to the care of the local authority. They can in fact adopt punitive measures. At the time of the study, magistrates had amongst their options

    i) An order for the parent or guardian to enter into
       recognisance to take proper care of the juvenile;

    ii) A hospital or guardianship order;
    iii) A fine;
    iv) An attendance centre order;
    v) A detention centre order;
    vi) Committal of young person of not less than fifteen
years old to the Crown Court with a view to Borstal
training being imposed;
    vii) Absolute Discharge;
    viii) Conditional Discharge subject to the condition
that he commits no offence during a period not exceeding
three years;
    ix) Supervision Order placing the juvenile under the
supervision of the local authority; and
    x) Care Order placing the child or young person in the
care of the local authority.

Unlike the Residential Supervision requirement in Scotland, the Care Order is not an order for residential care though that may indeed be the outcome. As with the Supervision Order, the decision as to what form supervision or care may take is the responsibility of the social services department.

The general point to be made however is that the conceptual ambiguity inherent in the control or the care of delinquent children is reflected in the availability to magistrates of different forms of proceedings (care or criminal) and different types of measures. Whether in practice there were any real differences between juvenile justice in Scotland and England was one of the questions we sought to examine empirically. Before turning to a consideration of the major questions considered in the study we wish to state our scepticism at a recent statement that suggests that 'the type of tribunal (juvenile or welfare tribunal) is largely unimportant. What is crucial is the philosophy underlying that tribunal and the ideology of its practitioners' (Morris and McIsaac 1978, p.111).

Our belief is that any examination of the 'ideology of practitioners' must of necessity be theoretically related to the construction or accomplishment of social institutions such as juvenile court or welfare tribunal.

The Present Study: Objectives

We refer to those factors which relate to children's 'needs' or 'interests' as welfare factors; thus the personal, social or environmental background of the child are considered to be 'welfare' factors. Statements which allude more to the offence and the nature of the child's involvement in it are referred to as judicial factors. These of course are rather vague and at the same time rather restrictive concepts. Indeed the potential for conceptual ambiguity underpinning systems of juvenile justice makes it difficult to separate welfare or judicial orientations, punishment or treatment, and care and control. However, we use the distinction to examine the practical accomplishment of juvenile justice within systems of which, in organisational and structural terms, one is more judicially oriented than the other.

First, given that panel members, in theory at least, only decide upon the need for compulsory measures of care and the form that such measures should take, a prime objective was to compare the extent to which panel members and magistrates deployed welfare factors in the decision-making process. Since magistrates must pay more attention to judicial considerations such as the nature of the offence and the degree of culpability of the offender, it was expected that welfare considerations would for them be less important. Once again though, as later analysis of the data confirmed, such ready distinctions between welfare and judicial considerations can not be readily drawn since how information about a child is used is determined by the frame of relevance adopted by the decision-maker.

Secondly, given the close association between the development of juvenile justice and social work with its emphasis on theories of human behaviour derived from a psychoanalytic base, we treated as an empirical question the extent to which a psychoanalytic framework was employed by panel members and magistrates. The involvement of social-work professionals in the selection and the training of panel members and magistrates suggested that it would be important. Indeed, a book recommended for use by panel members contains a chapter on 'Theories of Delinquency' almost exclusively devoted to psychoanalytic explanations of delinquent behaviour (Martin and Murray 1976).

Thirdly, because magistrates are obliged to consider the 'allegation issue' and because they can punish, we expected (and set out to examine this question empirically) that they would place greater importance than panel members on the question of personal responsibility, the seriousness of the offence and the need to protect society. This is of course in a sense the corollary of the first objective in that it relates more to a conceptual framework derived from 'judicial' ideology than a welfare one. In part, such considerations are also located within a theoretical framework which can be used to justify punishment. However, as we have seen there is no easy opposition of punishment and welfare. The purpose then was not simply to examine whether magistrates were more or less punitive than panel members but rather to examine how magistrates and panel members would resolve the potential for conceptual ambiguity of dealing with offences within a welfare ideology given the different organisational structures of the respective systems of juvenile justice.

Finally, since decision-making about delinquents in Scotland and England takes place within very different structural and organisational arrangements, a major objective was to determine whether any significant differences could be identified and what implications, if any, these had for the accomplishment of juvenile justice.

The concern here was to treat as an empirical question the significance of the different structures for the making of decisions about children who commit offences and not to make any *a priori* assumptions to the effect that the nature of the hearing had little bearing on the outcome (see Morris and McIsaac 1978).

The basic methodological problem was that of gaining access to individuals' own assumptions about delinquency causation and control without imposing too much of the researcher's own beliefs and values in the process of the research. The difficulty was compounded since, as we wished to examine the nature and process of the different types of hearing, we would be confronted by the fact that three (always in Scotland and generally in England) people would be involved in the decision-making process. That is, though our concern was with informal ideologies as espoused by individuals, it was apparent that we would have to recognise that the attempt to reach a decision was a collective and not simply an individual affair.

Sentencing Research: a review

Because of the similarities in sentencing problems in the context of the adult criminal justice system and the juvenile court, it was decided to refer to research relating to both. This is not of course to deny that there are differences between the processes involved in the sentencing of adults and of children, particularly in relation to the type of alternatives available. Where they are similar however is in the conflict between the potentially competing ideologies of welfare and of control. Grünhut, in developing the theme of the association between the juvenile and the adult courts suggests: 'Even the treatment of adult criminals has, in the principal approach rather than in legal forms and statutory provisions, been influenced by the experience gained in juvenile courts' (1956, p.1).

The predominant concern of much sentencing research has been to account for the apparent disparity in sentencing decisions (Hogarth 1971). The implication has generally been that 'disparity' is not desirable in as much as it is taken to indicate that, in some senses, 'justice' means something along the lines of 'treating like cases alike'.

But such a principle would have been comparatively easier to maintain within a classical framework for sentencing, and as has been pointed out 'the problem of sentencing disparity is closely related to the post-classical emphasis on individualised justice, which has regards to the needs of the individual offender, in contrast to the mechanical juridical emphasis on the nature of the offence' (Bottomley 1973, p.132).

'Treating like cases alike' actually tells us very little about the criteria which are to be adopted in deciding the 'likeness' of cases as it is merely a formal, logical imperative for the attainment of justice; it offers no account of 'likeness' which must be explained by reference to the material or substantial element in the notion of justice (Lloyd 1964; Perelman 1963). Under classical doctrine, with its emphasis on free will and responsibility, the 'likeness' of cases could be decided by reference to such criteria as the nature of the offence.

With the development and acceptance of individualised justice, the criteria by which cases can be said to be alike (the material element of justice) become 'need' criteria. That is, important factors as a basis for sentencing decisions are factors relating to the needs of individual offenders and not simply to what Green referred to as legal factors such as the type of offence, seriousness of offence or culpability of the offender (Green 1961). But there are two problems here which have significance for much sentencing research.

First, the development of individualised justice, of taking the offender's needs into consideration for the purposes of sentencing, has not wholly been at the expense of more traditional objectives in sentencing. Rather, the criminal justice system has become something of a hybrid in that sentencing decisions may well reflect punitive considerations as much as rehabilitative ones. The history of the development of juvenile justice in terms of the merits of court or tribunal, punishment or treatment has been in this respect a history of compromise (Morris and McIsaac 1978).

Difficulties in stating the objectives of the criminal justice system which would generally be accepted are then compounded by the development of rehabilitative considerations. As suggested by one commentator, the sentencer(s) may in fact have to make two types of decisions; a 'primary' and a 'secondary' decision (Thomas 1967). A 'primary' decision is the decision made as to what framework is the more appropriate for a sentencing decision, tariff or individualised justice. Once that decision has been made, a secondary decision has to be made as to what is the appropriate decision within the framework chosen.

Secondly, that offenders' needs are to be taken into consideration is by no means a straightforward principle because of the difficulty of establishing not just what offenders' needs generally are, but also what a particular offender's needs are. As we have seen, research into the 'causes' of crime or delinquency has been singularly unfruitful in providing objective criteria establishing the causes of delinquency or criminality. Consequently, there are no clear or agreed upon guidelines as to the 'needs' of offenders. Moreover, and certainly related to what has just been said, research into the 'effectiveness' of different types of rehabilitative measures has likewise been somewhat disappointing, adding to the very complexity of the sentencing task. (Indeed, the very lack of objective criteria about the 'causes' of delinquency has meant that formal systems of delinquency control are continually under review.)

Much of sentencing research, with notable exceptions, has largely focused on identifying factors which might explain the apparent disparity that appears in sentencing. It has become more than problematic simply to assert that sentencers lack uniformity or consistency, or that sentencing patterns reveal inequalities, because it is difficult to appreciate the factors the sentencer takes into consideration, the goals he hopes to achieve, and the reasons for his decision. Sentences which may, *prima facie*, indicate a degree of disparity may in fact be attributed to the unique circumstances associated with the case; on the other hand uniformity and consistency of sentencing may well be due to the ignoring of the unique features of different cases. The logical implication of the principle of 'treat like cases alike' is that cases that are unlike in important respects should be treated differently. *Prima facie* disparity or inconsistency may well reflect the acceptance of the premises on which indi-

vidualised justice is based. Once again the relevance of information for making decisions about children who commit offences
is to be treated as an empirical question.

The particular methodologies adopted by different researchers are determined by the search for factors to account for
'disparity'. Since our concern is to identify the significance of
frames of relevance for the decision-making process, the appropriateness or adequacy of methodological strategies employed
in earlier research is for us as important as the conclusions
reached.

What is particularly interesting then is that many researchers
have in fact claimed that disparity can only be explained by
reference to the human element though they had neither collected information on the interpretation of information by individual magistrates nor on the actual processes of the court
hearing and the communication involved. Yet the conclusion
often drawn has been that in the absence of any identifiable
factors disparity, or variation, can be attributed to some indefinable element such as the 'personality of the judge' even
though the methodologies employed only allowed conclusions
about how individuals make decisions to be made at the level of
oblique inference. As examples of such studies we would include Grünhut (1956) who referred to magisterial preference for
particular disposals; Mannheim, Spencer and Lynch (1957) who
identified 'intuitive assessment' as a prime factor; Hood (1962)
who speculated about the 'policies' of magistrates; and Patchett
and McLean (1965) who pointed to the differences in the
approaches adopted by magistrates as significant variables in
accounting for apparent disparity. Other studies where sentencing practice was the focus of inquiry and where similar
conclusions were reached would include Gaudet (1949) and
Green (1961).

In the Scottish Children's Hearing system, Morris and Mc-
Isaac (1978) argue that, despite the formal commitment to a
welfare philosophy, panel members and others in the system
make decisions on the basis of more classical and punitive
considerations. Panel members may in fact operate with a disguised form of tariff decision-making where considerations of
the offence, the child's involvement in it and so on become
relevant criteria.

The notion of the 'facts' of the case being objectively given
also ignores what Hogarth refers to as the 'selective perception'
of judges. That is, by adopting a methodological strategy that

is grounded in the assumption that sentencing decisions can be accounted for by simply analysing the information about the offence and/or offender, much sentencing research is insensitive to the way in which judges interpret such information. As has been noted elsewhere (Asquith 1977) such strategies treat the idea of what constitutes 'relevant' information as non-problematic. But a difficulty is that what the researcher chooses as his relevant independent variables may not be the same variables chosen for the purpose of sentencing. What we have suggested earlier is that information has to be assessed and interpreted in order to sift out what is relevant for the task at hand. However, the 'system of relevancies', to use the Schutzian notion (Schutz 1970), or the 'frames of relevance' of the researcher and subject will be different. The danger is that explanations of how sentencing decisions are made are premised more upon what the researcher rather than the sentencer determines to be relevant. The two purposes, that of sentencing and that of doing research into sentencing, are different.

Moreover, there is no guarantee that the only information employed for the purpose of sentencing is contained in the records or official sources. By designing methodologies to analyse what 'facts' are associated with decisions, researchers generally have omitted from their studies any consideration of information provided but not recorded, such as information gleaned in the course of discussion in court. Similarly, little consideration has been given to the question of how information is used. Most researches have been designed to examine 'what' questions and not 'how' questions, and in that sense it could be argued that much sentencing research has been primarily concerned with 'decisions' and not 'decision making'. Studies referred to earlier in this chapter for example were more concerned with the disparity in sentencing patterns between areas and courts but lacked an adequate methodological framework for examining sentencing as a decision-making process, in which the influence of individuals might best be examined. But as Hogarth rightly suggests 'The establishment of a statistical relationship between factors such as the severity of the crime and criminal record to the pattern of sentencing decisions made does not mean that these factors were consciously or even subsconsciously in the minds of the judges at the time of sentence' (1971, p.8).

Two important studies which attempted to examine sentencing in such a way as to correct these methodological inadequacies were conducted by Hood (1972) and Hogarth (1971) respectively. Both researchers were in agreement that disparity is a problem in sentencing; that previous sentencing research had been grounded in inadequate methodologies; and that, consequently, a new methodological alternative was required to study the theoretical basis of sentencing. Moreover, both investigations rest on the assumption that there are five important factors which affect sentencing decisions. These are

    i) the social, personal and judicial characteristics of the judges;

    ii) the attitudes of judges towards 'disposal';

    iii) the judges' perception of the nature of the offence and characteristics of the offenders;

    iv) the type of information considered relevant; and

    v) the controls or constraints exercised either by law, or by courts, or informally through local sentencing norms.

For Hood and Hogarth, the independent variable, or variables, cannot be located in the 'factual' make-up of the case *per se*. Rather cognition or perception becomes the independent variable; that is, it is the perception of information and facts assessed for the purpose of sentencing that directly bears on the sentencing decision. There are then no 'facts' which are relevant apart from their identification as such by those deciding on a sentence.

Hood, in attempting to elicit as much information as possible about the perception by magistrates of the information presented to them employed a battery of strategies which included simulated cases, self-completion questionnaires, the Eysenck Personality Inventory, conferences about actual cases, and attending court. The last tactic is particularly interesting if only for the fact that earlier researchers had argued that by not knowing the details about the courts included in a study, the researcher had the advantage of detachment (Mannheim et al. 1957). Hood identified three sets of variables which could potentially account for disparity in sentencing:

    i) Personal and social attributes;

    ii) Perceptions and attitudes; and

    iii) Factors associated with bench membership.

It is perhaps worth noting that despite his intention to offer a methodological framework adequate to account for the theoretical basis of sentencing, Hood's study nevertheless displays elements of the 'black box' model of sentencing research, though obviously to a lesser degree. He does gather independent information about the attitudes and perceptions of magistrates but nevertheless isolates factors, or groups of factors such as bench membership, which are then used to explain or account for sentencing practice through statistical association with actual sentencing decisions. However, he concluded that the research provided ample evidence 'that a method based on decision making in simulated cases can provide a realistic assessment of how magistrates actually behave in court' (1972, p.153).

The other study which sought to provide an alternative methodological framework, Hogarth's 'Sentencing as a Human Process', concentrated more on actual sentencing decisions than did Hood's study. The main objective in Hogarth's study was to explain the apparent inconsistency in sentencing practice amongst magistrates in Ontario. Variations in the use of particular measures 'appeared too large to be explained solely in terms of the differences in the types of cases appearing before the courts in different areas' (1971, p.12). He also makes clear his rejection of the 'black box' model of sentencing research when he asserts that 'this is a study of the sentencing behaviour of magistrates. It is concerned with *what* decisions different magistrates make, *how* they make them, and *why*' (1971, p.15). His research was designed therefore to explore the 'meaning' of sentencing as magistrates themselves experienced it and was logically committed to being based on explicit assumptions about how sentencing could be analysed. Whereas research such as that of Green and Gaudet inferred the existence of certain attitudes from sentencing behaviour, Hogarth assumed that prior to appointment magistrates already have certain opinions and beliefs which provide broad predispositions for specific attitudes the magistrate will later form in reference to his judicial role. As a result of their relationship to the demands of this judicial role and because of the dialectic between self-conception and these demands, magistrates develop a relatively stable and enduring set of judicial attitudes. Hogarth then defines judicial attitudes as 'a set of evaluative categories relevant to the judicial role which the individual magistrate has adopted (or learned) during his past experience, problems or ideas in his social world' (1971, p.100).

Wheeler et al. (1968) in a similar study had also argued that *prima facie* inconsistent sentencing or sentencing disparity could be seen to be rational given an examination of judicial penal philosophies.

Whereas the other studies had imputed the existence of attitudes from behaviour, specifically sentencing behaviour, the
conception of attitudes as evaluative categories necessarily entails a consideration of how information is processed by different magistrates with different attitudes. This in turn also demands a framework for studying attitudes and Hogarth distinguished between 'attitude scales' which are logically (theoretically) derived and those which are empirically (phenomeno-
logically) derived. In the former, the researcher, by making *a
priori* assumptions about the existence of certain attitudes,
thereby imposes his own evaluative categories on the categories
of those subjects in his research. The researcher is in danger of
substituting what has been referred to elsewhere as first-order
constructs by second-order constructs (see Cicourel 1968).

Hogarth's scales for measuring judicial attitudes, since he was
committed to a phenomenological method of scale construction, were developed by being based on statements which satisfied several clearly stated criteria (p.107) but which more specifically should be 'selected from the evaluative statements
actually used by the individuals involved, or from those that
have been made by well known persons in their environment'
(1971, p.106).

Hogarth's major conclusion, in relation to the penal philosophies of magistrates, was that whereas there may have been
wide variations in penal philosophies amongst magistrates,
individual magistrates nevertheless had a fairly consistent set of
beliefs influencing their penal philosophies. Thus, whereas
magistrates were inconsistent with each other, they were consistent within themselves; and once the purpose which magistrates subscribed to in sentencing – the internal consistency of
their thinking in respect of their judicial role – was known, the
whole of their penal philosophy could also be predicted. Moreover, he demonstrated that actual sentencing behaviour was
also significantly related to attitudes and 'the fact that variation
in sentencing behaviour was found to be associated with variations in the attitudes of magistrates concerned indicates that
the judicial process is not as uniform and impartial as many
people hope it would be. Indeed, it would appear that justice is a
very personal thing' (1971, p.365). Whereas earlier studies had
tended to view sentencing as a static entity or as irrational,
Hogarth views sentencing as 'a dynamic process in which the
facts of the cases, the constraints arising out of the law and the
social system and other features of the external world are inter-

preted, assimilated and made sense of in ways compatible with the attitudes of the magistrates concerned. Sentencing was shown to be a very human process' (1971, p.382).

The Present Study: Methods

To examine the processual nature of decision-making, there were several requirements that dictated the nature of the methodological strategies.

First, some means had to be devised so as to allow for genuine and valid comparisons to be made between panel members and juvenile magistrates in relation to decision-making. Given the very different organisational structures and official philosophies of the Children's Hearing system and the Juvenile Court, it was considered necessary to have a baseline for comparison between the two groups of subjects.

Secondly, one objective of the research was to examine the extent to which theoretical perspectives on criminality and delinquency provided 'available ideologies' from which the lay theories of delinquency and need were derived and employed by the subjects in the course of practical decision-making about children. The danger of a researcher simply identifying the existence of such ideologies, after they had undergone the metamorphosis of absorption into lay theories or ideologies, without involving the subjects themselves, is that he does in fact impose structure and organisation on the cognitive frameworks of his subjects.

Thirdly, as a direct consequence of the defects identified with 'black box' sentencing research, it was decided that the research should be actor oriented (a point which is related to the argument of the previous paragraph) – meaning that as far as possible in a study of practical decision-making an attempt should be made to assess how the decision-maker reaches a decision. Whereas in much sentencing research the factors identified in the background of the offender were treated as independent variables, it could be argued that by adopting an actor orientation the independent variable becomes the cognitive framework of the subject, though the dependent variable, the decision, remains the same. Similarly, an actor orientation is necessary in a research project committed to assessing the extent to which theoretical perspectives on criminality find their expression in the lay theories of delinquency and criminality espoused by those responsible for the identification of deviance or need.

Fourthly, most sentencing research had focused primarily on individual judges or magistrates but there had been few attempts to analyse the nature of collective decision-making. Since there must by law be three panel members present at a Children's Hearing and never less than two juvenile magistrates presiding in Juvenile Court, it is argued that any consideration of decision-making in these contexts must acknowledge the fact that decisions are ostensibly the outcome of a collective process. Whereas research into sentencing by magistrates in juvenile court had on occasion recognised the significance of the 'indefinable human element' the importance of interaction and discussion between magistrates had not been examined though this must undoubtedly have implications for the decision-making process. But an added factor was that since one of the objectives behind the introduction of the Children's Hearing system in Scotland and the further modification of the procedure of juvenile court in England was the promotion of informality, it was also important to evolve a strategy which would allow for some analysis to be made of the interaction and communication in the hearings as a whole. In Scotland especially, as recommended by the Kilbrandon Report, the informal proceedings of the Children's Hearing was adopted in order to allow parents and child to be more involved in the decision-making process. Consequently, to have tried to compare differences in decision-making between the respective systems without adopting a strategy which would accommodate a consideration of the relative contribution to the decision process of parents and children would have been to have ignored the very context in which decisions were made.

Finally, children's hearings and juvenile courts do not operate *in vacuo* but are part of a network of agencies providing specialist skills and facilities which not only serve to inform the decisions made by panel members and magistrates but which may also be involved in the actual implementation of that decision. Thus, the availability and nature of the facilities provided by such agencies as social work or social services departments, education departments, psychiatric and psychological services are not without significance for the making of decisions about children. Because of the potential influence of the services available in different areas, it was decided to conduct the research in complete administrative areas in an attempt as far as possible to control for national variability in services and facilities provided. This had an added advantage for examining collective decision-making. By concentrating on complete administrative areas, the samples of subjects were only drawn from one juvenile panel and one juvenile bench. In this way, the different permutations of subjects who presided at Children's Hearings and Court Hearings would only be composed of individuals who were members of the respective panel or bench.

In view of these constraints, the research could not be conducted employing a single methodological strategy but demanded a number of strategies. Phenomenological sociology and ethno-methodology, as revealed in Cicourel's work, proved to have limitations for this research. But this does not mean that phenomenological sociology played no part in the design of the research; its influence was twofold: it had an influence in the design of appropriate strategies for actor-orientation and it highlighted the relationship between theory and data, or methodology and results, by revealing how comments on, or accounts of, the world were inextricably linked to the constitutive rules employed by actors, whether subject or researcher.

Theoretical Foundations

Though examination of disparity as such is not an aim of this research, a prime factor in the eventual nature of the strategies evolved for the present project was the intention of being able to make statements about and comparisons of *how* decisions were made, to examine differences in decision-*making*, using a methodological framework adequate for that purpose.

Whereas a phenomenological or ethnomethodological approach would certainly allow for the 'tacit assumptions' or 'background expectancies' of different personnel involved in the decision-making process to be revealed, and consequently what implications these had for the processing of delinquents, it would not have allowed for easy comparison of two different systems of juvenile justice. This was espeically so because of the intention to examine the nature of interaction and communication between a number of individuals involved in making a decision and to acknowledge how diverse factors influenced such a decision. Though interpretive sociology criticises the positivistic bias of much sociological reasoning and rejects the method associated therewith as being inappropriate for the study of social phenomena, it is singularly lacking in the development of alternative methods. The ethnomethodologist (or 'anthropologist at home') seeks, in accordance with the Schutzian postulate of adequacy, to make his account of social behaviour compatible with the account of it given by those whose behaviour was the object of analysis. One of the failings, as we have seen, of positivistic sociology was that sociological concepts were second-order constructs; that is, they are constructs of the constructs used in commonsense and lay reasoning. But for present purposes, an important disadvantage of interpretive sociology was that there was no definitive statement as to how best one might render rationally visible the processes which make interaction possible. There are then two problems.

First, the postulate of adequacy associated with interpretive sociology comes close to suggesting that accurate accounts of social interaction can only be given by the actors involved in the interaction. The accuracy of any account given by a researcher is then determined by its compatibility with actors' accounts. But in some social situations, and perhaps in most of those in which more than one actor is involved, there may well be disagreement between the participants as to the accuracy of any account given of that social process. Moreover, it may not always be the case that actors themselves are aware of the tacit assumptions or background expectancies which allow them to accomplish the behaviour. Bearing in mind that this research set out to analyse decision-making in hearings involving as many as six or seven people, and involving information gleaned from a variety of reports and other sources, one must acknowledge the possibility of disagreement over the accuracy of any account as to how a decision was accomplished.

The second difficulty relates more to the lack of an articulated interpretive methodology. Perhaps the greatest contribution made by the interpretive perspective is that it has directed attention to the basis of professional theorisation as well as lay theorisation (see Schutz 1967; Giddens 1976). That is, not only does it focus on how lay actors account for or make sense of the world in lay terms but also how professionals such as sociologists account for the world in sociological terms. In accordance with the notion of 'reflexivity', interpretive sociology is committed to revealing the constitutive rules which make both lay and professional accounts of the world possible, thereby eroding the distinction between the lay or professional sociologist. Any account of the world whether lay or professional is then the product of the very processes which make the account possible. That is, the truth of such accounts lies not in their correspondence to some feature of an external or preconstituted world but rather is inextricably linked to the way (the method) in which the account was accomplished. Truth is then 'methodic' in character and no longer referential. The ontological and epistemological gap between theory and data is bridged, since, *ex hypothesi*, there are no data in the world independent of the theoretical assumptions or prescriptions guiding the researcher. But though this approach does warn of the dangers of dissociating accounts or conclusions from the way in which they were made, in other words ignoring the methodic character of accounts, interpretive sociology fails to postulate a methodology adequate to meet the strict demands of its maxims. The continual need to make visible the auspices under which research is made possible or accomplished in itself gives no indication of the methodology adequate for this purpose, and ethnomethodological studies are themselves not exempt from a critique in ethnomethodological terms. What may then be referred to as an 'ethnomethodological spiral' is established.

Whereas interpretive sociology provided few methodological prescriptions pertinent to the concerns of this research, phenomenological psychology, and in particular Kelly's theory of personal constructs, not only shared principles and theoretical foundations with the interpretative branch but also had the advantage of yielding recognised strategies and 'a number of techniques of investigation and measurement, which are closely tied to many of the assumptions in the main body of the theory' (Bannister and Mair 1968, p.32). The relationship between theory and method displayed in Kelly's theory of personal constructs was a crucial consideration for a study which purported to identify the assumptions and beliefs employed by social control agents in the practical accomplishment of juvenile justice. For Kelly, man was to be seen as an agent in the real sense of that word in that human nature was not merely determined by environment nor subject to physical or biochemical forces. This is indicated in the fundamental postulate of construct theory that 'a person's processes are psychologically channelised by the ways in which he anticipates events' (Bannister and Mair 1968, p.12).

The theory embodies a conception of a person as essentially anticipatory and predicting and not just responding to forces beyond his conscious control. A person can only anticipate events through his system of personal constructs and it is in the notion of a 'construct' that the key to the theory as a whole is to be found. Though Kelly did not deny the existence of a real or absolute world, of more importance was his claim that to operate in the world man has to make representations of it which he can then test in the course of his experiences in it. By 'representing' or 'construing' the world is meant the attempt to relate the pre-analytical diversity of phenomena into conceptual categories. It is through these representations or constructs that man gains knowledge of and acts in the world and since they are conceptual categories which do not simply refer to an external absolute reality they are subject to change in accordance with the experience of the individual. This is necessitated by the heuristic and pragmatic character of constructs.

Similarly, in personal construct theory, the events which man experiences cannot be absolutely apprehended but can only be conceptualised or appreciated by the constructions placed on them. Since events are not intrinsically meaningful, they are made meaningful or have meaning imposed on them by the individual only by reference to the system of constructs within which he subsumes them. Interpretations of events in the world are then subject to the differing construct systems employed by men to make sense of a world in which a degree of prediction and anticipation is a distinct advantage. The theoretical parallel with the notion of 'a frame of relevance' should be obvious.

Where personal construct theory does resemble interpretive sociology is in its presentation of a theoretical framework whose explanatory potential is directed not only at the psychological processes of man *qua* man but also man *qua* scientist or psychologist. Indeed the very reflexivity required by the theory means that personal construct theory is itself a form of construing that can be accounted for by personal construct theory. The basis of theorising of subject and psychologist is examined under the precepts of the theory. Thus, again, as in the sociological form of phenomenology, the onus is on the researcher to be aware that the constructs he employs in making sense of an individual's behaviour, though different from those available to the subject, are not necessarily any more authoritative. An assumption that Kelly makes is that 'whatever nature may be, or howsoever the quest for truth will turn out in the end, the events we face today are subject to as great a variety of constructions as our wits will enable us to contrive' (1970, p.1). This he then refers to as constructive alternativism whereby events may be construed in a number of ways by being subsumed under different construct systems amongst which may be included those of individual psychologists or different psychological perspectives. A merit of the theory which had direct relevance for this project is that though it was established in opposition to psychological determinism, the heuristic value of determinist accounts of behaviour is not rejected outright. In accord with the precept of 'constructive alternativism' personal construct theory is but one way of construing a world which may be construed in terms of other psychological theories and also of the theories of lay men. Personal construct theory allows of the 'truths' provided by other construct systems and reflects an acceptance of the 'methodic' character of truth associated with interpretive sociology (see Blum and McHugh 1971).

Moreover, there are clear implications for a project which seeks to examine the extent to which decision-makers in two systems of juvenile justice ascribe responsibility for delinquent behaviour. Personal construct theory neither makes nor is required to make any definitive commitment to a view of human nature as being either 'free' or 'determined' since 'free' and 'determined' are themselves the opposite poles of a construct. The free–determined construct is then a means of interpreting behaviour, whether in scientific or lay terms, and subjects are then free or determined only with respect to the standpoint or construct system employed by the observer. Thus, the theory avoids both an overdetermined view of man and also the doctrine of unlimited free will in postulating that man's contact with the world is mediated by the construct system he has evolved, whether he be experimenter or subject. Though the 'frame of relevance' of the experimenter and subject may be different, the basis of theorisation is essentially similar in the employment of a system of constructs.

Development of Instruments and Pilot Study

Because an actor-orientation was to be adopted we considered it important to involve personnel from the respective systems in the design of the instruments, and to gain further first-hand experience of the operation of juvenile justice. This was necessary in order to define instruments that required to be 'subjective' rather than 'objective' and which also, in Kelly's terms were to be 'life representative'. Consequently, the development of appropriate instruments was accomplished with the co-operation of magistrates and panel members and through a small pilot study conducted in two different areas. This involvement of personnel from the two systems in the design of the instruments was also continued after the fieldwork was completed when the researcher attended day conferences in both the study areas. This allowed for the presentation and discussion of some of his preliminary findings with both panel members and magistrates, a process which not only acknowledged the co-operation afforded by both groups but which at the same time had significant influence on the analysis of the data.

It had soon become obvious that what were seen to be the methodological requirements of the research could not be met adequately by adopting one particular technique. A number of techniques were then devised in a strategy which involved a considerable degree of what has been referred to as 'methodological triangulation' (Denzin 1978).

The main techniques, discussed below, were
    i) Case studies
   ii) Case reports
  iii) Interaction schedules

Case Studies. The first stage of the research was designed primarily to compare the extent to which different theoretical perspectives on criminality and delinquency provided available ideologies which were manifested in the working frames of relevance of panel members and juvenile magistrates. The main objective was to compare the extent to which a treatment philosophy or a judicial philosophy provided a conceptual framework for decision-making by panel members and magistrates respectively. But an added purpose was to compare the relative influence of each of the identified theoretical perspectives on delinquency whose premises rested on deterministic assumptions. A dual requirement of this element of the research then was that it be methodologically adequate to examine the ideological roots of the lay theories of delinquency employed by the decision-makers but also provide a baseline for comparison between panel members and juvenile magistrates. For these purposes, it was decided to use a number of case studies, containing basic information about an offender's background and the offence in which he was involved.

The techniques associated with personal construct theory, especially the Repertory Grid, have been subjected to many variations and modifications and, by using case studies, it was possible to utilise construct principles in designing the cases themselves. In trying to examine the differences in decision-making between personnel in two different systems of juvenile justice, the use of case studies, for the purposes of this stage of the research, eliminated the influence of technical rules and regulations which would apply to actual cases. At the same time, as Hood has commented (1972), the use of case studies introduces a further degree of control over the variability in information relating to specific cases. One argument, however, against the case-study method is of course that it is a technique which is artificial in the sense that it removes the subjects from their normal decision-making context, thereby ignoring the 'situated aspects' of decision-making (Hood 1972). (Acknowledging this caveat, the case studies only provided limited data and had of necessity to be supplemented by the other strategies described below.) But in terms of 'life representativeness',, the case studies were devised in such a way as to resemble realistically documents such as social enquiry reports. To this end, the researcher read a considerable number of reports made available to him by the Reporter to the Children's Hearings in the study area. Though each case study was to embody basic premises of the different theoretical perspectives identified earlier in this book (see chapters II and III), they were to be administered in a way that would not be too removed from the presentation of reports to the subjects in the making of decisions in actual cases.

In the case studies, the basic assumptions of each of the different types of causal explanations (psychoanalytic, biological, environmental, processual and behaviourist) were embodied in information relating to the child's background; in addition, this was balanced with information about the offence in which the child had been involved. (Thus, what we have referred to as a more judicial or legal ideology was also presented.) Five offences were depicted representing varying degrees of child involvement and varying degrees of seriousness. To control further for differences in cases, as in the research as a whole, only boys were referred to in the case studies.

Each of the case studies then were based on (a) a 'judicial' philosophy by which we mean a perspective on delinquency control in which such considerations as the personal responsibility of the offender and the consequences of the act are important; and (b) a 'welfare' philosophy in which the social, personal and environmental characteristics of the delinquent are more important considerations. These two models are obviously not mutually exclusive as the history of juvenile justice has indicated. And as we shall argue later in terms of the frames of relevance adopted by an individual they are not easy to separate conceptually. For the purpose of the research, each study contained a description of an offence and a statement of the social, personal and environmental characteristics of the child. Each case study was followed by a list of statements relating to 'welfare' factors derived from the respective causal theories we discussed and also statements relating to the child's personal involvement in the offence, the nature of the resultant harm, his awareness of right and wrong, his awareness of the consequences of his action and, on a broader level, the need for social protection. Copies of the Case Studies and a fuller description are contained in appendix I.

Case Reports. We have already argued that previous research into sentencing generally tended to ignore how information was selected as being relevant for the purpose of decision-making. But sentencing research had also failed to consider the influence of sentencers on each other's behaviour when the decision, theoretically at least, was the outcome of discussion between a number of magistrates. The Case Report Form was devised so as to allow conclusions to be made about how panel members and juvenile magistrates respectively judged information, and as far as possible to allow the researcher to make some comment on the collective nature of decisions, an objective which also involved an 'Interaction Schedule'.

Though we obviously cannot deny that known information about an offender is influential in making a decision as to how to deal with him, information is not intrinsically meaningful or relevant *per se*. It is only meaningful and relevant when it is treated as such by those responsible for making the decision. The search for those factors, either relating to the offence or background information, which can be said to be determinants of the resulting decision, has then to be conducted in such a way as to allow the researcher to examine how the information was interpreted and for what purpose. Thus, the important questions relate not simply to what information was used but also how and why it was used. In this respect, to appreciate decision-making, and not merely analyse decisions, it is important that the subject has the opportunity of indicating what influenced him in making a decision, and what was for him relevant information. A fundamental logical 'link' between information and a decision, as we have argued earlier, is the reason that the decision-maker gives for making the decision that he did. Though a number of people may employ the same information to reach what *prima facie* seems to be a similar decision, once the reasons for a decision have been established, it can be appreciated that very different decisions have in fact been made.

Since the underlying logic to this project was to consider the relative influence of welfare or judicial factors on decision-making in respect of children who commit offences, the difficulty of conceptually separating information relating to children's needs and that relating to the offences committed meant that it was therefore important to consider how panel members and magistrates themselves interpreted information.

But decisions are subject to a number of constraints other than the availability and quality of information on which decisions may be logically based, and these constraints are of two types. First, decisions may be restricted by statutory requirements. Green had also postulated that 'the statutory guide to the relative gravity of the various offences exerts a pronounced effect upon variations in sentences' (1961, p.32). Secondly, but just as importantly, decisions may be further restricted by the availability or non-availability of suitable resources by which appropriate treatment measures can be carried out. The principles underlying individualised treatment require that decisions be made in terms of an offender's needs rather than in terms of what he has done. Consequently, since offenders' needs are likely to vary considerably from offender to offender, different types of facilities are necessary to allow treatment measures to be realistically implemented. Where adequate resources or a variety of resources are not available, decisions cannot be implemented and the non-availability of resources, if known to the decision-maker, will necessitate that his decision be tailored accordingly.

From a list of factors generally associated with decision-making about delinquents and constructed with the help of magistrates and panel members, decision-makers were asked to indicate which factors were taken into consideration and how important these had been. For example, where the child's relationship with his father was considered to have been important, it would have added to the analysis of the use of information to have been able to allow the subject the opportunity to make some judgment of the factor. Thus, a child's relationship may be an important factor for making a decision and what we sought to analyse was the extent to which different factors were treated as important by magistrates and panel members. It was hoped that this simple approach would allow for some methodological progress to be made in research into decision-making unlike much sentencing research which had ignored which factors were relevant for the subject and how he judged those factors to be relevant given the objective he hoped to achieve. Four main categories of information were contained in the Case Reports. First, there were the different reports available in relation to which it was considered important to have some overall assessment of their importance for decision-making. Secondly, there were the 'background' or 'welfare' factors which, though less in number, were derived from the different theoretical perspectives in the case studies. Thirdly, there were the 'judicial' factors themselves as employed in the case studies but supplemented by information relating to the child's previous offence behaviour and previous contact with the juvenile justice system. Lastly, there was a residual category in which different types of information, which could not readily be incorporated into the other categories, were presented. Opportunity was also made available for the subjects to include factors which had not appeared on the Case Report.

After the list of factors, there were a number of questions which specifically focused on the reasons given by the panel member or juvenile magistrate for his decision, whether he agreed with it, and if not, why not and what would his decision have been.

In this way, we could examine the factors which were important and in what way they were important to the subject and also elicit his reasons for his decision. Though this could not be called phenomenological methodology, the design was nevertheless influenced by the phenomenological notion of intentionality. The primary methodological objective had again been to evolve a means whereby the frame of relevance of the subject would not be completely dominated by that of the researcher.

Interaction Schedules. As we have seen, a major disadvantage of research into sentencing is that there has been little attempt to provide information about what happened in court during the course of a hearing. The dangers associated with explanations of sentencing behaviour based on information extracted from official records alone have already been commented on (Hogarth 1971; Hood 1972), but few researchers have examined the process of decision-making in the hearing of a case. Though Hood (1972), for example, recognises the limitation of his games-theory approach, which he argues needs to be supplemented by information collected at court hearings, this actually occupies a minor part of the research. Others, as we have noted, even suggested that by having no knowledge of the courts and the hearings the researcher could in fact benefit by being 'detached'

(Mannheim et al. 1957). Even Hogarth, whose work was theoretically based on a phenomenological framework, derives his data from interviews, questionnaires and sentencing study sheets, and ignores altogether the nature of the discussion and interaction which provides the context for the hearing of a case.

To obtain this kind of information in the hearings, the original intention had been to tape-record the hearing of specific cases and then analyse the verbatim transcripts. But as permission could not be given in one of the areas where the main study was to be conducted, an alternative means of analysing the hearing transactions had to be found. After some deliberation, it was decided to use some form of interaction schedule on which to base the analysis of both *content* and *form* of the interaction in hearings. (By content is meant the nature of the discussion in relation to a case in a hearing; by form is meant the flow of discussion and communication between the different individuals involved in the decision-making process.) The Bales Scalogram (1950; 1951) was considered but it was rather limited in the scope and kind of information it could deal with, and was not particularly suited to examine the major hypotheses of the study. Consequently, without rejecting the concept of an interaction schedule, one was designed which was particularly suited: relatively simple to administer but at the same time capable of dealing with as much information from a discussion as possible.

It is a discussion of the main findings to which we now turn.

Chapter Six

ACCOUNTING FOR
DELINQUENCY

For comparative purposes, two complete administrative areas, one in Scotland and one in England, were chosen for the research. The restriction to one panel and one court area then means that no claims can be made as to the representativeness of the areas or of the subjects therein. Indeed, it is questionable whether any area or sample, however chosen or stratified, could ever be what might be called 'representative'. Because the desire is that panel members and juvenile magistrates should be representative of the community which they serve, any attempt to obtain samples representative on a national basis would inhibit the collection of information about the workings of the system in particular areas. Since each area, both panel and court, is characterised by the peculiar administrative and organisational arrangements of social and related services, as well as being serviced by a restricted number of panel members and magistrates respectively, additional variables would have been introduced to an analysis of decision-making. Indeed, the danger of seeking to obtain large samples that are representative of the national scene is that as much information is lost because of the attempt to be comprehensive.

Since we were concerned with the process of decision-making the danger of trying to be too comprehensive would have been to have ignored the peculiarities that exist within different administrative areas. Because the practice of juvenile justice is dependent upon local resources and expertise, and may also be a function of the nature of the delinquency problem, regional differences make it unlikely that a statement about juvenile justice on a national basis could meaningfully be made. Since one objective of the research was to examine situational and collective features of the decision-making process, to have crossed geographical and administrative boundaries would have restricted the kinds of comments that could be made.

A brief description of the respective areas now follows.

Scotland: the Panel Area

There were a number of important differences in the administrative arrangements between the panel and court area. In particular, whereas all the court hearings were held in the same
magistrates' court, during the day, the panel hearings met at
different locations and mainly in the evenings and in the after-
noons. There were in fact four different meeting places for the
panels, though any panel member might be required to attend
hearings at any of the four venues.

Another important difference between the two groups, i.e.
panel members and magistrates, is that because the new system
of juvenile justice in Scotland had only recently been introduced
(1971) the panel members were all first-time appointments.
There had, at the time of the research, been no turnover of
membership, though a number of the panel members were in
fact about to have their membership reviewed as their three-
year period of service (after which membership has to be reviewed) was almost completed. In general, however, and in
comparison with the juvenile court system, panel members had
less experience and were being offered training programmes
that themselves were only in the early stages of their evolution.

Table 1. Reports to Reporter

	Scotland	per 1000	Panel area	per 1000
1972	22,451	15.8	1,135	11.6
1973	28,448	20.1	1,439	14.5
1974	30,442	21.5	1,771	17.9

In terms of the cases dealt with by the panel members in the
study, there were several differences in the patterns of cases
referred over time to the Reporter at the national level, and
within the panel area itself, as shown in table 1. Whereas in 1972
and 1973, as well as later in 1974, the number of reports per
1,000 children at a national level was always greater than for the
panel area itself, both sets of figures showed an upward increase
in the rates of reports to Reporters. The majority of all reports
were for boys. Moreover, the number of offence referrals each
year increased both at national level and in the Panel Area, as
table 2 indicates.

The majority of referrals to the Reporter in any one year for

Scotland as a whole are for offence grounds. In 1972, for example, the 33,107 offence referrals constituted 92% of the total number of referrals. But whereas in that year, 58% of all referrals to the Reporter actually reached a Hearing, in the panel area, the corresponding figure was 63%. The greater proportion of offence referrals sent by the Reporter in the panel area to Hearings was repeated for 1973 and 1974, as can be seen. As for other grounds of referral, the proportions of cases referred to a hearing for Scotland and for the panel area were similar.

Table 2. Offence referrals

	To Reporter	To Hearing	% to Hearing
Scotland			
1972	33,107	19,260	58
1973	44,713	25,697	57
1974	47,933	26,473	55
Panel Area			
1972	1,519	971	63
1973	2,119	1,420	63
1974	2,457	1,523	61

However, as a proportion of all cases dealt with on offence grounds by the Hearings, marginally more residential supervision orders were made for the panel area than for Scotland as a whole. Of all disposals made in the panel area in 1972, 16.7% involved a residential supervision requirement, whereas the national figure was 15%. In 1973 and 1974, the figures for the proportion of residential supervision requirements in the panel area decreased to 12.5% and 9% respectively. What was particularly interesting about this was that the decrease occurred at a time when the numbers of residential orders being made also decreased nationally, but when the proportion of residential orders on offence grounds actually increased. What these figures suggest is that at least some *prima facie* significance may well be attached to offence behaviour in deciding upon residential care. In what way offence behaviour was considered significant was of course one of the questions the research was designed to study empirically.

The variation between the national figures and those for the panel area was indicative of the wide degree of variation in referral and disposal patterns between the different administrative areas of Scotland, as has already been noted. It is precisely because of such variation and because of the Kilbrandon argument that panels should be community based that, for the purposes of this research at least, to have ignored administrative and organisational boundaries would have been to distort any conclusions that may be drawn about decision-making.

England: the Juvenile Court

As we have already observed, the arrangements for court hearings were very different from those for panel hearings. All cases coming before the juvenile magistrates were heard in the same court buildings and in the mornings of the same three days each week. The complex which housed the Magistrates' Courts also housed the police headquarters for the area. Thus even in terms of the physical location (primarily the proximity of police offices) and the arrangements for convening juvenile courts, there was a marked difference from the Children's Hearings. Though the juvenile court in the pilot study was held in a less formal atmosphere, relatively speaking, the courtroom in the study area was structured architecturally in the traditional manner, with obvious implications for social relationships.

On occasion, 'extra' juvenile courts were convened *ex tempore* when it appeared that the work of the day would not be completed by the main juvenile court. Since, as a consequence of the selection process, all juvenile magistrates must also be magistrates in the adult courts, where the adult magistrates court had completed its business, those juvenile magistrates present could be called upon to sit as a juvenile court. What made this easier, was the fact that though three magistrates generally presided, on occasion only two did so.

Just as importantly in terms of the organisational differences between panel and court areas, whereas panel hearings dealt with very rarely more than six cases in any one session during the period of the research, as many as forty were arranged for court hearings. As a result, the court hearings tended to be somewhat shorter. (The implications of this will be discussed in more detail later.)

Whereas the statistics relating to the children dealt with by the Children's Hearings in the panel area were readily available, it proved exceedingly difficult to obtain similar information in respect of the study area in England. As a final resort, contact was made with the police in the court area, who were able to provide figures which, however, were not collated for the court area in the same manner as the Crime Statistics for England and Wales (see table 3).

What is apparent from them is that, like the panel area, and perhaps not surprisingly, the majority of children appearing in juvenile court were there on accusations of having committed criminal offences. This holds for both years prior to the research. Thus in both years, more than 90% of all charges were for offences. Similarly, the majority of children appearing in court were boys – 82% and 80% in 1972 and 1973 respectively. (The national figure for 1972 was rather higher, at 91%.)

Table 3. Court area

	offences	other reasons
1972	470	39
1973	578	36

Obviously one of the more significant differences between the Scottish and English systems lies in the measures available for dealing with children, since the English courts do have punitive measures available. It was for this reason, particularly with a view to providing a base line for comparability, that the Case Study method had been adopted in the attempt to examine the relative merits of types of information. The significance of such measures can be seen in terms of the decisions made in the court area (table 4).

In both years the fine was extensively used, though below the national figure of 50% in 1972 for all persons under 17. But what is obvious, even from a cursory examination of the figures, is that despite the emphasis in the official reports on supervision and care orders, and despite the introduction of care proceedings, more than 60% of all decisions were other than care or supervision orders.

Panel Members and Magistrates: a Profile

At the time of undertaking the research, there were 35 people registered as panel members in the Scottish study area and 33 people on the juvenile bench in the English one. Of the 35 panel members only two failed to participate in the research; in the

Table 4. Court area: decisions reached

	1972	%	1973	%
Fine	155	39.40	158	36.15
Care Order	44	11.20	62	14.20
Supervision Order	97	24.68	93	21.28
Attendance Centre	37	9.41	24	5.49
Committed to Crown Court	9	2.29	6	1.37
Absolute Discharge	7	1.78	8	1.83
Conditional Discharge	40	10.17	73	16.70
Detention	4	1.01	8	1.83
Binding Over	—	—	5	1.44
Total	393		437	

court area, of the 33 magistrates who were juvenile magistrates, two also did not participate in the research.

Because the samples were small as a consequence of the dictates of a research design which sought to examine certain aspects of collective decision-making and the organisational characteristics of complete areas, it is obviously unrealistic to relate the figures to national statistics. But as we have argued, it is the peculiarities of decision-making within complete areas with which we are concerned, not with the degree of representativeness between national and local profiles.

In the following section, we examine the comparability of the two samples prior to discussing the findings based on the first stage of the research employing the Case Study method.

Only in relation to three variables were there any significant differences between panel members and magistrates: age, 'experience of youth' and 'membership of a caring profession'.

In terms of age, panel members with an average age of 44 years were much younger than the magistrates included in the study whose average age was almost 53. Sixteen panel members but only two magistrates were under 40 years old; six panel members and seven magistrates were aged between 40 and 50; and eleven panel members were older than 50, though as many as 22 of the juvenile magistrates were so. The very different ages of the magistrates and panel members may well be a reflection of the selection processes within the different administrative structures. Panel members are selected only after they have applied for membership. Anyone may apply, but is required to go through a selection process usually involving members of social work departments, children's panel advisory groups and serving panel members. Since the panel is supposedly representative of the community, it was expected that a high proportion of younger people would apply. Though there is again variation between regions, the national figures reveal that in 1976 almost 44% of all panel members were under 40, two-thirds of whom were in the 30 to 40 age-group (Moody 1976).

The selection process for magistrates, however, is very different. Though the bench for a particular area is also meant to be representative (Magistrates' Association 1975), there is one important factor that bears on this. Only those magistrates who are adult magistrates are eligible for juvenile court membership. Thus, although personal qualities are also important, juvenile magistrates are chosen from the ranks of the bench as a whole and invited to sit on the juvenile bench. And since the only restriction on service in juvenile court is that the retiring age is 65, a high proportion of juvenile magistrates have long periods of service behind them.

Thus, whereas at the time of the study, the longest serving panel members had been on the panels for 3½ years, individual magistrates had served for as long as 18 years in the juvenile court and 21 years in the adult court.

The rather vague guidelines that refer to the criteria for selection to panel membership and juvenile bench membership suggest that dealing with children would be a distinct advantage. Nevertheless, in terms of their experience in youth work (e.g. youth club work, voluntary work etc.) many more panel members had such experience. This again may be partly attributed to the selection process and the criteria employed to identify 'suitable' panel members.

In both countries personal qualities and expertise at dealing with children were considered important criteria for either panel or bench membership. Yet when we examine the occupations of the two groups, we find a significant difference in terms of whether individuals were members of a caring profession or not. 'Caring profession' is a rather arbitrary category but we mean by it those occupations or professions where the individual is concerned with the health, welfare or education of children or of adults. In Moody's analysis of panel members in 1976 it was found, for example, that of all panel members in Scotland, 25% were teachers and almost 10% involved in medicine (Moody 1976). Twenty-two panel members but four magistrates were members of what we have called 'caring professions'.

Once again, because small samples are involved, a number of caveats have to be borne in mind in respect of interpretation and analysis. This is especially true in respect of the Case Studies. A baseline for comparison was needed and therefore panel members and magistrates completed the case studies individually with the result that only just over thirty were completed for each group. This was necessary, however, since we were also later to examine the extent to which the beliefs held by panel members and magistrates in general were related to the process of collective decision-making in the actual hearing situation. Whether the beliefs and assumptions held by individual subjects outside the context of a court or a panel hearing did influence the actual decision-making process was something that was to be tested empirically. And since Mannheim et al. (1957) and Hood (1972) have been criticised (p. 126) for their lack of rigorous observation in their research on sentencing, the significance of the results derived from the Case Studies can only be appreciated in relating them to later stages of our own study. By adopting an approach based on 'methodological triangulation' (Denzin 1978) no stage of the research should be assessed independently from the others.

Welfarism in Decision-Making

Earlier, different theories of punishment and crime were examined as providing 'available ideologies'. Similarly, we argued that the trend in juvenile justice had been increasingly towards a more welfare-oriented approach and one not based (at least primarily) on the conceptual framework of free-will and responsibility. Though criminology has never really reconciled the competing paradigms of determinism and free-will at the conceptual level, what was more important in the context of this research was to examine how these paradigms were incorporated into the frames of relevance of individuals given the responsibility for making decisions about children. This was especially so given that the administrative frameworks in Scotland and England are themselves founded upon different conceptual bases. That is, though panel hearings are concerned exclusively, at least in theory, with the needs and welfare of the child, court hearings are institutionally committed to questions of guilt and innocence (or in more colloquial language, 'whether he did it or not'). Because of this we expected that, even using the strategy of the simulated case study, panel members would ascribe much more importance to welfare considerations as a

basis for the making of decisions about children who commit
offences. That, not surprisingly, is precisely how it turned out.
Over all the five case studies and on the basis of the preferences
indicated by both panel members and magistrates, the difference in the importance attributed to welfare factors, the social,
economic and personal circumstances of the children was very
significant with panel members, treating such considerations as
more important than did their English counterparts. (Appendix
11 contains a fuller statement of the scores attained by panel
members and magistrates in respect of the case studies.)

This is perhaps the least surprising of the differences between
the two groups since the very nature of juvenile-court philosophy and proceedings, as a modified version of the ordinary courts of criminal law with summary jurisdiction, would
suggest that considerations of welfare would be considered of
lesser importance (but not irrelevant) by magistrates by virtue
of the demands of their judicial role.

In terms of the training offered to both the panel members and
magistrates, both received lectures and talks from members of
the different professions servicing the Hearings and Court systems respectively. Yet, as we have also seen, magistrates must
acquire some familiarity with the law and its application. The
training of panel members, far from being related to specific
problems of the law, more often than not is aimed at increasing
the individual's diagnostic and assessment skills (see Martin
and Murray 1976). This is not to suggest that there are no legal
requirements binding on panel members in the fulfilment of
their role and there has been a recent attack on the failure of
panel members to implement what are by any standards fairly
minimal statutory requirements (Martin et al. 1981). The point
however is that in the actual process of decision-making, quite
apart from the obligations incumbent on them to obey statutory
requirements, panel members are not required to take more
judicial considerations into account when reaching a decision.
This is not to say that the offence and the child's involvement
has no significance for panel members; as we shall argue later
such considerations do have importance for panel members but
are accommodated by them within a welfare frame of relevance.
That is, they may well be considered as elements to be taken
account of in the overall assessment of the child's needs with a
view to determining compulsory measures of care. Moreover, as
we shall again see later, the concern of panel members with the
welfare of the child does not mean that care measures are dis-

guised forms of punishment.

Conversely, the concern of magistrates in both the adult and juvenile court with the issue of intent and the availability of measures of a more overtly punitive nature suggest that they will be less inclined to view welfare considerations in isolation. Now none of this means that welfare provides no more than a rhetoric of treatment which legitimates in reality a more punitive form of juvenile justice (see May 1977); that needs more careful argument since even in the philosophical theories reviewed earlier punishment and treatment are not so readily distinguished as some commentators would lead us to believe. But for the purpose of this project, the assimilation of information about a child and the purposes to which it is put in the process of decision-making provided the empirical object of the inquiry.

But for present purposes, the fact that juvenile magistrates appear to ascribe less importance to what we have referred to as 'welfare' factors is perhaps not surprising from members of a system where the legal protection offered to the rights of individuals is underpinned by a conceptual framework on which considerations of punishment can be justified (see MacCormick 1974). And the fact that panel members are in more of a position to take *preventive* action would imply that welfare factors would in practice as well as in theory be extremely important.

What is also interesting is that there was also more agreement amongst the panel members than the magistrates as to the importance of welfare considerations. Not only did the welfare score for panel members indicate their greater commitment to identifying the needs of children, but there was also a much greater degree of agreement amongst them. That is, magistrates, as a group, were in less agreement as to the relative importance of welfare considerations. The greater importance attached by magistrates to judicial considerations such as the offence and the child's involvement in it has to be considered in the light of the fact that magistrates too found it difficult conceptually to separate 'needs' from 'deeds'. As one magistrate commented 'in some cases the child's involvement in the offence and the nature of the offence can be indicative of need and the lack of moral development. Our decisions have to somehow accommodate this'. The greater degree of concordance amongst panel members may well reflect the fact that in terms of the philosophy underpinning the Hearing system, offence behaviour *is* to be taken as indicative of need; for magistrates, however, the disparity may well be indicative of the fact that in terms of the system in which they operate, they can decide to treat offence behaviour as a manifestation of need or alternatively as the basis for a more punitive measure. More of this will be made later, but for the present it is worth noting that magistrates may have to make what Thomas (1970) calls a primary decision about the category into which any individual case falls and then a secondary decision about how to deal with the case. The separation of the adjudication of the allegation issue from final disposal in the Scottish system means that the panel members' role is not so circumscribed by such judicial concern and hence there is more agreement that welfare factors are important. This, however, as later stages of the research confirmed, does not preclude the possibility that panel members ascribe significance to considerations other than those of welfare.

Theories of Delinquency

The significance of the work of Cicourel (1968) in juvenile justice and more generally that of Kitsuse and Cicourel (1963) was to direct attention to the theories or definitions of delinquency espoused by the control agents. That is, they postulated the theories of delinquency employed by individuals within juvenile justice systems as crucial variables in the processing of cases and even in the construction of deviance or delinquent behaviour. Although such grand ambitions cannot be claimed for this project, one of the purposes was to identify the extent to which panel members and magistrates subscribed to particular accounts of delinquent behaviour and whether there were any significant differences between both groups. Thus, though it is perhaps no surprise that in general panel members appear to ascribe more relevance to 'welfare' considerations and to accounts of delinquent behaviour couched in deterministic terms, which particular accounts appeared to have more importance provided an equally significant empirical object of inquiry.

The five case studies each depicted social and personal background information about children in terms of broad deterministic accounts of delinquency aetiology; psychoanalytic, behaviourist, environmental, biological and processual determinism. As we have discussed earlier, theories of delinquency causation in general share a commitment to a deterministic framework in which the causes of delinquency have to be identified for the purpose of meaningful delinquency control; only when the cause of delinquency is identified can anything be done about it. However, despite the shared commitment to determinism, there is considerable variety in the kinds of events and circumstances identified as the cause of delinquency. Glover (1970) put it more succinctly in arguing that 'the determinist is not committed to the view that the causal laws governing human behaviour *must* be psychological, *must* be physiological, must be chemical or must be physical'. Though the lack of agreement at the philosophical level is itself interesting and warrants further consideration, the empirical object of the study was to consider how lay definitions of delinquency causation reflected the more orthodox theoretical positions. Of the different theories of delinquency, panel members ascribed much more importance to welfare considerations in the case based on the psychoanalytic perspective than in any other case, as can be seen in table 5.

Table 5. Mean welfare scores

	Panel	Court
Psychoanalytic determinism	7.9	9.7
Behaviourist determinism	8.0	9.6
Processual determinism	8.6	10.4
Biological determinism	9.0	10.9
Sociological determinism	9.7	10.6

(A lower figure indicates greater importance)

However, the importance ascribed to welfare factors in the psychoanalytic case was not so very different from the case based on behaviourist principles. The significance of this is apparent when the magistrates scores are considered. In terms of the difference between the two groups, panel members treated psychoanalytic and behaviourist considerations as more important than did the magistrates. That reflects the generally greater commitment overall to welfarism displayed by panel members. However, as for the panel members, there was no difference for magistrates in the way they treated the psychoanalytic and behaviourist in terms of importance and these were the two cases in which welfare factors were more important than for any other case. Thus, despite differences in emphasis, both these cases contained social and personal material about children which was seen by both magistrates and panel members to be important. This presents us with an intriguing possibility.

What is of extreme interest is that the two case studies in which the welfare statements are seen to be especially important are both based on theoretical frameworks in which delinquency aetiology and, by implication, its treatment can be said to relate to individuals. The apparent lack of substantial difference between how both groups construe these types of explanations may well be accounted for by the fact that both emphasise the importance of the home and parental relationships in the development and growth of a normal, healthy child. Delinquency in terms of psychoanalysis and behaviourism can in part be attributed to the breakdown in the normal processes of socialisation. Conversely, in terms of these perspectives, the object of treatment or welfare measures can be fairly readily identified, focusing either on the parents, children or both. Indeed, the policy changes in the field of child care in the 1960s were premised upon the family and the child being key variables in delinquency control. On a more practical level, the focusing of attention on the child and his family as in psychoanalytic and behavioural theories provides decision-makers with an obvious object for welfare measures unlike explanations which account for delinquency in rather broader social and political terms. Some weight is given to this speculation by the observation that for both groups relatively less importance was attached to the causal statement contained in the case study based on what we referred to as a sociological perspective (Case A). For panel members, it is in fact the case in which welfare considerations were seen to be least important.

There could be a number of reasons for this but perhaps not least is the fact that neither panel members nor magistrates, even if they wished, are in a position to effect any immediate and radical change in the social environment from which the child comes. Similarly, within the institutional setting of the hearing and court system, the information presented by the 'experts' (social workers, psychologists etc.), even where it does refer to social and environmental conditions, is primarily employed to account for the behaviour of the child or his relatives. It is, however, perhaps no coincidence that during the time of the research, a number of panels in different regions in Scotland were forming pressure groups not only in an attempt to acquire better resources for the hearing system but also to voice concern about the more social and political consequences of dealing with children from so-called deprived areas.

Within the confines of the decision-making process there is

then *prima facie* evidence to suggest that 'individualistic' accounts of delinquency are more pertinent as a basis for reaching a decision; this does not however preclude the possibility that broader social theories are nevertheless still considered relevant by such as panel members or magistrates but that the objectives are rather different and more long-term than those involved in dealing with a specific case.

But what also has to be remembered is that the ideological basis of social work and probation, both important influences within the respective systems, is located within a conceptual framework of determinism in which delinquency can be explained in terms of individual pathology. This is reflected in the importance of the role of social work in providing the respective systems with information about children.

As we have seen in chapter III, definitions of human action and behaviour in the more philosophical literature have to be assessed with reference to the concept of responsibility. In the next section, the relative importance ascribed to particular deterministic explanations will be related to an examination of how the issue of responsibility, amongst others, is accommodated within the frames of relevance espoused by panel members and magistrates.

Judicial Considerations

As a converse of the finding that welfare considerations are more important for panel members, magistrates generally ascribed much more importance to 'judicial factors'. (By 'judicial factors', as discussed earlier, is meant those considerations that related to the child's involvement in the offence, the seriousness of the offence and the issue of social protection.) What was interesting again was that conclusions about the general difference in importance ascribed by magistrates and panel members to judicial considerations have to be qualified in the light of *prima facie* agreement between both groups about particular judicial statements.

Since magistrates have of necessity to consider the facts of a case in a judicial setting modified from ordinary courts of criminal law, have at their disposal punitive sanctions, and since by virtue of their training they are committed to considering questions of intent and culpability, it is not unexpected that they will be more inclined than panel members to treat what we have loosely labelled judicial considerations as important criteria on which to base a decision. However, since an objective in the research was to examine in what way information is considered to be relevant for the purpose of decision-making and not simply what information was employed, a fuller assessment of the conclusions drawn from this stage of the research can only be formulated in the context of data derived from the other strategies employed.

Since in theory it could be argued that panel members should only be concerned with the needs of children and that magistrates have to take into consideration the wider needs of the community, we expected that magistrates would be much more concerned with the issue of social protection. Magistrates indeed did, at least on the basis of the case studies, treat social protection as much more important than did the panel members. And in interview magistrates stated that protecting society was a prime objective in dealing with children who commit offences. Overall, the differences between the scores attained were highly significant and in respect of each individual case study examined the differences were also significant. Though the difference in importance attached by the respective groups to questions of social protection was significant in Case E, both groups nevertheless viewed this case as the one in which social protection was more important than in any other case. As we have seen, Case E depicted an offence involving assault on the person and it would appear that for both groups this constitutes behaviour against which it is relatively important that society be given protection.

The conceptual ambiguity inherent in dealing with offence behaviour by means of welfare measures is nowhere more apparent than in cases involving offences which would within a system concerned more with punishment be considered to be the more serious or harmful types of offence. And even in the Scottish system, though it is often not referred to when favourable comments are made about Scottish juvenile justice, some of the more serious offences may have to be dealt with in court. The two-tiered system of juvenile justice in Scotland itself gives institutional recognition to the difficulty of dealing with offence behaviour in terms of welfare. And on a more informal level some panel members have on occasion themselves, in rather graphic language, alluded to the inappropriateness of the Hearing system for dealing with those '. . . best described as apprentice terrorists'. The distinct separation of adjudication of the facts of a case from the decision about the appropriate disposal may well create particular problems for panel members in actual hearings – we shall return to this later.

Morris and McIsaac (1978) suggest that, even in the hearing system in Scotland, panel members do appear to operate some kind of tariff system in which decisions are influenced by 'offence' and not 'need' considerations. This argument appears to have some merit when the importance of the harm caused by or the seriousness of the offence is examined, particularly in relation to Case E involving an assault on the person.

In relation to Case E, though magistrates generally were much more concerned with the seriousness of the offence, panel members and magistrates were agreed as to the importance of this factor for the purpose of decision-making. It would seem reasonable to suggest that there should be a relationship between social protection and the seriousness of the offence since it could be argued that the more serious the offence, the greater the need for social protection. Nor are such arguments lost on panel members. As one put it '(I) would be concerned about the seriousness and dangerousness of offences like taking and driving away a car or else assault with a booted foot'.

There would appear to be *prima facie* support at this early stage of the analysis, for claims that decisions made by panel members may well be made in accordance with some type of modified tariff principle. That is, decisions are made on the basis of the nature of the offence, the seriousness of the offence, the need for adequate social protection and other such considerations. On such an argument there would then appear to be little difference between the position of the panel member quoted above and the magistrate who states, in an explicitly punitive vein, that one must 'measure your punishment by the nature of the offence, the harm that results and how this affects others. Our main purpose is protection'. However, though both magistrates and panel members appear to agree as to the importance of Social Protection and Harm, these factors may well be important for different reasons. Whereas it did seem that both groups shared similar views about Social Protection and Harm, particularly in Case E, further analysis suggested that this might simply not be the case. When the individual Social Protection and Harm scores for Case E were correlated, we find an interesting difference between the two groups of subjects. Social Protection and Harm were significantly but inversely correlated in respect of the panel members' scores ($r = .360$, $p = .05$). For magistrates, the correlation was positive but did not even approach significance ($r = .022$). It would be too naive to suggest that the nature of the offence and its consequences were not associated, at least in the minds of panel members, with the need to protect society. Panel members in general will argue that in general the Hearings system does in effect offer some protection to society though not in as explicit a manner as the juvenile court. But in particular cases, their decision is usually not influenced by the nature of the offence and its consequences except insofar as it is indicative of the need for care. Thus 'sometimes the nature of the offence can display the extent of disturbance in a child or the child's background. But I certainly don't think that the decision should be weighted by the seriousness' (panel member).

The decision then ought not to be linked to the offence in terms of the harm that results nor in terms of the need to protect society. And with specific reference to Social Protection it certainly did seem that this was considered as more important for juvenile magistrates than for panel members. However, in terms of the 'frames of relevance' adopted by the members of the respective groups the significance of this for decision-making needs to be examined more fully in reference to later stages of the research. *In what way* it is relevant for decision-making is an empirical question. Is, for example, assault on the person more important because of the harmful consequences and the seriousness of such an offence or because such an offence is indicative of more serious levels of disturbance and so a greater need for intervention? What has to be remembered is that though panel members, in theory at least, ought not to be concerned with the seriousness of the offence in terms of punitive considerations, some offences are dealt with outside the Hearings system precisely because they are serious. The conceptual ambiguity of dealing with offence behaviour in terms of needs receives institutional expression in Scotland in the fact that children may be prosecuted for certain offences, some of which are considered serious.

Personal Responsibility

A crucial difference between the English and Scottish systems, and one that we have remarked upon more than once, is that magistrates are required on occasion to establish the facts of a case (i.e. did he do it?). In a system of justice based on a non-punitive treatment approach questions of responsibility would theoretically not arise. The position adopted, for example, by Wootton is that the concept of responsibility could and should be eliminated from a system of criminal justice, since intervention ought to be justified in terms of the causes of criminal behaviour. The concept of responsibility was in her view a theological and metaphysical abstraction. Children's Hearings, unlike the Juvenile Courts, are not courts of law. Since the functions of adjudication and of making decisions as to how to deal with children were separated in Scotland by Kilbrandon, panel members, at least in terms of the formal philosophy, only decide upon the need for care. Thus, since panel members are supposed to be concerned with the welfare of the child and his best interests and not with punishment, it could reasonably be expected that the issue of responsibility for an offence would be less important for the panel member than for the magistrate working within a system in which children can be punished and in which the issue of responsibility for an offence is important. This is, however, not to argue that panel members will, in terms of their own working frames of relevance, ignore considerations of responsibility.

We have already seen in discussing responsibility in general that important considerations for the ascription of responsibility were (a) whether the individual had intentionally committed the offence, (b) whether he knew what he was doing and that it was wrong and (c) whether he was aware of the consequences of his actions. Such considerations are significant in ordinary moral discourse in deciding on moral responsibility and in subjecting or exempting someone from blame or punishment. For the purpose of this project, one of the main objectives was to examine the extent to which panel members and magistrates agreed as to the importance of the concept of responsibility and the implications of this for the assessment and interpretation of information in the practical accomplishment of juvenile justice.

In terms of the formal philosophy underlying a social policy ultimately concerned with the welfare of children, deterministic assumptions are paramount. But in terms of the working ideologies or frames of relevance of individuals working within the spirit of that philosophy and responsible for its implementation there may well be what we have referred to as shifts in the frame of relevance (Asquith 1977) with important implications for the translation of social policy into practice. As we have already noted, Priestley et al. (1972) concluded on the basis of their research in the juvenile courts that it would be wrong to suggest that there exists a strong ideological consensus within members of the agencies involved in juvenile justice. Since magistrates are concerned with the level and the nature of involvement of a child in offence behaviour the notion of personal responsibility as a criterion in decision-making was of crucial significance for this project.

Not surprisingly, panel members were overall much less inclined to treat considerations of personal responsibility as important. (The overall difference was significant at .001.) What is particularly interesting is that the case in which panel members treated Personal Responsibility as most important was Case A (based on Sociological Determinism). We shall return to this but it is also worth noting at this juncture that in all cases magistrates ascribed more importance to this factor. When we come to what actually happened in the different types of hearings we shall also see that the significance of this factor was reflected in the 'content' and also influenced the 'form' of the discussion in court. That is, through the use of the case-study method, some preliminary speculations can be made about the extent to which different frames of relevance may influence the use of information and ultimately the decision as to how to deal with a child. What we also found was that when the individual scores for Harm, Social Protection and Personal Responsibility were correlated, there was an important difference between panel members and magistrates. That is, there is a much closer correlation between these factors for magistrates than there is for panel members. Not only then are magistrates more inclined to treat such considerations as more important than did panel members, but there was also a greater degree of association between them. Morris and McIsaac (1978), though they did not include panel members themselves in their research, argued that the statistical relationship between offence behaviour and disposal indicated the operation of some 'tariff principle'. The implication to be drawn here is that there may be some evidence to suggest that magistrates may well operate a system of tariff decision-making but that there is as yet little evidence to indicate that panel members do. Again, this discussion will be resumed in relation to the discussion of the 'content' and 'form' of decision-making.

Though the data relating to personal responsibility continue the trend of significantly different scores, they nevertheless conceal some interesting features which emerge when the constituent elements (Awareness of the Consequences, Awareness (of the difference between right and wrong) and Intentionality) were examined individually.

Again the difference overall between the magistrates' and the panel members' scores was highly significant in terms of Awareness of the difference between right and wrong though there were particular instances (in Case A and Case D) where there was no significant difference. But what was of considerable interest was that there was no difference at all (neither over all cases nor in respect of individual cases) in terms of Awareness of the Consequences. What this was matched by was the fact that though again there was a significant difference between the two groups over Intentionality, with panel members less concerned about this than the magistrates, this was accounted for largely by one case (Case C). In Case E, involving assault on the person, magistrates ascribed much more importance to this than did the panel members. In no other case is there any significant difference between the two. There is then generally little disagreement between panel members and magistrates as to the importance of intentionality for the purpose of decision-making. Thus, in the cases involving theft of a car (Case A), breaking into and damaging a school (Case B), breaking into a factory (Case C) and stealing from a departmental store, the issue of Intentionality was as important for panel members as it was for the magistrates. For all these cases, Awareness of the Consequences was also apparently as important for the magistrates as for the panel members. Only in Case E was there a significant difference with magistrates ascribing much more importance to this factor. The only preliminary interpretation that we can make of this is that, as we have seen, the degree of involvement in the actual planning or execution of such an offence would be important for those whose frame of relevance was founded mainly upon a judicial framework. What this must alert us to in our analysis is the possibility that apparent consensus between the groups of subjects actually conceals significant and fundamental reasons as to why certain factors are important. For example, though there is a degree of agreement between panel members and magistrates as to the importance of Intentionality, it is impossible to gauge in what way Intentionality is deemed important without locating it in the broader framework of the frames of relevance dominating decision-making by the two groups.

Case Studies:
Social Protection, Harm and Personal Responsibility

Even when the influence of different variables was taken into account, there was generally little difference of any note between the case-study scores. Only in a few instances were there significant differences. Of more interest for present purposes was the relationship between the different sets of scores and these are presented for the panel members in table 6.

Table 6. Panel Case Study scores: correlations

	Welfare	Social Protect.	Harm	Awareness	Consequences	Intentionality	Pers. Respons.
Welfare	—	−.405	−.509	−.623	−.254	−.483	−.744
Social Protect.		—	.2772	−.0088	−.3881	−.1231	1.203
Harm			—	−.0956	.0104	.1219	.012
Awareness				—	.3146	.0958	
Consequences					—	−.0531	

Significant correlations are in italic

There is no significant relationship between Intentionality and the other constituent elements of personal responsibility, Awareness (of the difference between right and wrong) and (Awareness of the) Consequences, which are themselves correlated significantly at the .05 level. We also found that longer-serving panel members treated Intentionality as more important than other factors and that the overall difference between panel members and magistrates in terms of the same factor was accounted for solely by one case. It would be unwise to conjecture as to the reason for the difference in importance attached to one constituent element of personal responsibility and not to the other two. Nevertheless, in discussion with panel members, what became obvious was that Awareness of the difference between right and wrong and Awareness of the consequences of behaviour were considered important indications of the child's character. That is, they were more important in terms of the way in which the child had been brought up and of the principles by which his behaviour was governed, rather than being specifically associated with the child's involvement in the offence. The notion of Intentionality, however, more readily locates attention on the child's actual involvement in the offence itself. This may account for the lack of relationship between Intentionality on the one hand and Awareness of consequences on the other. (The same factors in the court sample were all positively correlated.)

The greater importance attached to Intentionality may also be accounted for by the fact that panel members with longer experience did express concern that 'you become hard after a while'. The frustration expressed by the more experienced panel members at the lack of facilities, the continuing reappearance of a number of children, and the apparent increase in 'crime' might explain the importance with which they treat the actual involvement of the child in the offence. It was in expressing such concern that a number of panel members also thought that the restrictions placed on the length of membership of a panel was no bad thing. Certainly the panel members with the longest experience treated Harm, Social Protection and Intentionality all as more important than did those with less experience.

A similar conclusion could be drawn about magistrates since the longer a magistrate had operated in a juvenile court, it appeared to be the case that the more willing he was to treat Intentionality as important. The inference that could be drawn at this stage of the analysis is that with increasing experience in the juvenile court, magistrates more readily ascribe importance to Intentionality as a factor to be considered for the purpose of decision-making. We must stress that the actual differences in the scores were not significant but that the trends displayed paralleled the corresponding scores for panel members.

This was repeated when we also took experience in the adult court into consideration. Thus, it would appear that with increasing length of experience in both the juvenile and the adult court, the notion of Intentionality came to be treated as more important. The longest-serving panel members, who had obviously not had the length (nor the kind) of experience enjoyed by magistrates, also treated Intentionality as more important than their colleagues with less experience.

However, where this was also true of Social Protection and Harm for panel members, it was not so for magistrates, who revealed no consistent pattern in the importance they attached to these two factors. But for Personal Responsibility as a whole, though there is again a lack of significant differences, the more experience a magistrate had, the greater the importance ascribed. That is, personal responsibility would appear to tend to become more important as a factor in the judgment of juvenile magistrates as they gain more experience in court. At this juncture it is impossible to suggest that as magistrates gain experience they attach more importance to the notion of Personal Responsibility and therefore are more punitive. That does not logically follow and nor were the case studies designed to examine that. But it is perhaps worth bearing in mind that Lemon (1974) established that the first year of training did appear to inculcate punitive attitudes and instilled a necessary 'judicial attitude'. The training of magistrates does demand more familiarity with complex legal issues than for panel members, and the magistrate though working in a juvenile court is also a magistrate in the adult court where considerations of liability and fault are more explicitly significant. But institutionally whereas panel members are not required to decide such matters, magistrates even in the juvenile court have to determine 'whether he did it' and then 'what to do about it'. It is when we examine the correlations between the magistrates' scores that more consistency is revealed.

Table 7. Case Study scores: Court Area correlations

	Welfare	Social Protect.	Harm	Awareness	Consequences	Intentionality	Pers. Respons.
Welfare	—	−.454	−.617	−.804	−.620	−.657	−.866
Social Protect.		—	.2983	.1267	−.0371	−.0493	−.038
Harm			—	.2416	.1469	.3715	.299
Awareness				—	.6181	.4729	
Consequences					—	.3220	

Significant correlations are in italic

All three constituent elements of Personal Responsibility (Awareness, Consequences and Intentionality) were correlated significantly. In particular, the correlations (both positive) between the Awareness and Consequences factors, and the Awareness and Intentionality factors were both highly significant. Moreover, not unlike the Scottish figures, the Welfare score attained by the juvenile magistrates was negatively correlated with all other factors considered, and in all cases significantly so. Though the caveats associated with small-scale statistics have to be voiced once more, the strength of the correlations for these factors could not by any means be ignored.

Of particular relevance is the close inter-correlation of Awareness, Consequences and Intentionality. Whereas panel members had treated Intentionality differently from the other two factors, magistrates would appear to be more concerned with all three factors, and their importance for the purpose of decision-making. What remains unanswered at this stage of the analysis is whether the two factors of Awareness and Consequences are more obviously perceived by the magistrates as indicating the level and nature of the involvement of the children in offence behaviour; or whether, as appears to be the case for panel members, they are taken as indicative of the moral development of the child. That is, they tell more about the child generally than about the nature and degree of involvement in the offence. It could be argued that as magistrates operate within a framework of juvenile justice derived from criminal law in its application to adults (they do also, in fact, operate in adult courts) they will be more concerned with establishing the nature of a child's involvement in an offence. Such concerns are more obviously important in a system where amongst the measures available for dealing with children there are more overtly punitive options. The overall concern with personal responsibility and its constituent elements may well be a function of the fact that magistrates can and do punish but also of a system in which the protections and safeguards associated with natural justice or due process are more evident than in a welfare-oriented administrative tribunal such as the Children's Hearing system.

Though it approaches significance, the correlation between Harm and Social Protection as for the panel sample is not statistically significant. It was expected that it would be.

Discussion of the Findings from the Case Studies

There is thus strong evidence to suggest that panel members, at least as assessed by the case-study method, do indeed treat what we have referred to as 'welfare' factors as being of more importance than 'judicial factors'. The general reluctance of both magistrates and panel members to emphasise sociological, biological or processual information is counterbalanced by their preference for psychoanalytic and behaviourist factors. This is not unexpected as we had argued that the involvement of the social work and related professions in the provision of reports, in the hearing process itself, and also in the very selection process (in Scotland) meant that both panel members and magistrates would readily accommodate social-work typifications (see Asquith 1977; Smith 1977). The argument was only partially confirmed as magistrates treated the behaviourist perspective as more important than the others but the lack of difference between this and a psychoanalytically informed one suggests that the importance of these perspectives is that they highlight breakdown in the normal socialisation process as a causal factor in delinquency aetiology. In keeping with the underlying assumptions of a welfare philosophy it may well be that the ideological attractiveness of construing delinquency in such a way is that the objects of treatment or welfare measures are more readily identified. For that reason alone, sociological and biological factors may not be considered as relevant in as much as they are beyond the sphere of competence and effective action of control agents. It is precisely for this reason that the liberalism of the rehabilitative model has been criticised as being conservative and for fostering the developing 'psycho-social' expertise (Bean 1976).

Magistrates, again not unexpectedly, treat Social Protection as of more importance than do panel members though both are agreed that the case in which it is important is that involving assault on the person. Similarly, panel members do generally treat Harm as being less important than do magistrates, though this is subject to some qualification. In two cases (interestingly again Case E involving assault on the person) there is no real disagreement between both groups of subjects. Both treat Harm as important in Case E, the case in which Social Protection was most important. Thus, even panel members do appear to recognise the importance of such factors as Social Protection and Harm given certain circumstances.

Paradoxically in terms of 'personal responsibility', it is in Case E that the most significant difference in the scores is attained, with panel members treating this factor as relatively less important than in other cases. Thus, even though Harm and Social Protection are both considered important this does mean *prima facie* that they are as concerned about the nature of the child's involvement in the offence – *prima facie* because when the constituent elements of personal responsibility are analysed individually, though panel members and magistrates disagree as to the importance of such factors as Awareness of the difference between right and wrong and Intentionality, they do not differ materially in terms of the importance they attach to Awareness of the Consequences. Of the three factors, they are in agreement as to the relative importance of this factor and that of all the three factors in question; it is seen as less important than the others. What is important for our purposes is that Intentionality is not only treated as the most important of the three by the magistrates but that it is also most important for the panel members. And though the Intentionality score is significantly different overall, it is so only because of the very significant differences in relation to the assault case.

The importance of the notion of intent, of deliberateness of choice, is obvious in a system of delinquency control derived from the criminal law in its application to adults. But in a less judicial and more administrative form of tribunal, the signifi- cance of intentionality would seem to be diminished by the philosophical assumptions of a deterministic account of delin- quency. Yet, nevertheless, what we find here is that there is little disagreement between panel members and magistrates as to the importance of the notion. The limitations of the case- study method, though it does attempt to gauge individuals' perceptions of the importance of different kinds of factors, is that we are unable to relate our findings thus far to the actual decision-making process. In particular, the conceptual frame- works of determinism and free-will respectively are not readily reconcilable unless some form of compatibility thesis is adopt- ed. It is in the assessment of information and in the making of decisions about how to deal with children that shifts in frames of relevance will be better appreciated. This is not to argue that the material presented by the case method is not valid. Rather it is a part and a means of examining the different frames of relevance in operation in the practical accomplishment of juv- enile justice. What we have found in the case studies suggests that those who diametrically oppose welfare and punishment, or law enforcement and welfare ideologies, ignore the complex- ity of conceptual schemata as employed by the individuals who implement the philosophy underlying social policy. In particu- lar, the importance of 'intentionality' for both panel members and magistrates is that even within a system based on a deter- ministic philosophy, the possibility that panel members will on occasion operate within a frame of relevance incorporating the concepts of excuse, mitigation and leniency, as well as being overtly punitive, is not precluded. The fact that magistrates treat Personal Responsibility overall as more important, how- ever, suggests that we should be very wary of arguing that Intentionality and related factors are perceived by both groups of subjects as being important for the same reasons. We have already argued that the different perceptions of Awareness and Consequences are important for different reasons.

What we turn to now is an examination of the implications of the principal findings from this stage of the research for the making of decisions about actual cases. The conceptual ambiguity inherent in the welfare or treatment approach to dealing with children who commit offences means that any neat distinctions between different frames of relevance may be difficult to maintain. The merit of the case-study approach is that at the very least it identifies the conceptual complexity of delinquency control as mediated by the assumptions and philosophies of two groups of individuals operating within different control networks. We now wish to examine the relevance of this in a comparison of decision-making processes that are situated within very different administrative and organisational structures.

Chapter Seven

THE HEARING PROCESS:
DECISIONS IN COURT
AND PANEL HEARINGS

The Case Studies, as discussed in the previous chapter, provided a convenient comparative baseline for the research, but they were artificial and abstract in that they neither referred to real cases nor were subject to the contingencies associated with the hearing of cases. Moreover, given the theoretical thrust of the research, not to have developed some means of appraising how panel members and magistrates themselves treated information and what factors influenced actual decisions would have rendered the study open to the same criticisms that were made earlier (chapter IV) of what was referred to as 'traditional' sentencing research. In this chapter, the emphasis will be on analysing the data from the Case Reports and, in the next, what actually happened in court and hearings will be discussed.

There are three basic elements to a decision about children who commit offences: (a) Information; (b) Objectives and Goals; (c) Knowledge and Assumptions about delinquency. The discussion in the preceding chapter related to the analysis of the case studies in which the extent to which individual panel members and juvenile magistrates subscribed to the different available ideologies was examined. In the analysis of the case reports, the discussion will focus on (a) the factors deemed relevant by individuals in reaching decisions about children and (b) the reasons for such decisions. In that respect, the emphasis will be on (a) information and its use and (b) the objectives and goals panel members and magistrates sought to achieve with reference to the actual cases included in the study.

The concern with information and its use is twofold. First, in a system of individualised justice where decisions are based on the characteristics of individuals and not simply through the application of some general principle, decision-makers require a wealth of information. Secondly, how individuals interpret information can only be understood by appreciating the frames of relevance within which they operate and its use is in part determined by the objectives and goals which individuals seek to achieve. A danger of trying to analyse how decisions are made without examining the frames of relevance espoused by decision-makers is that relatively little can be discovered of the process of decision-making. The inadequacy of black-box sentencing research was precisely that it ignored the interpretive and selective activity of those persons with whom rested the responsibility for sentencing.

The information available to both panel members and magistrates is mainly verbal and written though there is another information source which we have elsewhere labelled 'paralinguistic' information (Asquith 1976). In the next chapter, we are to examine the nature of the discussion in the respective settings, but the prime consideration here is with what information both groups of subjects considered relevant for the purposes of reaching a decision about a child who has committed an offence.

In keeping with the logic of the research, the overall aim was to assess the relative influence of 'welfare' and 'judicial' ideologies in decision-making in the two systems. For the purposes of this stage of the research, a 'welfare' score was computed for each of the cases dealt with by the panel members and the magistrates, which once again allowed for some comparison to be made between the decision-making practices involved in the panel and the court.

There are difficulties with this method though it did allow for an examination of the factors that were considered important by the panel members and juvenile magistrates for the purpose of decision-making. In particular, such a method does not readily allow us to appreciate the logic-in-use in the making of decisions, in that it is a rather artificial means of analysing the process of decision-making. Moreover, such a method assumes that the resultant aggregate score is a true indicator of the influence of the relative contributions of the individual participants in that process. But the analysis will later include a discussion of the content and form of the decision-making process and as such will complement the data produced from the Case Reports. However, the merit of the case report method is that it allows the subjects to indicate which factors they considered to be important and in that respect, some progress has been made from that orientation to studying decision-making, which effectively ignored what information subjects considered important and how it influenced their decision.

With regard to 'how' information affected decisions, as has been argued, much of the logic of decision-making revolves around the reasons given by the subjects themselves for a decision. Though it is obviously important to appreciate which factors are used in decision-making, to ignore the reasons for a decision would be to ignore, as has been earlier suggested, the relationship between information, decision and frame of relevance. Merely to analyse decision-making by requesting the subjects to indicate which factors were important would be to expose oneself, albeit with minor modifications, to the very criticisms that have been made above of 'black box' sentencing research. Hence, in the Case Report forms the subjects were also asked to indicate the reasons for their decisions.

The Cases

The samples of actual cases used in the main study were again small, with 30 cases in the panel and 35 cases in the court area. But since each subject completed a Case Report form for each case involved in the study, this meant that 90 Case Report forms were completed by panel members, three for each case; 96 were completed by the juvenile magistrates, nine of the cases in court having been presided over by only two magistrates. The main reason for the small number of cases was the intention to analyse the process of decision-making in the respective systems in as much depth as possible, given the restrictions imposed by the fact that only one researcher was involved. Because a number of strategies were being employed in the research, this had the effect of making the collection of data a lengthy and time-consuming process. This was particularly problematic in the court, where magistrates often had to hear as many as thirty or forty cases at one sitting. Since we wished to examine the relative importance of 'welfare' or 'judicial' factors as judged by panel members or magistrates, only those cases where an offence had been committed and where the offender was male were considered suitable. To have included girls would have been to have added additional complexity to the analysis by introducing a further category of variables. Moreover, the cases had to involve 'fresh' charges. This was particularly important in the panel area where, under the terms of the 1968 Act, decisions made about children are subject to review by a panel before but no later than a year after the hearing. Review cases were thus not considered suitable because of the peculiar circumstances of such hearings. At each court or panel hearing, the first suitable case was chosen for the purposes of the study. Because of the criteria governing selection, this meant that in the panel area where there were as few as four cases at each hearing there were occasions when no suitable cases were available. The advantage however was that in both the panel and court area, during the course of the research as many as 200 hearings were attended during the collection of the data.

There were few differences of any significance between the two samples of panel and court cases. In terms of age (on average 13 years old) and the number of charges included in the referral there was no difference. There was however a significant difference ($p = .001$) in terms of whether the offender had any previous known offences. Only ten of the court cases had previous offences whereas nineteen of the panel cases had. We will discuss the significance of this later in the analysis but it is perhaps worth making one or two comments just now about trying to take such a piece of information into account. Given what has been referred to as the conceptual ambiguity of dealing with offenders in a welfare-oriented system, the significance a child's past history has for the practical accomplishment of juvenile justice is not immediately obvious. Any attempt to infer *how* a panel member or magistrate construes past record by analysing *what* factors were apparently important must be theoretically suspect where no attempt has been made to involve the individual's own interpretation in the analysis. Even in relation to the national statistics pertaining to Scotland the same ambivalence impedes meaningful interpretation of the increasing number of children who appear at a children's hearing on offence grounds, or at the very least those who are referred to the Reporter for those reasons. Is this because more children in 'need' are being picked up by the new system? Or is it because the new system is 'too soft', a factor in itself accounting for increasing crime figures? It is in the meaning given to such statistics that we more readily appreciate the convergence of panel and political ideology (see *Scotsman* 1978).

What was particularly interesting about the nature of the charges (in terms of which the samples were significantly different) was that five of the panel cases involved assault whereas none of the court cases were of this nature. The other cases in both samples were composed mainly of either theft or theft by housebreaking (burglary). Given that panel members appeared to be more concerned to adopt a judicial orientation in relation to the assault case in the case studies, this provided an ideal opportunity to identify what implications such an offence would have for the making of decisions in the process of the hearing.

Decision-making in Court and Panel Hearings

In the Case Study analysis, the major conclusion, and one that was surely not unexpected was that 'welfare' considerations were much more important for panel members than for magistrates. On the basis of the analysis of the information deemed relevant for the purpose of decision-making in actual cases exactly the same conclusion can be drawn. Overall, in terms of commitment to a 'welfare' frame of relevance, the scores attained by the panel members were significantly higher $(p > .001)$. Again, such a conclusion is perhaps not surprising in relation to a global statement about panel members and magistrates overall and the more interesting data come when the nature of the offences involved are taken into consideration and when the specific factors deemed important by the respective groups are identified.

It has been suggested that panel members, though theoretically concerned only with the needs of children, do in fact operate some kind of tariff principle. That is, decisions are influenced by the kind of offence, its seriousness, and so on. Morris and McIsaac (1978) argue that the conceptual ambiguity underlying the control of children who commit offences within a welfare framework is reflected in the fact that the panel members operate within a retributive or more explicit punishment/non-treatment orientation than intended by the legislation. However, we argued earlier that such claims were made on the basis of a methodological framework in which the frame of relevance revealed more of the researcher's objectives and goals than of the subject's. There was little evidence in this study to support the claim that a hidden tariff system was operated by the panel members.

It would be wrong to suggest that no panel member ever reached decisions with tariff considerations in mind. Morris and McIsaac (1978) have made their views on this well known. Indeed one panel member in the study did confess that: 'I'd be inclined to think some offences more serious than others. My decision has to reflect something of that'. But the general conclusion drawn from the 90 panel-member case-reports is that tariff principles did not influence the decisions studied here.

When controls were maintained for the type of offence, the number of charges and the number of previous offences, panel members and juvenile magistrates were in disagreement about the importance of 'welfare' with magistrates treating it as less important. In all instances the 'between' scores were significantly different. However, the importance attached by panel members to 'welfare' was not influenced significantly whether one or more charges were involved in the referral, whether the child had a previous offence history or not, or whether the case involved theft, theft by housebreaking or assault. It has to be said that the same held for magistrates though the trend was for the 'welfare' scores to be lower for cases involving more than one charge and previous offence history.

Again though the scores were not significantly different, panel members in fact, in cases in which children had had some previous offence history and in the cases involving assault, took the 'welfare' of the child more into account. The fact that when controls are maintained for prior offence history and type of case, more importance is attached to welfare factors in cases with one or more previous offences and in assault cases suggests at least that the importance of these categories is not simply that they provide the basis for a more punitive orientation. For panel members operating within a more overtly welfare-oriented system of juvenile justice, this may well indicate a greater need for intervention, rather than provide the basis for some form of penal calculus. Morris (1974) has also acknowledged that the more 'serious' the offence committed by a child, the more serious might be his needs. What this highlights once again is the necessity of appreciating for what reasons and with what objectives in mind, individuals reach decisions about children who commit offences. This is because the conceptual complexity of separating 'needs' from 'deeds' is reflected in the semantics of delinquency control, which are riven with ambiguity. The danger of ignoring the interpretive activity of the control agent is that possible shifts in the frames of relevance are ignored in the analysis. It also identifies the vagueness of such freely used concepts as 'seriousness'. The measure of such notions has to be determined by reference to the information deemed relevant by the decision-maker and the objectives he hopes to realise.

In the case-study analysis, it was found that the assault case was the one in which 'welfare' was less important for panel members who indeed treated that case in much the same way as had the juvenile magistrates. This was at least *prima facie* evidence that panel members may well operate some kind of tariff and indeed retributive principle. Yet, in the actual cases before hearings, the panel members treated perpetrators of assault more in terms of welfare than they did the perpetrators of other offences, so no conclusion can be drawn to the effect that a tariff or retributive principle is being operated here. And as we shall see, the reasons given by panel members for the decisions they reached contain no explicit references to retributive or punitive sanctions of any kind. This does not mean that the type of offence is not important but rather that greater recognition has to be given to the importance it has for the decision-maker. Even Morris and McIsaac (1978) recognise that the ambiguity in attempting to deal with offenders by principles associated with social welfare may allow for 'seriousness' to be defined in terms of the child's needs and not his deeds.

In the case studies, magistrates did attach much more importance to more judicially oriented considerations than the panel members and it begins to appear that this might also be true with actual cases. The juvenile magistrates operate within an organisational and structural context derived ultimately from a court of criminal law, whereas panel members operate within a system more exclusively concerned with the identification and meeting of needs. The legal ideology that characterises the juvenile court is epitomised by the fact that magistrates must not only decide on how best to deal with a child but also on whether the child did in fact commit the offence or not. Panel members have no such jurisdiction.

Age and Responsibility

As noted above, there was no significant difference between the ages of the children in the panel and court samples. However, the age of the child would appear to be an important factor for juvenile magistrates as it was closely (and negatively) correlated with the 'welfare' score ($n = 96$; $p = .001$). In other words, juvenile magistrates attached more importance to 'judicial' than 'welfare' factors in the case of older children. In a system in which legal responsibility is still an important concern it is to be expected that the older a child is, the more will his capacity for responsibility for what he has done be a relevant ground in deciding what to do about him. And, as Bottoms observed (see chapter 1), the recommendations for modification of the juvenile court which were incorporated into the 1969 Act in

England were made on the premise that the individual-patho-
logy model of delinquency was more appropriate for younger
than for older children. It was on such an argument that the
distinction between care and criminal proceedings was drawn.
Moreover, what has to be remembered is that, unlike panel
members, juvenile magistrates may apply explicitly punitive
measures. Juvenile magistrates are required to make what
Thomas (1970) calls primary and secondary decisions. That is,
they have to decide first of all whether a case is to be dealt with
mainly in terms of welfare measures on the one hand or punitive
and judicially oriented measures on the other. The age of the
child will then not be unimportant in such respects and only
after the primary decision is made can it be decided what to do
with the child. In some cases, e.g. road traffic offences, the
magistrates' choice as to how to deal with a case is statutorily
prescribed, leaving them with little choice in the primary decision. No such limitation is imposed on the panel member who
is in formal terms at least only concerned with the possibility of
compulsory measures of care. In that respect, the child's age is of
less significance for the panel member and this was reflected in
the lack of association between age and the importance ascribed
to 'welfare'. The emphasis on the individual in terms of responsibility is a feature also of the specific factors deemed relevant by
magistrates.

Relevant Information

Welfare Items. Over the 90 panel and 96 case reports completed
by the panel members and magistrates there was very little
difference in the volume of information employed for the purpose of decision-making. As well as being asked to indicate
which items were important both groups were required to indicate how important specific items were for them in helping
them to reach a decision. Only the more significant of these are
included in table 8.

In general, there were in fact few significant differences in the
importance ascribed to specific factors by panel members and
magistrates. Both groups agree on the importance of such factors as the child's relationship with his father, mother and
siblings, home conditions and parental discipline, all of which
are treated as having considerable importance. In the case
studies, both panel members and magistrates attached most
importance to the information in the case studies which referred to parental discipline and to the child's relationships with

Table 8. Mean weighted scores

	$\bar{x}$		
Factors treated as important	Panel	Court	p
5. Relationship with father	1.8777	1.5376	
6. Relationship with mother	1.6222	1.3548	
7. Relationship with siblings	0.611	0.333	
8. Family unit	1.7333	1.1075	.005
9. Financial position of family	0.6	0.6989	
10. Broken home	0.3777	0.5483	
11. Child's character	1.6555	1.1505	.02
12. Area of residence	0.4555	0.5376	
13. Home conditions	1.311	1.4301	
14. Associates	1.188	0.6021	.001
15. Parents in trouble	0.1222	0.129	
16. Treated as delinquent	0.1555	0.0215	
17. Leisure time	1.0111	0.7096	
19. Parental discipline	1.688	1.5376	
35. S.W. relationship to family	0.8222	0.3655	.01

significant adults. Where they did disagree, however, was in relation to the family unit, the child's character and the child's associates.

What is particularly interesting about these differences is that they refer either to the child or to his family. The reorganisation of social work in both countries had been based on a re-conceptualisation of the ideological foundation of social-work practice as much as the need for greater access to social services for the community. The notion of generic social work had relocated the focus on the family as a unit rather than on individuals. What is perhaps surprising about these significant differences is that it would appear that juvenile magistrates attach less importance to the social and personal characteristics of the child and his family than do panel members.

Panel members and magistrates also differed significantly in the importance they ascribed to the social worker's relationship with the family, this being more important for the Scottish group. A reason for this may well be that in the Scottish system of juvenile justice, and certainly in the panel area studied, social workers who are either known to the family or who have prepared the social work report are encouraged to attend the hearing. Panel members can therefore more readily appreciate for themselves the relationship of the social worker with the family. In the court area, the function of social-work represent-ation to the court was fulfilled by a social worker seconded full-time for that purpose. Only occasionally were those who wrote the reports actually present in court. The presence at a hearing of a social worker with knowledge of a family is a feature of Scottish juvenile justice which one might expect to have implications for what actually takes place during a hear-ing. But as we shall see later, this did not appear to be the case. What also may account for how the social worker's relationship to the family is viewed is that there was a much closer relation-ship between the social workers and the panel members than existed in the court area. Indeed magistrates felt, and expressed, some concern at the expansion of social-work powers at the cost of their own.

Significantly, both panel members and juvenile magistrates agreed on the relative unimportance of Area of Residence, though in most instances the children of both samples of cases came from the more deprived of the areas within the panel and the court jurisdictions. This does not however of itself imply that the Area of Residence is altogether unimportant or irrelev-ant. In the case-study analysis the emphasis on individualistic explanations was identified and in relation to the actual cases here the same interpretation may need to be made. That is, within the institutional setting of the panel and court hearings, based on a welfare or treatment philosophy to a lesser or greater degree, the nature and extent of intervention required to deal with problems of social deprivation is beyond the sphere of influence of panel members and magistrates. Both the formal philosophy of the respective systems and the informal philo-sophies of panel members and magistrates in accomplishing decisions are premised on the commitment to individualistic explanations of behavioural problems. This is perhaps not sur-prising since the focus of assessment with a view to either preventive or curative measures is a child and not broader social and political considerations.

Social Work and School Reports. In all the panel cases some form of social work and school report was available to the panel members, and in England they were available in all but two cases.

Similar importance was ascribed to social work and school reports by both panel members and magistrates. But with re-spect to how informative they were thought to be, there was in fact a very significant difference ($p = .001$). Whereas 64 magistrates considered the reports to be very informative only 39 panel members did so. Magistrates therefore consider social-work reports just as important but more informative than do the panel members. One obvious explanation could be that the quality of the reports south of the border is better than in Scotland. However, the very different administrative and structural characteristics of the two systems may be more important contributory factors. Panel members, unlike juvenile magistrates, may, and in most cases do, have all reports for a case a number of days before the actual hearing. They are therefore able to assimilate the information contained therein and to employ it as the basis for discussion or exploring certain aspects of a child's background during the actual hearing. The magistrates only receive the reports after a finding of guilt has been made and after the pertinent facts of the offence and the case have been discussed in court. Panel members are therefore more directly involved at a personal level in the diagnosis and identification of needs than are juvenile magistrates, many of whom expressed concern at the delegation of real discretionary power away from the courts to the local social-services department. Panel members may themselves therefore be more willing to disagree with basic information contained in reports, and they also have the opportunity of exploring particular concerns further in the actual hearing. For that reason, they may find social work reports less informative and less important than magistrates.

Others have noted (Morris and McIsaac 1978) that panel members rarely disagree with the recommendations made by social workers. Certainly, in our study, on only 11 occasions did panel members disagree with the social worker's recommendation. However, since choices have to be made only on three general types of decision, that is discharge, supervision at home, or residential supervision, there is rather little room for disagreement anyway. What may be more important for panel members is not agreement with the decision but agreement as to the reasons for the decision. We have argued elsewhere that the danger of analysing decision-making from statistical information about outcome is that *prima facie* similar decisions may be founded upon very different assessments of information and very different objectives. Certainly where there is a greater range of measures available, more disagreement could be expected between individuals, and in this study magistrates disagreed with the social-work recommendation on no less than thirty occasions.

There was no disagreement of any significance either in relation to the importance or the informativeness of the school reports. It became obvious from discussions, with the panel members and magistrates that they felt that school reports were extremely important but that the quality of report provided was generally poor. In both the study areas, dissatisfaction centred around the fact that school reports were written on stereotyped forms. They were generally thought to be of little value other than providing basic information about the child's school performance.

Parents and Children in the Hearing. Panel members and magistrates were asked to indicate how important, if at all, they considered the attitudes of the key individuals in the actual hearing to be. For panel members, the attitude of the father, mother and child were very much more important than for the magistrates ($p = .02$, .001 respectively).

It would certainly appear that the attitudes of mother, father and child in the hearing are a more influential determinant in the panel than in the court setting. Open and informal discussion was seen as being one of the benefits of an administrative style system of juvenile justice (Kilbrandon 1964), as well as the possibility of parental participation in the decision-making process. It certainly appears to be the case that panel members do in fact ascribe more importance to the role and contribution of parents and children in the children's hearings. We shall see later that the nature of the contributions made by parents and children in the hearing is very different from that of parents and children in court. But for the present, it is perhaps worth speculating as to possible reasons for the difference in importance ascribed by the panel members and the magistrates to the presentation of the parents and children. Magistrates in interview suggested that appearance at court should be something that had 'a salutary effect' on the parents and children. Moreover, they were concerned that proper respect be shown by them to the bench. Now whereas one or two panel members felt that their colleagues were not formal enough in the panel hearing, most of them felt that the atmosphere was more conducive to discussion than the court type of hearing.

Two comments can be made. First, panel members may consider the participation of the parents and children in the actual discussion of the case as a crucial source of information. Secondly, for this very reason, and given that the structure of the Hearings system in Scotland allows the panel member to participate more fully in the diagnosis and assessment of a case, the way in which the parents and children present themselves may be taken to reflect wider considerations, e.g. how the parents relate to the child or to each other and so on. But it certainly appeared from the court and panel hearings attended by the researcher that parents and children are given a greater opportunity to be involved in a discussion with panel members than with magistrates.

Judicial Items. Again on the basis of the case studies, panel members appeared to treat Social Protection, Seriousness/Harm, Awareness of Wrong and Intentionality as less important than do magistrates. From table 9, the list of judicial items considered important for the making of decisions about actual cases again reveals great differences on these factors.

Table 9. Mean weighted scores of factors treated as important

	Panel	Court	*p*
Social Protection	0.33	0.75	0.01
Harm	0.10	0.30	0.05
Seriousness	0.43	0.86	0.02
Awareness of Wrong	0.93	1.20	0.05
Awareness of Consequences	0.52	0.73	0.05
Intentionality	0.48	1.00	0.01

In the simulated cases, there was no difference in the importance ascribed to Awareness of the Consequences and in the actual cases that is in fact the only factor in terms of which there is no disagreement between panel members and magistrates. For magistrates, Social Protection, Harm, Seriousness, Awareness of Wrong and Intentionality are all much more important than for panel members and this despite the fact that a number of the cases in the panel sample had involved assault. Earlier, the age of the child was identified as being a crucial factor for magistrates in terms of the ascription of responsibility for behaviour. What is now apparent is that the notion of intentionality in offence behaviour is of prime significance for magistrates and may well be influential in determining whether and how much a child may be punished. Certainly, one of the most

important, and significant, differences between the two groups
is in relation to the notion of Intentionality. In the preceding
chapter, the lack of difference between the two groups in terms
of Awareness of the Consequences in conjunction with the very
different treatment of intentionality was taken to suggest,
prima facie, differing frames of relevance. Similarly, whereas
there was a close relationship between Consequences, Awareness of Wrong and Intentionality for magistrates, for panel
members there was no such threefold association. The argument has been that magistrates are much more concerned with
the degree and nature of involvement in specific offences whereas panel members were much more concerned to appraise the
child's moral development and general awareness of misbe-
haviour. Certainly, this appears to receive some support from
the evidence of the actual cases, where again the question of
intent is a crucial determinant of magistrates' decisions. Given
that magistrates can and do punish, they are logically required
to be more concerned with the question of intent in order to
inflict punishment justly. And in practice, the procedure, and
indeed philosophy, of the juvenile court is premised upon the
significance of the issue of intent for a form of proceedings
derived from criminal law. When the reasons for the decisions
made are examined later in this chapter the implications of the
way in which panel members and magistrates respectively treat
Social Protection, Seriousness, Intentionality and so on will be
seen to provide further evidence that different frames of relevance are employed.

The nature of the offence was again very much more important for the court sample than for the panel. And magistrates
were found to be much more concerned than panel members
with the child's involvement in offence behaviour.

It would perhaps be rather easy at this juncture to suggest that
there is then no evidence at all to suggest that panel members do
operate a tariff principle. However, when the type of offence, the
number of charges and the number of previous offences are held
constant (see appendix II) what is remarkable is that between
the court and panel there were in fact very few significant
differences in the importance given to Social Protection,
Seriousness, Harm, Awareness of wrong, Awareness of Consequences and Intentionality. Moreover, for panel members
social protection and seriousness were in fact significantly more
important for decision-making in relation to cases with more
than one charge than for those with only one involved. How

then might this be best explained? Is it indicative of some form of tariff decision-making? The danger of such premature conjecture is that it lends itself to the same criticism of superficiality as those claims about the punitive orientations of panel members founded on analyses of the statistical associations of decisions with the variables deemed relevant by the researcher. Similarly, as our philosophical and historical discussion showed, there is no simple dichotomy between punishment and treatment, or free-will and determinism. Rather, the development of juvenile justice has been characterised by continual attempts to reconcile welfare and punitive objectives. And as we have argued earlier, in terms of the available ideologies, it is perfectly feasible for an individual to be concerned about the serious nature of offending and the need to offer society protection without being committed to punishment. Put in another way, it seems perfectly reasonable for someone to have a concern for societal protection and the nature of the offence, but nevertheless to adopt a working frame of relevance in which children do not conceptually belong to those categories of individuals who may rightly be punished. When we come to consider the reasons given for decisions we shall argue that there is considerable evidence to support this claim.

From our analysis it therefore appears that generally speaking there is relatively little disagreement between panel members and magistrates over the importance of the number of offences, the nature of the offence and whether the child had previous offences. What matters however is the way in which these are considered to be important. It is in appreciating the overarching frame of relevance espoused by individuals and derived from competing available ideologies that the reasons for the importance of particular sets of information can best be acknowledged. Earlier, the objectives and goals espoused by the decision-maker were identified as a crucial element in decision-making. It is to this that we now turn.

Reasons for Decisions

After each Case Report was completed in which panel members and magistrates indicated the importance of specific factors, they were then asked to indicate what the main reasons were for the decision. An interesting feature of this exercise was that since individual panel members were asked to indicate their reason for the decision, it was obvious that apparently similar decisions were made on the basis of very different reasons and

considerations as between different individuals at a panel or
court hearing. We shall return to this at the end of the chapter,
but here we present a list of the main categories of reason stated
by panel members and magistrates in support of the decisions
made in actual cases (see table 10).

Table 10. Reasons stated in support of decisions made.

	Panel	Court
Family and child welfare oriented reasons	111	64
Home/area conditions	2	12
Schooling	25	1
Reports	—	8
Nature of offence and child's involvement	23	16
Past record	7	17
Past disposals/measures	11	4
Punitive objects	—	23

A number of inferences can be made from these figures. First,
juvenile magistrates would appear to justify decisions in terms
of punitive objectives more often than the panel members and
would likewise appear to be less concerned about welfare objectives. Nevertheless, panel members do also seem to have
considered the nature of the offence and the child's involvement
in it more than did their court counterparts. Secondly, magistrates have stated in a number of cases that the reports and
information contained therein were important determinants of
and reasons for the decisions made whereas the panel members
did not justify their decisions in this way at all.

Panel members would appear to take welfare objectives into
consideration much more than the magistrates, since they made
much more frequent reference to welfare and family-oriented
factors than did the magistrates. It is significant in view of our
earlier discussions that though the overall figures are different,
magistrates and panel members both stated that parental control is an important reason for a decision (21 and 28 times
respectively). Similarly, the low priority given to area conditions is also reminiscent of the fact that the case study which
was indicated as providing the least important welfare factors
was that in which environmental causes were presented. A
possible explanation of the apparent lack of emphasis on welfare
objectives in the reasons magistrates gave for their decisions

may well relate to the different sources of information in the respective systems. We shall see later the very different inter-actional processes at work within the court and panel hearings. But we have already seen that the various forms of report are available to the panel members over a much longer period than to the magistrates. This may explain the lesser emphasis placed on welfare objectives by juvenile magistrates, as well as the importance they attach to reports as a whole. However, what also has to be taken into consideration is that, unlike panel members, the juvenile magistrates can avail themselves of more explicitly punitive measures.

Of the reasons given by panel members for their decisions, there were more than 40 references to the nature of the offence and the child's involvement in it, the child's past record and any measures the child may have previously experienced. There were, however, no explicit references to punishment in any of the forms discussed earlier. All decisions by panel members appeared therefore to have been reached with the child's inter-est and welfare in mind. But of the 61 references made by juvenile magistrates to those same factors (nature of the offence etc.) there were 23 reasons given which contained some refer-ence to punitive considerations. Since magistrates can, and do, punish, a distinction was drawn between those cases in which the final outcome was either a supervision or a care order and those in which it was a fine, or a discharge, or an order for committal to an attendance or detention centre.

In cases where the decision involved a care or supervision order, welfare factors were deemed more important by magis-trates than in the cases where the decisions had been a fine, committal to an attendance centre or detention centre (the case report means were 61.6 and 43.2 respectively, $p = .001$). An inference that could be made is that there is then, at least for the juvenile magistrates, a clear relationship between the actual decision and the factors taken into consideration. That is, where the final outcome is a care or supervision order there is a much greater emphasis on welfare factors; whilst where the outcome is more explicitly punitive, there is greater emphasis on what we have termed 'judicial fctors'. It would then appear that there are two conceptually different frames of relevance in operation: in one, children are construed as legally, if not morally, respons-ible for their behaviour and as therefore being eligible for punishment; in the other, the relevance of information about a child's social and personal circumstances is inextricably linked to a decision to commit a child to the care of the local social services. However, as we suggested at the beginning, such frames of relevance are ideal-typical in that the difficulty of separating them conceptually may be reflected in the reasons given for a decision. It is also reflected in the fact that there is no clear dichotomy between punishment and treatment in the first place.

There did appear to be evidence of conceptual ambiguity in the magistrates' reasons for decisions. The most clear-cut reasons were those which did in fact refer to a care or supervision order. In all cases, the reasons were primarily to benefit the child or the family by offering them social work and related services. The only evidence of possible conceptual ambiguity was displayed in a number of cases where reasons given revealed a mixture of punitive and welfare considerations. That is, the child was to be punished but only as a means of promoting his welfare or serving his best interests. Certainly the 'available ideology' of the compatibility thesis would support utilitarian justifications of punishment/treatment. Amongst the reasons given by juvenile magistrates (see appendix 1) utilitarian justifications are prevalent and include the deterrence of the offender, the prevention of crime, and the protection of the public. It was expected that more explicit reference would be made to social protection, but its omission may be due to the fact that juvenile magistrates, as revealed in discussion generally, accept social protection as an overriding objective in any case. There are few explicit references to retribution; but the greater concern of juvenile magistrates with those judicial factors of intentionality and the nature of the offence, as well as the simple fact that they decide not simply whether but also to what extent punishment should be invoked, means that in those cases in which punitive sanctions are invoked their decisions are founded on a blend of retributive and utilitarian justifications. As Gordon states, the criminal law is a blend of the utilitarian and the deontological (1967).

Perhaps the most important points to draw from this section are that juvenile magistrates seem capable of maintaining fairly discrete frames of relevance depending on whether punitive (either punishment/non-treatment or punishment/treatment) or welfare objectives are to be invoked. In addition, and unlike the panel members, they may legitimately avail themselves of punitive sanctions. What, then, of the apparent emphasis by panel members on 'judicial factors'?

What is particularly interesting about the reasons given by panel members is that all of their references to the judicial or allied factors related specifically to information about the offence and the child's involvement in it. Yet there were no overt references made to punitive objectives in the reasons for the decisions. That is, though judicial and allied factors did appear to form the basis for decision-making in some instances, the objectives which panel members sought to achieve did not include any overt reference to punishment, though there were references made to information such as the seriousness of the offence, the triviality of the offence and so on. The magistrates, on the other hand, stated as important objectives in those cases involving punitive sanctions the wish to give a short, sharp shock; to deter the offender; to prevent crime; and to protect the public.

Discussion in the Light of the Case Reports. On the basis of the case studies and case reports, the panel members and magistrates do not appear to attach the same importance to the notion of Intentionality. Where children are not held morally responsible, they may not justifiably be subjected to punishment. This has been one of the arguments that has underpinned the development of criminal law away from a purely retributive system of justice. In the juvenile court, magistrates do appear to operate within a retributive framework to the extent that they reach their decisions bearing in mind the principles of consistency and proportionality – at least in reference to those cases which, either on account of statutorily prescribed guidelines or because of seriousness, are the subject of punitive sanctions. They are thereby able to separate conceptually the different frames of relevance underpinning punishment and treatment, in part because the structural and constitutional arrangements of juvenile justice in England allow them to do so. The crucial and central category accommodated within these different frames of relevance is that of moral responsibility, whereby those who may be punished can be distinguished from those who may not.

In Scotland, the organisational and structural arrangement is such that the notion of criminal responsibility does still apply, with appropriate standards of evidence and proof. This however applies only within the court structure, since children in Scotland may still be prosecuted – but only in court. Similarly, where children deny the grounds of referral, their case is referred to the Sheriff for adjudication. The separation of the functions of adjudication and disposal neatly epitomises the supposed in-compatibility of a legal with a welfare ideology.

The fact that, in 90 reasons given for decisions by panel members, there are no explicit references to punishment whether of the punishment/treatment or punishment/non-treatment kind is perhaps then not unexpected within a system which is based upon a deterministic conception of delinquency. On the basis of the case-study and case-report analysis the conclusion has to be that this is because of the very different way in which panel members and juvenile magistrates accommodate the crucial concept of Intentionality. Since panel members appear to treat this notion as less important than do magistrates it is not surprising that there are fewer explicit references to the differing ideologies of punishment.

Consequently, this will have important implications for the interpretation of information about the child's background and his actual involvement in the offence. Magistrates are more concerned to establish responsibility or fault for specific offences – indeed that is one of their functions. They are also required on occasion to operate some form of tariff system to determine the extent to which children should be subjected to punishment whether for punishment/treatment considerations or for non-treatment/punishment considerations. Panel members, however, though not concerned to the same extent as magistrates with responsibility and fault for specific offences appear to be more concerned with whether the child is able generally to appreciate the difference between right and wrong, or to acknowledge what consequences impinge on untoward behaviour. Thus a child's past record (see above) may well be important for panel members, operating within a conceptual framework of need, in the attempt to construct as reasonable an assessment as possible of whether and to what degree a child is in need of compulsory measures of care. Morris argues (1976) that offence behaviour has an important bearing on decisions reached by panel members in that there is a relationship between such factors as the seriousness of the offence and the disposal reached. We agree with her in part. But it is methodologically naive to infer from the identification of a relationship between certain factors in a case and the final outcome *how* people interpret those factors or in what frame of relevance. That would tell us about the researcher's, not the subject's, view of the relevance of the information. The reasons given by panel members themselves are necessary to assessing the relevance to them of information.

Nevertheless, despite the lack of concern with responsibility in the sense of moral responsibility, it would be naive to suggest that panel members operated only within a frame of relevance underpinned by the conceptual framework of need. In everyday life, for the purpose of ascribing blame or responsibility it makes a difference whether or not an act had to occur and the designation of conformity or deviance depends on this commonsense consideration. The very language of treatment and the technical language of need is not necessarily accommodated within ordinary everyday language in which the notion of fault, right or wrong, is important. Panel members obviously do make a distinction between those cases in which the referral involves an offence and those cases which would formerly have been called care and protection cases. They appear to do so in a number of ways.

Information and its Use. When offence criteria become relevant determinants of decisions, then information about the personal, social and environmental background of children may assume a different significance. Information may then be used not for 'explanation' as such but in terms of 'mitigation'. Thus, decisions to put on supervision in the community may be determined not simply by the need for care but because 'it would be unfair to send him to a List D school, especially after what he has been through at home'. Similarly, panel members confess that there are cases when leniency is called for, a concept which it is difficult to accommodate within a process of decision-making theoretically designed to meet need.

Interestingly enough, a similar confusion in frames of relevance also occurs in the juvenile court though not necessarily in the magistrates' minds. We shall have more to say about the contribution of the lawyer to the actual hearing of a case but we note that in the cases where lawyers were involved, the mean case-report score was lower than for children not legally represented. Lawyers, in presenting information to the court about a child (see below) spend a considerable deal of time discussing the nature and circumstances of the offence and the child's involvement in it. Moreover, it appears that information about the child's social, personal and environmental characteristics are used by way of mitigation. That is, the information is employed as a means of asking for leniency and as an explanation of the child's appearance in court. The concentration by lawyers in presenting their case on such factors as the offence, the nature of the child's involvement and the nature of the offence may well be reflected in the fact that the mean case-report score for such cases was 43.3 compared with 50.6 for those without legal representation.

In the juvenile court, the magistrates do have the opportunity to decide upon measures which are based upon overt punitive considerations. The panel members do not, and we wish to argue that the fact that they may on occasion accept the validity of notions such as leniency and mitigation reflects an inability to operate entirely within a frame of relevance based purely on assumptions about the causes of delinquency and the needs of children. On occasion 'you have to be lenient – some offence referrals are just trivial' (panel member). That panel members do differentiate between those who commit offences and those who appear at a panel hearing for other reasons is also indicated in another way.

Use of Resources. One of the implications of the development of the treatment model in juvenile justice was that the distinction between offender and child in need of care for other reasons should be eroded. Consequently, the resources, especially the residential establishments, were to provide facilities to meet the needs of children who have been referred to the panel system on both offence and other grounds. However, not all panel members are able to maintain the lack of distinction between offenders and other children, simply because the offender is a child who has broken a law. As a result, some panel members are dissatisfied – mainly because of the 'contamination' theory – that they have to commit children in need of care to the same establishment as that to which they send offenders. In this respect, there is then agreement between some panel members and magistrates who wish to keep delinquents and other children separate because, as the following quotations suggest,

> One is on the slippery path to crime and the other is in need of care and protection. (magistrate)
> . . . it's the good ones who would be corrupted. Especially those who are in need of care and protection are likely to be most vulnerable. (magistrate)

One panel member in fact argued that

> I'd like to be able to select the List D school – according to degrees of badness, i.e. make schools graded according to degree of badness of the offender. Then allow the child to come up through them in different stages.

Panel members, however are more intimately involved in the

decision-making process than magistrates and the fact that there does seem to be confusion in frames of relevance due to the conceptual ambiguity raises a further intriguing question. Hogarth (1971) criticised earlier sentencing research for ignoring the penal philosophy of the judge. What we in turn suggested earlier was that sentencing, or at least decision-making in juvenile court and panel hearing, is in fact a collective process. The issue that this presents then is the possibility that *prima facie* similar decisions in fact rest on different interpretations of information, are made with different objectives in mind and with different conceptions of what available resources are for. Where there is ambiguity or ambivalence in the working ideologies of the decision-makers, then the decision to send to a List D school can be made by those different panel members on the basis of very different considerations. The conflict traced earlier in this book between different models of delinquency causation may then be reflected in lay assumptions about what use is to be made of supervision, List D schools, Care Orders etc. Despite the change of name, for example, in Scotland, a number of residential establishments still have the reputation (at least in the eyes of some panel members) of dealing with particularly tough boys.

Though Platt (1975) is surely correct in highlighting the tacit assumptions of those responsible for implementing systems of social control, what must surely be of importance is how individuals collectively reach a decision. The argument in the next chapter will be in fact that one of the crucial differences between a panel and a court hearing is the way the search for information is conducted. This will also require a discussion of the degree to which individuals, who presumably do not completely share the same frame of relevance, work together in the task of decision-making.

Punishment. As we have seen, amongst the reasons given by panel members for their decisions made there were over 40 references to the nature of the offence, the child's involvement in it, the past record of the child and the previous measures experienced by the child. There were, however, no explicit references made to punishment of any kind. That is, children were not seen as appropriate objects on whom could be inflicted either retributive (punishment/non-treatment) or punishment/ treatment measures. This is at least the inference we make in the analysis so far, though we do argue that the significance for panel members of Awareness, Consequences and Intentionality may suggest that they are more concerned with the moral development of the child. We might then have expected some allusions to the fact that punishment measures could be influential in the fostering of the appropriate moral and intellectual development in children. As suggested by a panel member in discussion: 'Punishment after all can be an effective means of treatment'. But the fact that formally panel members ought not to seek punitive objectives may inhibit explicit reference being made to them in a statement of the reasons for a decision.

It would, however, be more than foolish to deny that panel members may on occasion, for what they determine to be serious offences, seek punitive objectives. This is particularly so with reference to those youths whom they describe as the 'thugs', 'hooligan element' or 'young crooks'. One panel member, for example, when asked to consider whether the panels ought to have more punitive sanctions amongst the options available graphically expressed his feelings thus: 'Make no mistake about it, there will require to be very stern measures introduced involving the police if the present Hearing system is to be really effective in dealing with the group of adolescents who can aptly be described as apprentice terrorists' (*Glasgow Herald* 1976). Similarly, panel members may wish to deter other children from delinquent behaviour. There is here, of course, no incompatibility between belief in welfare or treatment on the one hand, and the need to deter on the other, though even this may be expressed rather ambiguously: 'Deterrence comes into it in the overall pattern of the Children's Hearings. We try to deter the child as a means to an end – not simply deterrence for its own sake'. Again in the next chapter this will be discussed since we will be concerned not simply with what information is sought and used in a children's hearing, but also how it is sought and used. In particular, the symbolic use of the hearing itself as one means of inculcating appropriate attitudes in children who have committed offences will be discussed.

How individuals conceive of the resources available and the use to which they may be put has to be taken into consideration in analysing decisions. Thus, in many cases panel members and magistrates agree that those who have committed offences should not be put in the same residential establishment as children who have experienced other problems. And though not as explicitly as magistrates, panel members will confess their decision to send a child to a List D school has been influenced by what the child has done; or that the decision to put on supervision at home, rather than sending him to a List D school, has been determined by considerations of leniency and mitigation rather than being directly related to any objective assessment of the child's needs. In that respect, the 'trivial' nature of much offence behaviour may be underpinned by the same logic by which offences are considered serious. That is, just as some panel members may feel that certain offences are too serious to be dealt with them then, so they complain that many offences are trivial and do not warrant an appearance at a Children's Hearing.

The practical accomplishment of juvenile justice in general is a very complicated affair and the making of a decision in particular has to be analysed with reference to the frames of relevance adopted by individual decision-makers. That is, how information is employed in the decision-making process is as important as what specific items are selected as important. Earlier, available ideologies of delinquency control were identified and the ambiguity between punishment and treatment noted as characteristic of philosophies of crime control. With specific reference to how these are displayed in the frames of relevance revealed by panel members and magistrates, the practical accomplishment of juvenile justice in the panel and court area confirms that in practice no easy dichotomy between punishment and treatment or 'welfare' and 'judicial' ideologies is maintained. Panel members have to resolve the conceptual ambiguity inherent in dealing with offenders by welfare measures within a system based, at least theoretically, on a conceptual framework of determinism. This does not mean however that they are not concerned at all with traditional considerations such as deterrence or social protection. Magistrates employ a more overtly 'judicial' orientation in which intent and responsibility are central features and in which punishment is a legitimate product of their deliberations. Again, however, this does not mean that they are not concerned with the welfare of children. But the difference between the panel and court system is that whereas panel members have to reconcile a welfare philosophy within a system for dealing with offenders where they are not concerned with punishment or with questions of criminal intent, magistrates are able formally to distinguish cases requiring welfare measures and those in which children can justly be punished.

The organisational differences in the court and panel type of hearing have been referred to continually. In the following chap-

Chapter Eight

THE HEARING PROCESS:
FORM AND CONTENT

As we have noted previously, Morris and McIsaac (1978) state that in terms of decision-making 'the type of tribunal (juvenile court or welfare tribunal) is largely unimportant. What is crucial is the philosophy underlying that tribunal and the ideology of its practitioners'. On the basis of the research here reported, such a conclusion is unwarranted and the main point to be made in this chapter is that in practice (since the philosophy of the tribunal and the ideology of the practitioners cannot be separated from the practice) the court and administrative tribunal are very different forms of proceedings. Any analysis of decision-making about children who commit offences must accommodate consideration of the processes by which information is assimilated and interpreted by individuals working within a particular organisational and administrative structure. The juvenile court hearing is different from the tribunal form of hearing since the decision-making process is influenced by the need to reconcile within a single administrative and organisational structure the competing ideologies of welfare and punishment. Recent rejection (see Morris et al. 1980 and Black 1979) of the administrative tribunal as an inappropriate forum for making decisions about offenders is perhaps too hasty and premised upon unwarranted assumptions about the lack of difference in decision-making in the respective systems of juvenile justice. Our conclusion is that the court and panel hearing are different in terms of 'form' (the major patterns of communication) and 'content' (what was actually discussed).

The methodological difficulties in gauging the nature of the interaction in actual hearings was compounded by the fact that in England the court hearing, by its very nature, did not allow for communication of a kind comparable to that in the panel hearings. Indeed, it was on such considerations, amongst others, that the Kilbrandon Committee had itself rejected the juvenile court since it did not allow for a decision-making process consonant with the need to take the welfare and needs of the child into account. As we have already seen, according to the Kilbrandon philosophy to define delinquency itself in legalistic or judicial terms was inappropriate. Delinquency was conceived as a behavioural condition requiring diagnosis, assessment and treatment. It is on such a philosophy that rest perhaps the greatest differences between the Scottish and English systems. The Children's Hearing is no court of law; questions of disputed fact have to be referred to court since adjudication is outside the jurisdiction of the hearing; punitive measures are not legitimately available; the child and his parents have no right to legal representation. Moreover, it is the case that panel members and magistrates are both respectively lay members of the community. Nevertheless, a further feature of the English system is that a magistrate can only be elected to the juvenile bench if he/she is already a member of the bench in the adult court.

Because the juvenile court is a modified version of a court of criminal law, there are further differences that merit attention and which, as we have seen, have no small bearing on the decision-making practices adopted.

Form

Formality of the Court. One of the intentions behind the 1969 Children and Young Persons Act had been to promote a system of court procedure that was more informal than had hitherto been the practice. However, in the court area included in the study, the physical and architectural structure of the court was such as to make informal communication well nigh impossible. The courtroom, though fairly new and purpose built, was laid out traditionally with a raised dais for the bench, seating for the clerk and specific arrangements for social work, probation and other official personnel. Parents and children had their own allotted location which, interestingly, was some distance from the seating allocated to the social and probation services.

Not only was the physical structure of the court fairly formal, but so too was the very nature of the hearing process: the procedure adopted for the hearings was generally very formalised with the different participants having their roles rigorously circumscribed by convention and ritual. In particular, parents and children were only allowed to speak at certain points in the proceedings and only then at the instance or with the permission of the bench for the day. The prosecutors, the lawyers, social workers and probation officers only rarely failed to follow the conventional practices governing speech. The interesting empirical question posed by this was whether the form of the hearing actually influenced the content of the decision-making process.

The very form of questioning itself was different between the panel and court hearings (as indeed it was between the court areas involved in the pilot study). All questions from the bench were directed through the chairman of the day. This may at first sight appear a rather trivial matter but it did in fact prove to have considerable significance in determining the nature of the proceedings.

The contrast of all this with the panel hearings is rather obvious inasmuch as all hearings were, as far as possible, conducted in 'round-table' fashion, with all (panel members, parents and children) alledgedly equally participating members. In general (though not always) the panel hearings attended (more than 200) were less formal than the court hearings. A point that has to be made here is that no criticism is being directed at any individual or group of panel members or magistrates. The research was concerned with the sociological implications of different decision-making processes and did not have criticism as an objective.

Adjournment. Unfortunately, on a number of occasions the bench actually adjourned, a practice that is common in the court area and not restricted to the period of study. This in itself was a crucial difference between the two systems because it invariably involved the magistrates reading reports (panel members have reports at least four days prior to the hearing). Also, it meant that at least in some cases part of the discussion was not heard by parents, children, social workers, probation officers and others involved in a case. It was incidentally also not heard by the researcher 'in the interests of justice'.

Police Prosecutor. Children's hearings in Scotland must not be held in buildings associated with the police and the police themselves have no formal authority to attend a hearing. In the main study area in England, the person responsible for conducting the prosecution of cases was in fact a uniformed police inspector. Again, as we shall see, the police prosecutor occupied a particularly important role in the hearing process which, by virtue of the conventional practices adopted in that area, he was able to fulfil without there being any continued 'interaction' with the bench. What this is indicative of is the fact that the police, not just as prosecutor but also more generally, are important agents in the administration of juvenile justice in England and Wales. The dissatisfaction expressed by a number of magistrates at the loss of their powers to the social services is paralleled by their concern that the police who are 'real servants of their court' have numerous restrictions placed on their activities as a result of the 1969 Act. Similarly, the separation of probation and social work has lead some magistrates to conclude that probation officers rightly show more allegiance and loyalty to court than do social workers whose loyalty is often seen to rest with their client, irrespective of obligations to the court.

The close working-relationship between the magistracy and the police may well reflect the fact that both groups share similar predominantly judicial ideologies. Thus, the apparent conceptual ambiguity between judicial and welfare considerations is expressed institutionally in the form of a social-control network where the different bodies involved do not share similar frames of relevance. That is, they may differ as to the relevance of information about a case since they operate on what are essentially different conceptions of the phenomenon (delinquency) and how to deal with it. How this influenced the decision-making process was of course an object of empirical inquiry for this project.

For all the above reasons, the different types of hearing structure made a comparative analysis in one sense somewhat difficult. On the other hand, from the perspective of the parents, children and other particiants in the hearing, the relative lack of discussion in the court was itself a significant feature of the court process and one which characterised it as very different from the Scottish administrative type of tribunal. The point to be made is that the nature of the hearing, whether court or panel hearing, is itself an important variable in the decision-making process. Because of the different agencies involved at the hearing stage of decision-making, there are crucial differences in what is discussed and in the use to which these discussions are put. Morris and McIsaac's conclusion about the lack of difference is not tenable on the basis of the evidence from this project.

Form: Court Hearings

The first question addressed was whether there was in fact, as had been intended by Kilbrandon, more free and open discussion in panel as opposed to court hearings. What actually constitutes 'free' and 'open' discussion is difficult to define clearly but the form of analysis adopted concentrated on the contributions made to the decision-making process by various people and in particular the parents and the children involved. The first measure, using a modified version of Bales' Interaction Schedule, was rather crude but provided an initial baseline from which to develop a comparative analysis.

By noting the statements made by and to magistrates and by and to panel members, we were able to get a rather simplistic profile of the form of the discussion in the respective types of hearing.

Perhaps what should be pointed out first is that children's hearings were significantly longer affairs than court hearings with much greater levels of discussion. Whereas hearings averaged out around 45 minutes (with some much longer), court hearings lasted on average little more than 20 minutes. This has to be further qualified by the facts that (a) there are rarely more than five hearings at any one sitting of the Scottish panel; in the period in which the research was conducted in England there were occasions when more than 40 cases constituted the work of the day; and (b) that cases in England often involved all parties of the offence being dealt with in the course of a single hearing. For these reasons, it is perhaps no surprise to find that panel hearings were longer and appeared to involve greater discussion. Thus it seems that the Scottish hearing system allows for greater exploration of cases. This has a number of implications for the way in which information is sought, and how it is used.

Table 11 presents the 'form' of the discussion and the contributions to and by the magistrates in the hearing of court cases.

Table 11. 'Form' as proportion of total discussion.

$n=$	By magistrates to:						
	Child	Parents	Magis- trates	Clerk	Social worker	Police	Lawyer
159	45	23	5	11	3	4	—

$n=$	To magistrates by:					
	Child	Parents	Clerk	Social worker	Police	Lawyer
915	6	10	1	4	40	37

(The figures are percentages of the total amount of discussion initiated by and addressed to magistrates.) A number of rather obvious points can be drawn from this table. First, very little discussion actually takes place between magistrates themselves. As we have argued (1977), since information is not intrinsically relevant (i.e. it has to be assessed and interpreted according to the individual's frame of relevance), in the absence of discussion with each other what may appear to be a decision that is the outcome of collective behaviour is no more than the product of very different assumptions about the causes of delinquency and how to control it. Secondly, very little of the discussion is actually initiated by the magistrates; rather more is directed to them and, of crucial importance, the main contributors are the police and lawyers (where these are actually involved).

The Police Prosecutor. In the study area in England, the prosecutor, a uniformed police inspector, had considerable influence on the nature of the interaction in the courtroom. In all cases, the greater part of the prosecutor's contribution to the discussion took place at the beginning of the hearing when he presented information concerning the child and the offence in question to the bench. Paradoxically, though the prosecutor presented considerable information to the bench, as can be seen above, the bench rarely questioned him as regards this information and overall there is in fact little communication from the bench to one who is a key figure in the whole process. The ritualistic nature of the processing of cases in the court allows different participants to present information to the bench at appropriate times without themselves necessarily being addressed to any great extent by the bench. The police prosecutor in the fulfilment of his role was then merely operating according to the conventional practices of the court. The significance of this will become more apparent when the data relating to the 'content' of the prosecutor's contribution is later presented. That is, both in terms of the 'form' of his contribution and in terms of the 'content' of that contribution, his participation was a crucial variable in determining the practical accomplishment of juvenile justice in the hearing.

Parents and Children. Whereas the bench directed a considerable proportion of its statements, mainly in the form of questions, in all cases to the youth, the youth's contribution to the bench only constituted a small part of the discussion. Similarly, parents that were in court with their children were addressed more by the bench than they themselves addressed the bench. What this rather crude means of measurement of the interaction in the court hearing suggests is that there is very little opportunity for 'free' discussion. This seems especially so when one also considers the fact that, whereas the statements to the child and his parents by the bench involved the greater part of the discussion, the statements to the police involved a much smaller part; conversely, whereas the joint contribution made by the child and his parents to the bench only accounted for a minimal part of the total discussion to the bench, that of the police and the solicitor together involved almost all of the discussion with the bench. The nature of the lawyers' involvement will be discussed later, when this will be assessed in relation to the actual content and presentation of the solicitor.

Again, the ritualistic nature of the court hearing may account for the form of the discussion in that, though questions may have been directed at the children and their parents, fuller replies or descriptions of their involvement and backgrounds are actually given by the police, or on occasion by the lawyer. Not unexpectedly, as we shall see, the content of the police contribution to the bench is heavily 'judicial', which, when added to the low level of youth or parental participation, offers little opportunity for discussing the child's needs or interests. The police concern with establishing the nature of the involvement of the child and the offence in which he was involved means that the predominant frame of relevance is not solely a welfare one.

Social Worker. What the table also shows is that the social worker or, possibly in England, the probation officer, takes little part in the actual discussion of a child's case. Social-work participation accounted for very little of the discussion. Two other factors make this low level of contribution a matter of interest. First, the social-work interest in a case or potential case is usually the responsibility of a representative of the social services department, and not necessarily the social worker who is or may be responsible for the case. In the court area there was in fact a post of Court Duty Officer. Consequently, the social worker in court would not usually have first-hand information about the case. Secondly, and related to the first, because of the derivation of juvenile court from an ordinary summary court, the juvenile court fundamentally remains a court of law. Therefore, no report or information about a child's background may be offered to the court until the facts have been established or accepted. This means that, in view of the lack of involvement of the social worker in the discussion, the magistrates' only opportunity for assimilating social-work information is by the reading of reports which can only be presented after the facts of a case have been accepted or established. This was done either in court or in adjournment and essentially meant that little time was available, and it is perhaps not without significance that the magistrates found social-work reports generally very informative and very important. The fact that not only the social worker's contribution was small but also that the bench addressed itself to the social worker in a very limited manner would mean a greater reliance on written information in view of the lack of opportunity for questioning it.

Because of the erosion of magistrates' power in the decision-making process in England, the lower level of social-work involvement may reflect a practice in which the nature of the 'treatment' decision is the responsibility of the social-services department and not of the magistracy, who must only decide whether a child needs compulsory measures of care. Magistrates do not have the responsibility of deciding what form these measures should take. But perhaps the main point that could be made here is that in relation to the contribution of the social worker, the magistrates rely mainly on written social-work information.

One further comment that can be made is that the Clerk of the Court appears to play only a small part in the proceedings. Yet the low contribution made by him to the bench must not be used as a basis for arguing that his is not an important role. His role is important in informing the magistrates of the statutory limits within which they can operate and generally keeping them advised of the law. What can be said is that much of his involvement with the magistrates actually takes place in the adjourning room. Thus what he had to say was not available for inclusion in the research. More importantly, however, this also meant that it is not available for public hearing in the open court. Whereas it is possible for panel members to adjourn or ask for a period of discussion in the absence of the parents or children, this very rarely happens in practice. Only in one panel area, in the North of Scotland, is the researcher aware of the availability of an adjournment room, but even here most of the panel members felt its use would be contrary to the spirit of the Kilbrandon philosophy.

Form: Panel

The most obvious difference in the nature of the hearing between Scotland and England is the absence of a police prosecutor and lawyer, and the role played by the Reporter to the Hearings rather than by a Clerk of Court. But there were other more interesting differences which were not accounted for simply by the absence of certain participants in the juvenile court (see table 12; figures are again percentages of total discussion).

Table 12

n=	Statements *by* panel members *to*:			
	Child	Parents	Other panel members	Social worker
3118	64	27	6	3

n=	Statements *to* members *by*:		
	Child	Parents	Social worker
2815	54	36	5

A striking feature of the differences in the interaction in the court and panel hearings respectively (at least for the cases studied in the research) was the far greater volume of discussion. Some consideration must, however, be given to the fact that the magistrates in many cases, as in general practice, did in fact adjourn to discuss certain cases. However, since the intention was to gauge courtroom and hearing activity respectively, the fact that magistrates did on occasion retire is not without significance for the discussion about the difference in levels of interaction between Scotland and England.

Parents and Children. Over all cases, the difference in the volume of interaction was highly significant. Moreover, the distribution of the volume of interaction in Scotland was markedly different from that in England. As with England's magistrates, a considerable part of the comments and questions made *by* panel members to others in the hearing were directed to the youth and his parents. But unlike the form of the parallel type of discussion in England the child and the parents together contributed most of the discussion *to* the panel members, children making the greater contribution. Whilst the greater part of the discussion in the court was accounted for by the participation of the police prosecutor and legal representative, in the panel hearings it was in fact the children and parents who accounted for much of the interaction.

Whereas in court, the rather formal atmosphere and ritualised process did not allow for open discussion involving the parents and the children, in the panel hearings they did appear to take an active part in the decision-making process. Moreover, all three panel members in each hearing were involved more immediately in the hearing than were individual magistrates, a fact reflected in the much greater level of communication.

Social Worker. Since the social-work report is available to panel members some days before the actual hearing of a case, the search for information is fundamentally different from that of the court hearing, where only a short time is available for the assimilation of written social-work information. The social-work report in Scotland may be used by panel members as a basis for introduction to the discussion. Because of the greater opportunity for discussion, and the freedom of the child and parents to enter into the proceedings of the hearing, social-work information can be challenged in a way that is not so possible in the more adversarially oriented juvenile court structure.

Nevertheless, though reports, as we have seen, were not considered to be so generally informative in Scotland and despite the greater opportunity for discussion at the actual hearing, social-work participation in the interaction, surprisingly, was almost as low as it was in the juvenile court. It would be unfair to suggest that this low participation is simply the fault of the social-work representatives since panel members seem to direct little of the discussion specifically to them. In many respects this is unfortunate, especially since in the majority of cases included in the research the social worker actually involved in the case or who had written the report was usually present. In view of the intentions of the 1968 Social Work (Scotland) Act, social workers were generally expected to attend the hearings. Thus, unlike the situation in England there was as much opportunity to discuss with the social worker the contents of his report as to read the reports themselves. The main question directed to the social worker was of the nature 'Have you anything to add to your report?' It is perhaps more surprising that this should be so in Scotland since the decision as to the need for compulsory measures of care may well include recognition of the qualities of the social worker, as we have seen, and the nature of his report. Nevertheless, most of the responses showed agreement with the recommendation of the social worker.

Despite their apparent lack of involvement in actual hearings, social workers were nevertheless considered by many panel members to be extremely important: 'I wouldn't like to be without the Social Work recommendation – also the social worker has to be asked his opinion in the hearing. I don't like hearings where a social worker is not introduced to the discussion' (panel member). We might have expected, however, that social workers would have taken more initiative in the actual discussion of the case and of their social-work report.

The conclusion is nevertheless that the panel hearings did allow for a more open form of discussion. In particular, the parents and children were able to contribute more to the actual discussion in what appeared to us to be a more informal and free atmosphere than existed in the juvenile court in the study area.

In summary then, even on the basis of a rather crude means of assessment, it would appear that parents and children in the Scottish system do become involved more in the discussion; that social workers however in both systems contribute little to the actual hearing process; and that the discussion in the English juvenile court is dominated by the police and solicitors. What is just as important as the actual 'form' of the interaction process, if not more so, is what is actually discussed by the different personnel involved and it is to 'content' that we now turn.

Content

The marked difference between panel members and magistrates *vis-à-vis* 'welfare' and 'judicial' factors was repeated in the actual content of the respective hearings.

Not only do the discussions in a panel hearing have a very different form from a court hearing but also a very different content in that there is overall a significantly greater preoccupation with welfare considerations.

Even a cursory glance at table 13, which depicts the content scores (using the modified version of Bales' Interaction Schedule) will reveal the extent of the difference in the actual nature of the discussion in the panel and court hearings. Moreover, this global difference is reflected in the role played in the discussions by the various participants, though it has to be remembered that key individuals were inhibited in court from contributing to the discussion by virtue of the ritualistic and rather conventional-ised nature of decision-making.

Table 13. Mean content scores.

	Panel	Court
To panel members and magistrates	72.2	27.8
By panel members and magistrates	72.3	15.7
Overall discussion	72.2	26.0

(The greater the score the more emphasis placed on 'welfare')

Content: Panel Members

Overall panel members were much more concerned than juven-ile magistrates to discuss 'welfare' factors though there did appear to be no little attention paid to 'judicial' considerations such as the circumstances of the offence. Panel members who were also chairmen in the hearing had a much lower content score (63.2) than did their colleagues. This may well be ac-counted for by the fact that in the area included in the study it was the practice for chairmen to begin the discussion by ad-dressing the child about the offence.

The 'content' would therefore be influenced by the inclusion of 'judicial' factors as a result of the chairman's role. For reasons that may also be associated with the role of chairman, these panel members also took a greater part in discussion of a case than did those who were not chairmen. That is, not only did chairmen comment more than their colleagues on judicial fac-tors such as the child's involvement in the offence, but they also, in view of their role, took a much greater part in the discussion.

Priestley et al. (1977, p.90) noted that 'magistrates . . . pursue the personal dimensions of offence behaviour in two further ways. First by asking for explanations. "Why did you do this?" is asked so frequently and receives so few replies that its use seems at first sight to be merely rhetorical. But there is a serious purpose to be discovered behind it. The "causes" of criminal behaviour are often discussed in the reports submitted by pro-bation officers and social workers, but magistrates also appear to be genuinely in search of explanations direct from the horse's mouth.' What is particularly interesting about this quotation is that panel members, in their capacity as chairmen, also often initiate proceedings in the hearing by asking the child why he did it. That is, the child is also given the opportunity to present his reasons for his behaviour and in this way much of the early part of the hearings for the cases in the study was focused on the child's reasons for his involvement. This is, however, not to suggest that the relevance of such considerations is the same for panel chairmen as for the magistrates. Indeed, as we concluded on the basis of the analysis of the case studies and Case Reports, the importance of the child's involvement in the offence may be taken as being more indicative of the child's moral development than of considerations of intent and responsibility. What makes this more problematic, however, is the possibility that panel members may even consider that the child who deliberately commits an offence, particularly if it is serious in its consequences, may be more in need than the child who is 'easily led' or 'weak-willed' or who is in need of different measures. In addition, the content of the discussion was not affected significantly by whether the children involved had any previous offences recorded nor by the number of charges laid against the child. Similarly, the child's age appeared to have little effect on the nature of the discussion. That is, even controlling for such considerations, the discussion by panel members was predominantly about the social, personal and environmental circumstances of the child. However, the child's age can be important in the decision-making process, and especially so when the child is approaching the age at which he can legitimately be dealt with by the court. Panel members will confess to being aware that the fifteen-year-old will soon be under the jurisdiction of the court and allowing this to influence the nature of the decision ('we'll discharge the case because he'll soon go to court anyway') or the presentation of the decision ('we'll discharge the case this time but remember, it's the court for you next time, my lad').

Only in one type of case was the discussion dominated by 'judicial' considerations – assault cases. We had already seen from the case studies that cases involving assault appeared to pose particular problems for panel members working within a system based on a welfare philosophy. Though on the basis of data from the previous chapter there is no explicit reference to the wish to punish a child in any of the reasons given for the decision, this does not mean that the decision-maker may not experience a degree of conceptual ambiguity in trying to distinguish offence and need considerations. The advantage the magistrate has is that the ambiguity is recognised in the very institutional framework within which he operates where he can legitimately punish. Nevertheless, the emphasis on judicial considerations by panel members in such as assault cases cannot be taken to suggest the adoption of a 'tariff' principle, though, as we shall see, it may have implications for how a child is dealt with in the hearing itself.

An examination of the relative influence of the individual factors provides further evidence to support the claim that panel members are indeed much more concerned with the social, personal and environmental circumstances of the child. The significance of the following major factors discussed, is in the way the list relates to other parts of the analysis:

    Schooling
    Circumstances of the offence
    Disposal measure
    Associates/friends
    Use of leisure time
    Motives/reasons for the offence
    Parental discipline
    Career prospects
    Home supervision

What is particularly interesting about the list is that most items relate specifically to the child either in terms of his involvement in the offence or in terms of his personal circumstances, e.g. schooling, leisure time, etc.

The fact that 'the circumstances of the offence' and the child's reasons for the offence appear high in the set of factors discussed by the panel members has to be analysed in the light of the other factors that were considered important enough to be discussed often. Magistrates for example discuss the same 'judicial' factors but very rarely discuss, at least in open court, more 'welfare' oriented considerations. Thus it would appear that panel members, who operate more than do magistrates within a welfare frame of relevance, seek to interpret such factors in such a way as to give a fuller picture of the child's problems. They do not concern themselves so much with the specific act or offence in abstraction from the child's general behavioural problems.

It is perhaps no surprise that the most often discussed factor, in view of its importance in the Case Reports, was 'Schooling'. In discussion with the researcher and in presenting reasons for their decisions, panel members identified truancy and school

difficulties with delinquency and other behaviour problems
generally. Indeed some of the magistrates even conceived of
'truancy' as 'delinquency'.

An important aspect of the list of factors actually discussed is
that considerable discussion took place with reference to the
decision itself. The disposal of the case was one of the most
discussed features of a hearing and a crucial difference from the
court where this was rarely, if at all, discussed in the open
hearing. It would therefore appear that a panel hearing, by its
very nature, allows parents and children to have the opportunity
of at least being aware of the kind of decision being contem-
plated by the panel members, if not completely involved in the
discussion of it. In commenting on the merits of the Children's
Hearing system, one panel member felt:

> we are lay people who have to endure the same stresses as
> people we're trying to help . . . I can speak the same language
> that the child and parents speak. The informality must help
> in reducing the strain and allow parents, the children, to be
> involved in all aspects of the case;

and another remarked:

> what happens in the hearing is as important as the decision
> we reach . . . if parents can leave the room feeling less
> aggrieved, less hostile and with some dignity, we've
> achieved something. We at least try to win them over to see
> what we are doing – this must surely be better than the
> court.

What panel members then appear to seek is an atmosphere
which allows the parents and children to participate even to the
extent of involving them in discussion about the most appropriate means of disposal. When we examine the findings for the
court hearings we shall see that not only does less discussion
take place but that it also covers a smaller range of topics.

Content: Court Cases

The main factors discussed in court were as follows: Circumstances of offence; Reasons/motives; Seriousness of offence. As
we can see this is a much more limited list than the corresponding one for panel hearings. Any other factors were referred to
only minimally by the magistrates. This reflects both the concentration of magistrates on more judicially oriented factors
and also the much lower level of discussion in the hearing of a
case in the court area. The obvious difference from the panel
hearings is that there is in fact little discussion by the magis-

trates of factors other than judicial ones and even then, the chairman is almost the only contributor from the bench. This is not to say that other factors are not discussed. There are two reasons for this. First, the research was bedevilled by the fact that the magistrates often adjourned, which meant that that stage in the hearing was not available for analysis.

Secondly, what these figures represent are the factors mentioned in the statements made by panel members and juvenile magistrates respectively. They do not contain any reference to statements made by others. Indeed, the differences in the content and form of the discussion of cases by panel members and magistrates point to more fundamental issues relating to the nature, the source and the use made of information available to those responsible for making decisions in the two systems. In particular, the more formalised and ritualistic nature of the juvenile court allows personnel other than magistrates themselves to determine the nature of the information provided.

We suggested above that panel hearings did allow for more open discussion involving both parents and child. What is equally important, however, is the nature of the participation by these key figures and it is to a consideration of this that we now turn.

Parents and Children

We have seen that the overall content was significantly different as between the panel and the court samples. The greater emphasis placed on welfare factors by panel members appears to be reflected in the content of the children's and parents' contributions to the discussion, as in the comments directed to them by the panel members. For panel members, the content of the discussion to the child and to the parents was heavily 'welfare' oriented. In other words, the greater part of the discussion with the child and his parents focused more on the child's social, personal and environmental circumstances than on more judicial aspects of the case.

But just as important was the fact that the welfare content of the actual contributions to the discussions by parents and by children was also high. They too were prepared to discuss the child's background and not just concentrate on the offence.

Table 14 presents data relating to the content and form of the involvement of parents and children in the panel hearing. We can see that parents and children in panel hearings are active participants in that they contribute a lot to a panel discussion

Table 14

		Content	Form
Child	To panel	60.5	53.5
	To child by panel	62.5	64.3
Parents	To panel	82.9	35.8
	To parents by panel	83.5	27.8

(form) but that they also focus more exclusively on welfare factors in their discussion. This does not necessarily mean that they themselves are committed to welfare frames of relevance. As we argued earlier in this research, the language of therapy or treatment is not readily compatible with ordinary, common-sense moral discourse. Similarly, though the aim was to achieve a panel membership that was both suitable and representative, Mapstone (1972) argues that if membership were truly representative then the attitudes and beliefs expressed by panel members would be more reactionary, conservative and punitive. For Mapstone, the attitudes to crime and delinquency expressed by the general Scottish public are not those which would necessarily lead to the successful selection of particular individuals. But the main point to be made here is that no *a priori* assumptions about parents' and children's assumptions about justice and delinquency control can be made; empirical research is necessary to establish the tacit assumptions commonly held by different sections of the community. The influence of the Calvinist ethic on Scottish morality suggests that any inference as to the extent to which the parents and children in this study are committed to a welfare ideology has to be treated with caution (Asquith 1977).

In all probability the greater concentration of parents and children on welfare factors may be attributable to a variety of reasons, not least that their contributions are determined by what panel members wish to discuss. But whatever the reasons, the greater part of the discussion in panel hearings was accounted for by the children and parents discussing welfare aspects of the case whereas in the court hearings discussion was dominated by the police prosecutor and the legal representative.

Panel Members and Magistrates

As all questions from the bench were directed through the chairman for the day, there was little interaction in court amongst magistrates. There may obviously have been more in the confines of the retiral room, but in the courtroom itself it was negligible. Of the interaction that did take place between the magistrates, the physical separation of the bench from the body of the court made it difficult for the researcher, and undoubtedly for the child and his family, to hear what was actually said. But more surprising is that within the more informal structure of the children's hearing, though panel members did discuss features of a case with the child and the parents, there was little actual communication between panel members during a hearing. This does not mean, of course, that individual panel members ignored the interaction of other panel members, but that there was little attempt to test each other more precisely about impressions of what were considered relevant pieces of information and why.

This raises an intriguing possibility. In both systems, individual panel members and magistrates do, of course, on occasion disagree with the actual decision reached about a child; the decision need not be unanimous since a majority is sufficient. There is then explicit disagreement expressed about the decision. However, just because a decision is *prima facie* unanimous, this does not necessarily mean that the decision has been reached on the basis of the same information, on a similar interpretation of the information available, or with the same objectives in mind. We have already seen that between the two groups there is considerable disagreement as to the importance of a welfare frame of relevance, and there is sufficient evidence to suggest that within groups, especially amongst the panel, the welfare orientation is qualified in a number of respects, e.g. by considerations of leniency, mitigation etc. One of the main arguments in this book is that information is only relevant insofar as it is assessed within a particular frame of relevance. Yet it has been seen that in the actual hearings and the process of decision-making there is very little communication amongst panel members and magistrates prior to the reaching of the decision. Operating then with possibly different assumptions about the causes of delinquency, the most appropriate measures of delinquency control and about the functions of the available resources, apparent consensus and unanimity may well conceal greater disagreements than actual agreement. The process of decision-making in both the court and the panel hearings is theoretically a collective enterprise. What earlier research into 'penal philosophies' and 'the human element in sentencing' (see chapter v) ignored was that decision-making, especially in the lower courts, was a collective process and that the making of a decision was a complex social accomplishment involving a number of people.

The interesting question that this raises, but which we cannot investigate in detail here, is whether in fact parents and children themselves, who may well operate within more judicially oriented frames of relevance (i.e. more concerned with intentionality, responsibility, fairness, etc.), actually truly become involved in the decision-making process. We have already seen that at least one panel member felt that a merit of the Scottish system of juvenile justice was that parents and children could become fully involved in the decision-making process. Thus, parents may ostensibly agree with the decision, but for reasons little to do with welfare consideration. An example would be where a child was sent to a List D school by panel members ('because he needs a structured environment') and where the parents agreed with the decision ('because it's no more than he deserves').

Legal Representation

The importance of including this in the analysis is that (i) the question of legal representation epitomises much of the conflict we have attempted to identify between what we called judicial and welfare modes of thought and has implications for claims that children in the Scottish Hearings system should be legally represented (Martin, Fox and Murray (1981) have recently pointed to major concerns about the apparent lack of recognition given even to the few statutory requirements that do exist in the Scottish system); (ii) it also has implications for the confused state of the right of appeal against a decision made by a children's hearing in Scotland (Grant 1976; Gordon 1976) where the right of appeal against a decision made by lay persons actually rests with the judiciary.

It was difficult to make meaningful interpretations of most of the content of court discussion because of the simple fact that so little actually took place in the court areas. Nevertheless, some comment can be made on those cases where children were legally represented.

The most interesting feature of the representation of children in the few cases in this study is the significance of the solicitor's contribution in the hearing of a case. In all the cases where a child was represented legally, the child himself made no actual

contribution to the discussion, the greater part of which, in all
but one of the cases, was accounted for by the participation of
the lawyer. Moreover, the overall form of the lawyer's contribution in the study cases was as much as 64.0% reflected in the
fact that in such cases, police interaction in addressing the
bench was much lower. The situation as regards cases where
there was no legal representation was that the police contribution overall was significantly greater.

But whereas the greater part of the discussion to the bench is
made by the legal representative of the child, it was important to
consider not only the 'form' of the lawyer's contribution but
also the 'content'.

Over all the cases where legal representatives were involved,
the content indicated a rather greater emphasis on 'judicial'
factors than on 'welfare' ones. What is equally interesting is that
these cases involved a greater volume of interaction directed to
the bench than in the cases where there had been no legal
representation. Thus, where there was legal representation,
there was overall a greater volume of discussion directed to the
bench, the greater part of which was offered by the lawyer. This
discussion however focused more on the offence information
than on the child's welfare. The main concern of the lawyer was
with clarifying the nature of the child's involvement in the
offence. What observation at the hearing of the cases afforded
was the opportunity to appreciate the use of the information
made by the lawyer and though it would be more than unfair to
suggest that the lawyer did not take the child's welfare into
consideration, some comment can be made at this juncture on
his presentation of information.

On occasions where the child's background characteristics
were revealed to the court by the lawyer, this was used not to
construct an argument relating to the child's needs or interests
in arguing for an appropriate disposal of the case. Rather, it was
used within the court predominantly as the basis for an argument for the modification of any sentence intended by the
magistrates. The 'modification' usually took the form of asking
the court to show leniency or to accept the mitigating circumstances of the child's background, such as coming from a deprived area, poor family, etc. That is, though background and
'need' information was being used, its use was determined more
by a conceptual framework espousing legal and judicial values
with its greater emphasis on notions of responsibility and culpability. The concepts of mitigation, excuse and leniency are

more readily located within a frame of relevance based on responsibility and punishment rather than on one of need. But
with the shift in frames of relevance from 'need' to 'offence'
criteria, there will also occur a subtle shift in the interpretation
of the personal, social and environmental characteristics of
children who commit offences. Legal and judicial ideology highlights notions of intent.

Since there remains a right of appeal to a Sheriff in Scotland, it
is important to consider the extent to which judicial and welfare
modes of thought are compatible within the same system of
juvenile justice. Elsewhere we have argued that judicial review
of welfare decisions about children is problematic, a claim supported by the fact that the judiciary themselves are in disagreement over when to allow an appeal (Asquith 1979). The point is
that in the juvenile court system, the presentation of information by a solicitor about a child, though it may make reference
to *prima facie* welfare considerations, is founded upon a predominantly judicially oriented frame of relevance. Accordingly,
the interpretation of information about the child's social and
background characteristics is made within a judicial frame of
relevance in which leniency and mitigation form part of the
conceptual configuration. Interestingly enough, a number of
panel members also operated with such concepts indicating
that they did not subscribe completely to welfare considerations. But one wonders whether the involvement of the legal
profession within the framework of the Children's Hearing system, albeit in the interests of the child, would alter the practical
accomplishment of juvenile justice.

On a wider level, this has as much significance for the acceptance of a system of juvenile justice based on welfare by the
community. Criticisms of softness and unfairness, as with
leniency, may be made by those who, for their part, view delinquency control in terms of punishment and justice.

As regards legal representation in particular, an important
feature of the legally represented cases in England, without
exception, was that the contribution made to the bench by
children was absolutely nil, whilst parents only made a contribution in one of the cases. And yet the bench initiates little
interaction with the lawyer, whose role in the structure of the
court proceedings was fairly rigidly determined by convention.
Consequently, there was an allotted time at which it was appropriate for him to present his information before the court, and as
such he did not even require to be invited by the bench to speak.

But more importantly, the presence of the lawyer, who may have only seen the child just before the hearing, would appear to obviate the need for the child and his parents, if present, to speak and present their own case. As can be seen, children and parents contributed very little to the discussion.

Police

Where there was no legal representation, the greater volume of statements to the bench was, not surprisingly, made by the police prosecutor whose duty it was not only to present information about the child's involvement in the offence but also about his background. Although the police made a large contribution to the discussion *to* the bench in all the cases, only little of the discussion from the bench was directed to the police prosecutor. Similarly, the statements directed to the lawyer (in the cases where one was involved) by the magistrates was almost negligible. Neither the prosecution nor the defence required to be introduced into the discussion by the bench since, despite the hopes of the 1969 Children and Young Persons Act, it was expected that they knew when was the appropriate time to speak. That is, the 1969 Children and Young Persons Act had not removed the air of ritualism associated with the adversarial nature of criminal justice. Certainly, informality would be difficult to achieve in a system where uniformed police operated, where the bench was physically removed from the body of the court, and where children and parents could only speak when requested or with permission from the bench.

By comparison with the court hearing, we would argue then that, on the basis of the evidence available to us so far, there does appear to be more scope for the involvement of the children and parents in the discussion in a panel hearing. In terms of the 'form' of the discussion in the panel hearings and the court hearings, the Scottish system allows for greater involvement of the parents and children. And in terms of the 'content', panel members pay more attention in the discussion of a case to welfare factors, lending support to similar conclusions drawn from other parts of the research.

Symbolic Character of Hearings

It is perhaps worth commenting at this juncture on how appearance before a court or a panel may be used as a symbolic reminder to the child that he has done wrong. Earlier it was argued that symbolic denunciation of offence behaviour was associated

with traditional theories of punishment, in its pure form, more
than with treatment or welfare considerations. Indeed, one of
the arguments made by early advocates of the Scottish system
was that it would allow for the eradication of the stigma associated with court appearance.

In the court area, the participation of key personnel in the
hearing is circumscribed by a fairly stereotyped protocol for
court hearings. Much of what Carlen (1976) has had to say about
magistrates' justice could be seen in the study court where
formalism and the 'majesty' of the court served to prevent
normal social intercourse. The magistrates themselves also
argued that the very appearance of a child before a court should
be sufficient to 'bring home to him just what he has done'; or
'have a salutary effect on the child'; or should 'deter others'.
That is not to be completely unexpected in a system of justice
where punishment of children is still a recognised, legitimate
objective.

But what was interesting was that panel members may have
also evolved their own informal strategies for conducting hearings of offence cases. We have noted the ambivalence of panel
members over the difficulty they experience in separating the
relevance of 'offence' and 'need' information. This is perhaps
easier for magistrates in a system which recognises that punishment is a legitimate aim. Panel members do confess to differ-
entiating between children who appear for offence reasons and
those who appear for other grounds, in that those who offend
have broken the law. It would appear to be such an approach to
delinquency control which underlies the demands by some
panel members for the provision of separate establishments for
offenders and non-offenders and for more powers to deal with
'hard cases'.

Even where the use of punishment is not explicitly stated, the
shift in the frame of relevance to one which attaches more
emphasis to offence criteria also has implications for the way in
which the hearing itself is conducted. The fact that delinquents
have committed an offence and have broken the law also determines the posture adopted towards offenders by panel members.
Bean (1976) has noted the fallacy of moral neutrality claimed by
the proponents of the treatment approach and has suggested
how moral evaluation mediates the diagnostic terminology.
The commonsense distinction between delinquents and other
children who appear before a hearing is also reflected in the
adoption of a moral posture by panel members. This is not only

in reference to those children who are the 'real delinquents' or the 'serious offenders', but occurs regularly in any instance where an offence has been committed. The hearing is used as a symbolic reminder to the child that he has done wrong and serves the function of delineating the parameters of delinquency and conformity. In an attempt to bring home to the child 'the seriousness of what he has done', panel members may deliberately take steps to endow the hearing with an air of formality, despite the promise of the Act. Indeed, some panel members feel that hearings ought generally to be more formal affairs so that not only children who appear before the hearings but also the wider public may acknowledge the seriousness of an appearance on offence grounds. Tactics adopted in an attempt to make the decision more formal vary between panel members and different panels, but include such strategies as lecturing and evoking a sense of shame. Despite the formal intention of the legislation, there are elements in children's hearings more generally associated with forms of 'degradation ceremonies'. What is particularly interesting about such tactics is that they may even be employed where considerations of need are paramount or even where a decision has been made to discharge a case, and are not reserved for cases which are conceived as being more serious in terms of offence behaviour. Even where punishment is not an explicitly stated aim, this does not rule out the use of shame, its moral and social analogue.

Amongst the reasons given by panel members for decisions there was no explicit reference to punishment whether it be in terms of pure punishment or punishment/treatment. However, in the summing up by the chairman, children are warned about their behaviour, lectured about the seriousness of appearance before a panel, and even on occasion threatened with possible committal to a List D school. Thus the public announcement of a decision to the child and to his parents, even, it would appear, where children are to be discharged, is often accompanied by warnings about the possible consequence of further offence behaviour.

It has not been possible, given the scope and limitations of this research, to subject the hearing process, whether it be in a court or a panel system, to a complete analysis. However, the significance of the present analysis has been to identify important features of the process of juvenile justice within a structure and setting derived from a court of summary jurisdiction and one which is best described as a form of administrative tribunal.

By examining important aspects of the actual hearings, we have been able to make some comment on the practical accomplishment of a welfare philosophy within different administrative structures. It was in terms of the absence of such information that we criticised earlier approaches to sentencing research.

The search for information on which to base decisions is influenced as much by how information is sought as it is by what information is available. Indeed, a key theme in the theoretical framework employed in this research has been that information about a child has no meaning independent of the processes by which it is produced (by, for example, report writers) and the use which is made of it. Decisions about children who commit offences are theoretically the outcome of the organisation and assessment of information based on the individual's knowledge about resources, treatment and behavioural problems, and on the objectives he hopes to attain. Moreover the search for 'relevant' information in a hearing is not an individual enterprise but a collective process circumscribed by the more social and symbolic features of different types of hearings. With regard to the 'form' and 'content' of the respective panel and court hearings the claim that the type of hearing is not important is one that is not substantiated on the basis of the evidence from this research. A court and a panel hearing are essentially different social processes involving different individuals from a variety of backgrounds with resultant implications for the way in which information is sought and indeed used.

One additional feature of the differences between the two systems is not simply what information is available but also when it is available. In the juvenile court, where the search for information is more overtly circumscribed by formality and ritual, reports about children from the various agencies cannot be seen by the magistrates prior to a finding of guilt or the acceptance of guilt by the child. In one sense it could not be otherwise since the child in the terms of criminal law is not technically guilty of an offence until the facts of the charge have been established. The effect of this is that reports have to be read either in court or in adjournment with the result that magistrates only have a limited time to assimilate the material contained within them. Panel members, however, have reports available a number of days before a hearing and therefore can familiarise themselves with the material and can employ this as a 'springboard' for further discussion. This obviously gives rise to a number of legal implications about the protection of children who have not yet had the grounds of referral established. But it also is significant in the implications this practice has for the decision-making process as a whole. One of these is that there appeared to be different types of decision-making by panel members which can be crudely labelled 'backward' and 'forward' decision-making. The labels themselves are not as important as the social practices they denote.

But as regards the decision-making process, with the availability of reports prior to the hearing of a case, panel members may reach some tentative conclusion as to what the decision should be in a particular case. Perhaps this is particularly so when the panel member adopts a more offence-oriented frame of relevance since the bulk of the 'relevant' information will already be available to him (e.g. police charge-sheets, grounds of referrals etc.). This may not only apply to individuals but to panel members as a group who may reach some tacit agreement as to what should be done and how the hearing should be constructed and proceed. What we refer to as 'backward' decision-making is that approach in which decisions are tentatively reached in advance of a hearing and where the hearing is used to obtain information that will serve to justify that decision. It is 'backward' since the search for information is dictated by a decision already tentatively reached. As we have argued above, panel members, where offence or judicial considerations are important, may also decide prior to a hearing to adopt particular approaches such as lecturing, including shame, or employing the 'sword of Damocles' with veiled threats. The hearing then takes on a more symbolic role than perhaps might be expected in an administrative tribunal.

'Forward' decision-making can be seen as an approach to decision-making that is more logical inasmuch as it is characterised by the attempt to assess all information prior to the reaching of a decision which is then the conclusion to a wide-based search for information. It is then justified by reference to specific sets of 'relevant' information, leading to specific conclusions about a child's needs and the most appropriate measure to meet these. The contribution of parents and children in this form of decision-making is important because the greater level of communication within a panel hearing may well mean that they can indeed influence the decision or at the very least be involved in the whole process. In that respect, the panel hearing is a much more open process than a court hearing and one that is as democratic as it can be. But the general point to be made is that within a system of justice based upon a welfare philosophy, the availability of information prior to the actual hearing influences the decision-making process. Doubts may still be raised about the justice of social-work and other reports being available prior to the actual hearing and the charge made that even minimal statutory requirements are being ignored (Martin, Fox and Murray, 1981) may require further consideration of the extent to which children do receive legal protection within the system as a whole. On the other hand, in the court system where, theoretically at least, children receive more legal and judicial protection, the involvement of police and lawyers within a court structure renders the search for information and more importantly the use made of it a very different enterprise. With more reliance being placed on written reports and the statements by prosecutors and lawyers the hearing of a case is sociologically fundamentally different with the predominant frame of relevance being judicially oriented and the assimilation of information being primarily determined by this. Perhaps the difference between the two types of hearings reflects no more than the attempt to reconcile within different organisational structures the often conflicting demands of welfarism and punishment, of 'offence' and 'need' considerations. The hearing of offence cases in actual hearings, as opposed to the use of case studies, may well force into the open the conceptual ambiguity of trying to deal with child offenders by a welfare philosophy as indicated by subtle shifts in the frame of relevance adopted and by the use made of the hearing itself.

The general conclusion to be drawn from all this is that at the very least it is unwise to divorce the nature of the hearing, whether it be court or panel type of hearing, from the decision-making process as a whole. The relevance of information has to be seen in the context of who provides the information, how it is used and the objectives espoused by those responsible for making decisions. In that respect, the children's hearing and the juvenile court provide very different contexts for the practical accomplishment of juvenile justice.

One further point can be made. Juvenile justice is often seen as being accomplished within 'systems' such as the 'Scottish' or 'English' system. And indeed there has been a recent attempt to present a national profile of Scottish juvenile justice (Martin, Fox and Murray, 1981). Yet, it could be argued that because of the way in which decision-makers (panel members or magistrates) are selected and trained for their task and because of the conventional organisational and administrative practices that arise within different regions, there is not *a* system of juvenile justice but a number of different local arrangements. Thus, though this research was conducted on a comparative basis in England and Scotland it would be perfectly reasonable and theoretically appropriate to compare the accomplishment of justice for children between areas within Scotland or within England. It would be unwise, for example, to make *a priori* assumptions about the juvenile justice in Strathclyde or in London on the basis either of the two areas discussed in this research or on the basis of a national profile (as in Martin, Fox and Murray, 1981). For that reason, any attempt to assess or evaluate how a 'system' of juvenile justice is working cannot be made alone by an examination of official crime-statistics. These are themselves the product of and dependent upon the selective and interpretive activity of law-enforcement personnel and render statistical comparisons between or within countries very dubious. The merit of the phenomenological approach, though we could not follow its dictates fully in this research, is that it points to the need to treat statistics as 'topics' for research and not as 'resources' to be employed by the researcher. Despite the claim of some commentators (Martin, Fox and Murray, 1981) statistics are not useless for the committed phenomenologist but rather are important sociological artefacts. It is hoped that this study has pointed to important sociological differences between a court and a tribunal approach to the making of decisions about children who commit offences. And in that respect, it should contribute to our understanding of the different processes involved in dealing with such children and to a recognition that official statistics, at the end of the day, have to be analysed in the context of the selective and interpretative activity of key officials such as magistrates or panel members. To return to the theme of chapter 11, analyses of social policy, such as the implementation of legislative statements relating to delinquency control, can only benefit from the recognition of the significance of the actor's perspective in determining the practical realisation of formal policy statements.

Chapter Nine

CHILDREN AND JUSTICE:
A REAPPRAISAL

After a summary, there are two objectives in this final chapter. These are to examine: (i) the sociological implications of some of the 'return to justice' proposals, and (ii) the relationship between preferred forms of delinquency control and much broader social and political considerations. The two objectives are related since any analysis of how juvenile justice is accomplished has to be analysed in reference to wider social and political developments.

Summary

The difficulty of resolving the conceptual ambiguity of a 'welfare' and a 'judicial' ideology finds institutional expression in most systems of justice for children. Even in Scotland, despite the fact that the Children's Hearings are based upon a more overtly welfare ideology, the Hearings do not have a monopoly over delinquency control since children can still be prosecuted; the age of criminal responsibility remains at eight; children can still go to court to have the facts established; and (neatly reflecting the ambiguity and compromise between a welfare and judicial ideology) the right of appeal against a decision made by a Children's Hearing is to a sheriff in the first instance. The historical trend, until recently, in justice for children has been away from conceiving of the delinquent as a responsible individual and towards causal and deterministic accounts of delinquent action. A recurring feature though has been that almost every system in western industrialised societies, no matter how committed theoretically to a welfare approach, retains some form of judicial involvement. The Scottish system is no exception.

The main assumption underlying this book is that how people conceive of delinquency in part determines what they do about it. That holds true both for formal policy statements and for the lay theories of delinquency and crime maintained by those responsible for the implementation of policy formulations. The empirical study reported here is an attempt to analyse the translation of social policy into actual practice within court and panel forms of decision-making. In particular, the main objective was to examine the extent to which decisions made about children who offend by those operating within the two systems reflected and were based on the competing judicial and welfare ideologies. The empirical study therefore included an analysis of the frames of relevance adopted by lay panel members and lay magistrates in the practical accomplishment of justice, the extent to which these contained elements of the different ideologies, and the implications these frames of relevance had for the assessment and use of information as well as what was revealed about the different organisational structures in question.

Actual decision-making in a court or panel hearing is a collective process involving other magistrates or other panel members, parents, children and other appropriate personnel. It involves exchanges of information both written and verbal in a rather formal setting. And with particular reference to the panel members, the symbolic use made of the hearing itself suggests that they ascribe more importance to the fact that the child had done wrong than had been expected. In terms of the analysis of the situated aspect of decision-making and the logic-in-use (Cicourel 1968) of the decision-makers our approach may even then not have been sufficiently sensitive for what is a socially constructed event. There is more to a hearing, whether it be a court or a panel hearing, than simply the sum of the different perspectives employed.

In general terms it would appear that the panel members ascribe more importance to welfare considerations than do the more judicially oriented magistrates. The frames of relevance espoused by the panel members were predominantly concerned with the social, environmental and personal characteristics of the children. Nevertheless, in terms of the 'available ideologies' of delinquent explanation, both panel members and magistrates agreed to the extent that both groups treated individualistic types of explanation as more important than more sociologically based explanations. We suggested that this may well be due to the fact that the welfare approach to delinquency has developed generally within the context of the development of social, and particularly social casework, services. Thus, it is perhaps not surprising that individualistic types of explanation will inform panel members' and juvenile magistrates' decision-making. However, this may be accounted for by other means. First, individualistic explanations may relate more easily to questions of responsibility and thus provide more acceptable excusing criteria than do sociological forms of explanation where the theoretical links between cause, responsibility and behaviour are less readily drawn. Criminology contains many theories of criminal behaviour where the significance of deterministic assumptions for questions of rationality and criminal responsibility are not clearly articulated. It is easier to see the rationale behind exempting someone from responsibility on the basis that, for example, he is mentally defective than on the basis of widespread social deprivation. Second, it is much easier to tackle the problems of individuals than the problems of areas or of societies, at least within the confines of a criminal justice system.

But though panel members were more concerned with welfare than judicial considerations, they did nevertheless indicate that they agreed with magistrates on certain issues. In particular, in the case study stage of the research, Intentionality was almost equally important for both groups of subjects, though for juvenile magistrates this was also correlated significantly with the other personal responsibility factors, Awareness and Consequences.

In the Case Report section however, despite the earlier *prima facie* agreement about the importance of Intentionality, panel members' decisions were based more on welfare criteria and included no explicit reference to punishment. Magistrates however did, and legitimately so given their role, state their desire to punish amongst the reasons for their decision and were much more concerned with judicial considerations. The implication is that the importance of specific considerations, such as Intentionality, has to be gauged in the context of the frame of relevance predominantly and generally employed. Thus, where the frame of relevance is derived from welfare considerations, the concern may be made with the moral development of the child rather than any desire to establish fault or guilt. Similarly the importance for individuals of such factors as previous offence involvement or the number of charges cannot simply be taken to indicate that panel members or magistrates are thereby committed to a punitive philosophy or a tariff approach to decision-making. There is some ambiguity however amongst panel members for whom leniency and mitigation seem to be pertinent concepts.

Institutionally, the welfare and judicial ideologies are more neatly separated for the juvenile magistrates than for panel members in that they are legitimately concerned with the issue of guilt or responsibility (and are permitted to punish) but they can also decide whether a child is in need or not. There are thus stages in the proceedings where 'offence' or 'need' considerations can be divorced. For panel members, the position is more complex since theoretically they are only concerned with the need for a compulsory measure of care and their allusions to 'offence' considerations are more subtle than is the case with magistrates. The ambiguity of 'judicial' and 'welfare' ideologies is perhaps more keenly experienced within an administrative system of juvenile justice in which panel members are not formally concerned with the issue of responsibility. Nevertheless, it is an important concept in ordinary moral discourse and though not overtly 'judicial' in their orientation, panel members nevertheless still distinguish between those who have committed offences and those who have not.

This is particularly so in the hearing of actual cases: First, there is much more discussion in panel hearings than in court hearings and this relates more to welfare than judicial considerations. Secondly, in panel hearings, parents and children themselves have more opportunity to be involved and there is evidence to suggest that their part in the discussion also focuses more on the social and personal characteristics of the child. Thirdly, the search for and use made of information in a panel hearing is very different from the court hearing where reports are read in court and where the police prosecutor and the lawyer are significant persons in the way they provide information and in the information they provide.

But what is interesting is that despite the more informal approach in the panel hearing, panel members do on occasion adopt moral tactics which serve to differentiate between offenders and non-offenders. The symbolic use of the hearing and the adoption of moral postures serve to impress on the child, without in any way being overtly punitive, that he has done wrong.

Panel members and juvenile magistrates, on the basis of this study, employ very different frames of relevance. More concerned with welfare considerations, panel members will interpret information and reports about offenders generally in terms of the need for care rather than in terms of what he has done. Nevertheless, they may well still make subtle distinctions between those who have committed an offence and those who have not in keeping with ordinary moral discourse.

The greater emphasis in training given to judicial and legalistic matters, the structure of the court and the very fact that they also operate in adult courts of criminal law, means that juvenile magistrates will be more disposed to operate within a frame of relevance in which the concept of responsibility is central in the process of assimilating the various types of information available.

Moreover, the relationships between the different agencies involved in the social control network may well reflect allegiance to dominant frames of relevance. Thus, it was certainly the case that in the juvenile court, there is a far closer working relationship between the magistrates and the police than there is between the panel members and the police in Scotland; in the panel area, there is on the other hand, evidence to suggest that there is more of a shared approach to delinquency control between panel members and social workers than is the case with magistrates who have 'lost power to the social services'. The general point to be drawn from this is that basic differences, as between panel members and magistrates, in the ascription of relevance to even *prima facie* similar information may involve very different social and organisational structures in which agencies such as the police or social work departments have to compete in terms of some hierarchy of relevance. Thus, in the court area, the close working relationship between the police, the lawyer and the magistrates during the court is founded upon the fact that the language they employ to describe and explain delinquent acts is essentially a shared one in which information about social and personal considerations is assessed in terms of a predominantly judicial orientation.

For the purpose of decision-making the relevance of information, the use made of it and what are seen to be the legitimate sources of information are all inextricably linked in the processes that allow justice for children to be practically accomplished. The phenomenological perspective directs attention to the organisational and social structure within which decisions are made as it does to the frames of relevance or operational philosophies employed by key individuals. Any suggestions for change or modification to a particular form of decision-making have then to be appraised with respect to the implications that these may have for the structure of the decision-making process as a whole.

Legal Transplanting

As we have seen the 'return to justice' movement advocates a reversal in policy for delinquents away from a welfare-oriented approach in which individuals such as magistrates and panel members are given considerable discretion to a more court-based system in which decisions will be subject to strict judicial scrutiny and in which legal representation is to be a necessary component. The proposals are made in the belief that the exercise of discretion within a welfare perspective allows for intervention that may not only ignore basic principles of natural justice but also be unjustifiable in the first place because of the theoretical inadequacy of current theories of delinquency causation. Only in a system of strict judicial and legal control can children's rights be protected and justice realised. The solution then is, both to adopt a punitive non-treatment approach and to apply the principles of legality in the effort to check what are seen to be the excesses of wide discretionary powers.

With specific reference to the Children's Hearing system, concern at the lack of protection is voiced by Martin *et al.* (1981) who, on the basis of a recent study, have argued that even the few statutory requirements that govern decision-making are being ignored. And there has also been more general concern that some means of protection may need to be offered to children in a system where they may be potentially subject to compulsory measures of care which may involve their being taken from home (Asquith 1979). The problem is of course to determine what form such protection or representation may take without altering the very nature of the system as a whole and it is in this respect that the study reported here has some relevance. Recommendations for representation of children usually mean legal representation but it is difficult to conceive what role could be devised for a lawyer operating within a system of justice for children based on the philosophy of the Kilbrandon Report. There are a number of reasons for this, all of which point to the basic incompatibility of legal and welfare ideologies.

Contrary to commonly held assumptions about the Scottish system of justice for children, decisions reached by panel members are subject to judicial review and rule of law. Where the parents or children decide to challenge a decision, their appeal is heard by the sheriff. What is intriguing about this is that the Kilbrandon Report rejected the judiciary as appropriate to make decisions about the welfare of children on the grounds that their training and expertise were more suited to questions of adjudication than the disposal of cases. Yet, recognising that children should have the protection of the law, the right to hear appeals was in fact vested in the judiciary. Appeals can be made on two grounds, referred to as appeals on law (relating to the competence of the procedure followed in the decision-making process) and appeals on merit (relating to the substance or appropriateness of the decision). A number of points can be made. First, there are in fact very few appeals anyway. In 1974, whereas there had been over 14,000 disposals made there were only 28 appeals. Second, the few appeals that were successful are usually appeals on law where procedural incompetence is claimed. Gordon (1976) has suggested that it is only to be expected that appeals would be more about the procedure adopted than the merit of the actual decision. Third, but perhaps most importantly, the judiciary are themselves in dispute over whether they should be concerned with the merit of the decision (is this the right decision?) or whether they should only be involved in questions of law (has the decision been reached in a right and proper manner). That is, some sheriffs have argued that they are not competent to judge the propriety of the decision itself since they are not qualified in questions of welfare. What all this crystallises is the basic incompatibility of legal and judicial ideology with matters of welfare and anticipates the difficulties to be encountered in identifying just what form of protection for children could be accommodated within the Children's Hearing system.

If the representative were to be a lawyer then it could be argued that this would fundamentally alter the process of decision-making with the introduction, as in the juvenile court, of an individual for whom welfare is a secondary concern and whose orienting philosophy is alien to the spirit of the 1968 Act. Further, one of the crucial differences between the court and panel hearing is the facility of the latter for open discussion in which children and parents are key participants. Yet in court where children are legally represented, the contribution of parents and children is reduced dramatically with the lawyer presenting what appear to him to be salient elements of the case. The prsentation of the 'facts' of the case or information about a child's social, personal and environmental circumstances by an individual with legal training and expertise would demand the restructuring of the very process whereby information is interpreted and assimilated. In the interest of promoting the rights of

children, which would in all probability mean providing children with protection against procedural injustices (Gordon
1976), both the 'form' and 'content' would be essentially modified. The conflict of law and welfare is neatly summed up by
Campbell (1975) who argues:

> Without for the moment asking which system of ideas
> should take precedence when they conflict (i.e. law and
> welfare), it can be argued that those involved in exercising
> discretion within the Hearing system should see their de-
> cisions both as those of an impartial judge whose concern is
> with appropriate penalties under the law and those of pater-
> nalistic diagnosticians, or social medicine men whose con-
> cern is for the children's welfare.

The paradox, however, identified by Campbell, is that if the
child's representative were an expert in child welfare, this form
of representation would in no way appease those who consider
welfare in practice and in theory to be basically unjust. The
conceptual ambiguity inherent in debates about the provision of
welfare is of direct relevance for questions about who appro-
priately may represent a child and what his role might be. The
dilemma has not gone unnoticed by panel members themselves
and the solution is seen by some to involve neither a legally nor
a welfare-trained representative but rather a 'panel of appeal'
composed of lay panel members.

No attempt is being made here to suggest a preferred solution.
That would both be inappropriate and outside the terms of our
research. Rather, the point is to identify the sociological consequences of attempts to check discretionary decision-making
through a form of representation, in particular legal representation, for the network of relationships and agencies within the
decision-making process. Even in the juvenile court system the
incompatibility of legal and welfare modes of thought is reflected in the very different use made of information about children's
backgrounds. A fortiori, the practical accomplishment of justice
in the panel hearings could not accommodate overt judicial or
legal involvement without a radical reordering of the social and
organisational structure in the context of which decisions are
reached. The pursuit of justice and the promotion of children's
rights has to involve more than simply institutional transplants
in which elements of one system are grafted on to another. The
wider implication of this discussion is that what is at stake is
not just how best to promote children's rights and achieve
justice but is rather what rights are to be promoted and what

kind of justice is being pursued. The danger is that the procedural rights of children may well be enhanced by providing checks and controls within a system of delinquency control without in any way affecting the material social circumstances in which children find themselves and which may well be a contributory factor in their being caught up in formal processes of social control. That is, the promotion of children's rights and the pursuit of justice demands more than simply 'tinkering' with the processes of control. What is required is a truly critical reappraisal of the relationship of systems of justice for children to the society in which they are located. The practical accomplishment of decision-making by control agents has to be articulated to wider sociological concerns if not only the procedural but also the more substantial rights of children are to be realised.

Children and Justice

In the practical accomplishment of juvenile justice, the focus of inquiry has to be the selective and interpretative activity of key personnel in the determination of information as relevant for the purposes of decision-making. This however does not mean that the sociological enterprise from this perspective should be limited simply to the identification of different ways of construing the world or parts of it, for our purposes delinquency. Indeed, one of the criticisms often made of phenomenological theory is that of 'ideological relativism'. That is, that individuals see the world differently and there are as many views of the world as there are individuals in it. With reference to the research reported here, it could be argued that all that has been presented is an analysis of how significant individuals within the social control network view the world. However this ignores cardinal features of the phenomenological enterprise. First, views of the world are shared. For example, though there may be a number of ideologies about how to control delinquency, assumptions about what delinquency is and what approach to adopt towards it will be shared by those who adhere to a broadly similar ideology. Second, again with specific reference to delinquency control, only particular ideological orientations come to be incorporated into either formal policy statements or the informal ideologies espoused by those responsible for translating policy into practice. It is for such reasons that Smith (1981) can argue that an examination of the informal working ideologies of individual actors can reveal much about the social and bureaucratic structure within which they operate. The merit of the phenomenological approach is that, as well as identifying what in the literature have been variously described as 'ideologies', 'working ideologies', 'operational philosophies', or 'frames of relevance', it also points to the need to account for the fact that only certain views of the world are ascribed legitimacy. Empirical research and more abstract theorising are far from mutually exclusive and a truly critical analysis of juvenile justice can move forward only by maintaining a dialectic between the two.

It almost goes without saying that there is no consensus as to what delinquency is, how it comes about or what to do about it. The fact that systems of juvenile justice are continually under review is testimony to that. Nevertheless, a number of what Pearson (1975) refers to as 'constancies' can be traced throughout the historical development of justice for children. Some of these can be identified in the way in which both panel members and magistrates ascribe relevance to information about a given child. Whereas panel members subscribed more to a welfare orientation than did magistrates who were more concerned with judicial considerations, they did however share things in common. Both groups operated predominantly on what we might refer to as individualistic explanations of delinquency as we have seen. For magistrates operating more in 'judicial' terms, the offender was an individual essentially responsible, possibly punishable and for whom social circumstances could be taken to mitigate potentially severe decisions. For panel members, the explanations of delinquency that were favoured tended to be those in which the causal factors in delinquency were seen to be associated with the individual or his immediate environment, whether social or physical. Both agreed to the extent that delinquency was an individualistic phenomenon and that the appropriate measures – whether punishment or treatment – were to be applied to the individual.

Indeed, in terms of the ideologies available to magistrates and panel members, the training programmes of both are suffused with explanations of delinquency from an individualistic perspective. Thus, in terms of the training programme, the ideologies available to panel members are heavily deterministic and predominately locate the causal factors of crime in the child or his immediate environment (see Martin and Murray 1976). For magistrates, though the training programme did obviously include contributions from social workers, psychiatrists and allied professionals, a much greater emphasis than in Scotland was placed on legal and judicial considerations in which individual responsibility is a key concept. Magistrates are even encouraged to infer the level of intent from the nature and seriousness of the offence (Sanders 1973).

This does no more than reflect the fact that despite continual review of systems of control, the idea that delinquency is an individualistic phenomenon, in terms of causation and control, is firmly enshrined in the various strategies adopted for dealing with those children who commit offences. Formal systems of control have therefore attempted to seek a balance between an approach that treats the offender as responsible and potentially liable to overtly non-treatment/punishment measures on the one hand and an approach that sought change in the individual through treatment/non-punishment measures. Again Bean (1976) captures the significance of this nicely as well as pointing to the importance of social work more recently by referring to those who provide welfare to offenders as 'psycho-social' experts. Certain conceptions of delinquency receive more legitimacy than others and the notion of it being an essentially individualistic phenomenon is firmly rooted in the practical accomplishment of juvenile justice.

Moreover, delinquency is also generally construed as a lower-working-class phenomenon. It has been a matter of historical contingency that those who get caught up in the formal processes of social control are generally those who are working class, poor, living in deprived areas, unemployed and so on. The current trend towards more retributive and judicially based forms of juvenile justice no doubt anticipates a move back to some form of liberalism, such has been the history of justice for children. In the field of crime control generally, developments have been characterised by pendulum-like movements swinging between punishment and rather more liberal measures. Formal policy statements and the practical accomplishment of juvenile justice are both riven with ambiguity, an almost logical consequence of attempts to reconcile philosophies of control that in the abstract are based upon very different principles. But there is a greater danger and that is that by continuing to formulate policies in this incremental, piecemeal fashion, major social institutions such as juvenile-justice systems may well serve to perpetuate the very conditions that contribute to the problem of delinquency. Whether in the form of punishment or a welfare philosophy, delinquency is conceived of as an individualistic, working-class phenomenon and delinquency control is therefore seen to be essentially a problem of dealing with individuals. Murphy (1973, p.169) argues: 'Institutions of punishment are, in the absence of major social change, to be resisted by all who take human rights as mostly serious, i.e. regard them as genuine guides for action and not merely rhetorical devices which allow people to morally sanctify institutions which in fact can only be defended on grounds of social *expediency*'. And more recently, King (1981, p.132) has put it thus: 'Punishment does not provide effective social control where the causes of anti-social behaviour are rooted deep in the structure of the social system'. Both these comments relate specifically to punishment but the argument applies equally well to welfare philosophies which concentrate 'help' or 'care' on the individual offender whilst ignoring the social-structural and economic position in which he finds himself.

No criticism is here being directed against panel members or magistrates. Indeed, they generally recognise that broader sociological and political considerations are important factors and there have been suggestions that they should themselves form political pressure groups advocating recognition of the wider aspects of delinquency. Such action would have to be outside the confines of the criminal and juvenile justice systems. The danger is that the conceptions of delinquency and the controls that are contained in formal policy statements and the translation of these into practice within a system of justice, far from getting at the root causes of the problem, may well perpetuate the 'structural injustices' (Harris 1972) of society. That is, through the ideologies of delinquency control that come to dominate official thinking, systems of juvenile justice can be seen as only one of the means by which particular forms of social and economic arrangements are maintained. By concentrating on the individual, attention is deflected from the way in which a certain social and economic structure sustains the very phenomenon that juvenile-justice systems, and in particular the decision-makers whether they be magistrates or panel members, are required to deal with. For such reasons we believe that a phenomenological approach is of considerable practical relevance (despite the claim of its critics) in that it fosters the need to analyse the social and structural origins of ideologies of delinquency, and analyses of the practical accomplishment of justice for children have to be appraised in relation to the function it may serve in leaving unchallenged basic social injustice. Social institutions such as systems of delinquency control, whether premised upon punishment or welfare, where they operate in terms of a philosophy which ignores basic social and economic injustices merely continue to 'blame the victim'.

The pursuit of justice and the promotion of the rights of children has usually meant modifying the decision-making process in the attempt to achieve greater procedural equality and is less concerned with the substantial rights of children in terms of taking steps that will truly serve their best interests. If there is genuine concern about the rights of children and their long-term welfare then greater concern has to be directed at the material conditions of social life in which children who offend find themselves. The ideologies of delinquency control and the social institutions through which these find expression must bear some relationship to the way in which opportunities in life are distributed. Those who make decisions about children are granted a fair degree of power to intervene in the lives of the young. If the ideologies they espouse bear little relationship to social and economic reality (see Murphy 1973), then the pursuit of justice may well be inhibited. Since the 1908 Children Act there have been no truly radical alternative forms of justice for children (despite what is often said about the Scottish system) inasmuch as all proposals have operated generally on a philosophy that has shown more concern with the individual offender and measures designed to 'change' him. To ignore basic social and economic inequality whilst promoting greater procedural equality inhibits the realisation of the rights of children and may well achieve a degree of justice within a system of control which has all the hallmarks of material injustice. Perhaps King (1981) should have the last word when he states: 'Many of the present debates about the welfare of children, their rights and their interests are distractions, drawing attention away from concern over the way in which power is distributed and exercised'.

APPENDIX I

i) CASE STUDIES

Case Study A

James Green, 99 Lowvale Road, Hightown Estate, Charington (age 14)

James lives with his parents and sisters in a council house in Hightown Estate, where there is a high level of anti-social behaviour. Many of the houses have been damaged as a result of vandalism and James' own house has been without electricity for some months because the family were unable to pay the bill. His father has been unemployed for four months and this may also explain the recently incurred rent arrears. As with many families in the area, the Greens are receiving assistance from the social services department.

School reports indicate that James is not without ability, but that he lacks the motivation to concentrate on his studies and eagerly awaits the day, two years hence, when he can leave school to find a job.

According to the social worker, the financial and living circumstances of the family have been creating strain in the relationships between the different individuals in the household. James may therefore not be receiving the guidance and control he needs.

Recreational facilities in the area are of a poor quality and indeed most have been closed due to vandalism and gang fights. James spends most of his time with his friends just walking about the streets with no particular purpose in mind. The majority of his friends are known to the police. He shares his father's and associates' distrust of authority, especially the police, who are seen as patrolling the Estate in order to 'pick up' youths like James at the slightest chance. However, his association with local gang elements is giving rise to concern, in that prior to the Greens' move to the Estate, some three years ago, he had never been in trouble with the police.

He states that the offence was committed by him in company

with his friends, all of whom wanted to go to Hopkirk to see their football team, Armingham Thistle, play. Since none of them had sufficient money to pay their fares to the game, James suggested that they 'arrange' their own transport. He knew of a man whose family were on holiday and that the man himself worked nightshift. When he was at work his car was left unattended outside the house. On the night they wanted to leave for the match, James organised two of his friends to keep watch while he and another stole the car. He knew how to cross the ignition wires with silver paper and so did not need the appropriate key. Entry to the car was just as simple, since the quarterlight was easily forced with a screwdriver. After the match and on their way home, they decided that it would be best to abandon the car and in doing so, drove it through a fence into an orchard. The car was considerably damaged and would cost £400 to repair.

Although they made off at the time, they were later apprehended by the police who were given a description of the boys by a witness to the crash.

1. He was well aware that what he was doing was against the law.
2. He comes from an area where there is a high level of antisocial behaviour.
3. His family is in a bad financial position.
4. He should have anticipated the consequences of being caught.
5. Living conditions generally are extremely poor in the estate.
6. Society has a right to protection.
7. James initiated and planned the whole affair.
8. His associates have been in trouble with the police previously.
9. The incident resulted in considerable damage to property.
10. There are no recreational facilities in the estate.

Case Study B
William Black, Fotheringham Children's Home (age 13)

Willie was removed from his parental home at the age of five on the advice of the social worker who was involved with the family. His father was a chronic alcoholic who was unable to give the necessary emotional support to his wife who was virtually left to raise Willie and his younger brothers on her own. Mr Black's alcoholism also meant that he could not provide the material requisites for bringing up his family. Due to financial and emotional pressures, Mrs Black had a nervous breakdown when Willie was only about one year old. While she was in hospital, all her children were looked after in separate foster homes, and Willie apparently experienced his separation from his mother as most traumatic. When Mrs Black returned from hospital, it took Willie some time to settle down and he began to behave in an extremely aggressive manner towards his mother. This situation improved slightly with time but deteriorated again when Mrs Black left home because she felt her husband's excessive drinking was becoming too much for her. The children were once more split up and sent to Children's Homes temporarily.

Mrs Black returned after a period of one year but the social worker decided that, because she was still showing signs of her nervous condition, she was unable and apparently unwilling to care for her children or to show them love and affection, the children should therefore be removed from the parental home on a permanent basis.

For different reasons, some administrative and some arising from Willie's own personal problems, he has been taken care of in various homes. In this way, and as a result of his enforced separation from his mother, he has experienced rejection in many different forms.

According to the report from the house in which Willie is at present, he is something of a problem. He attaches himself to no one in particular but forms shallow relationships with anyone who happens to be available. Moreover, his behaviour shows various signs of regression, including bedwetting. He does not seem to have sufficient self control but rather acts on impulse and for immediate gratification. Nor does he accept the most ordinary discipline, but is easily frustrated if he does not get his own way. His school report emphasises the disruptive effect his behaviour has on the rest of the class.

Willie says that it was not his idea to break into the school but that he was asked by some of his friends to go with them. This he decided to do, although he did state to the social worker that he knew it was wrong to do so. Once inside the school, however, Willie took an active part in the destruction that followed, and actually led the others to what seemed to them to be a music room. In this class room they hammered tape recorders and musical instruments with billiard cues taken from the games room. Generally, they ran through the school continuing to destroy property.

When they came to the science laboratories, they broke a considerable amount of apparatus before they found a cupboard containing methylated spirit. This they used to start a small fire with some jotters, but when the fire got out of hand they left the school premises and stood at the perimeter fence, waiting until the fire brigade came. Total cost of the damage to the school was £12,000.

1. He was not forced to go with his friends but went through choice.
2. Extensive damage resulted from the fire.
3. In his formative years, his life was spent in an unstable home environment.
4. He knows the difference between right and wrong.
5. Consideration must be given to the protection of public property.
6. Since he was five, he has been in the care of the local authority in a Children's Home.
7. He well knew what would happen if he were caught.
8. He is only able to form superficial relationships with others.
9. On several occasions, he has experienced rejection.
10. He acts on impulse and is easily frustrated.

Case Study C
Jimmy James, 4 Provost Road, Lamington (age 15)

Last year Jimmy was placed under the supervision of the social services department for his part in a fight between rival football supporters in which a youth was stabbed quite seriously. The present offence occurred while he was still under supervision.

Since he was dealt with for the last offence, far from benefiting from his period of supervision, Jimmy's behaviour has deteriorated considerably. His previous offence, up to which he had never been in trouble before, came as quite a shock to his parents, who are both well known in the area, his father being a prominent member of the church. Apparently, since then they have used the name 'delinquent' in addressing Jimmy any time he does not comply with their wishes. They also require him to be in at nine o'clock although his sister is allowed to stay out longer because she is more 'trustworthy'.

At school, where he was doing quite well before this first offence, the teacher would refer to him as a young tearaway in front of the class and repeatedly warns the other children that they will turn out like Jimmy James if they do not keep out of trouble. Jimmy has reacted in a way which he thinks shows his contempt – by living up to his delinquent tag. He now bullies other young children at school and has started associating with a crowd of boys who are constantly in trouble with the police. Since then his former friends have been prohibited by their parents from meeting him and as a result he has tended to seek companionship amongst an anti-social element in the area. He has been blamed at school and in the neighbourhood for things of which he had no knowledge, but which were readily attributed to him because of his reputation.

The police are keeping a close watch on him and he is amongst the first to be 'picked up' and questioned when an offence has occurred. Perhaps as a result of this, he now frequents the adjacent housing estate in which his new-found friends live and in which anti-social behaviour is readily entered upon. He has adopted their dress of denim jacket, jeans and boots in preference to his school blazer and more casual clothes. His parents now feel that he is incapable of spending money wisely on clothes and so have reduced the amount he gets as an allowance.

He and his friend had made up their minds to break into a factory which was quite near their home. Although the factory had closed down some time ago, it was left standing intact until the new owners arrived. Guard patrols make regular rounds in the property immediately surrounding the factory. Jimmy and his friend therefore had to watch the factory for two or three weeks prior to the offence, in order that they could work out the safest time to break into the factory, without risk of being caught. Since the factory had been engaged in the manufacture of plumbing equipment, lead was extensively used and some deposits of it remained scattered about the factory floor. It was the lead which Jimmy and his mate were after, since they could sell it below market price to local scrap dealers without too many questions being asked as to its origins. They were both aware of the risks involved but felt sure that they could get away with it.

They cut through the mesh fence surrounding the factory with wire clippers and made their way to a side door where the friend used a steel ruler to open a Yale lock. Once inside, it was an easy matter to collect the lead and put it into a sack, but as they were doing this they heard the sound of a patrol, with a dog, making a tour of inspection of the factory. Both made a dash for the fence and only managed to scramble over it without being caught, but not before a patrolman saw them and was later able to give their description to the police. Not only did they fail to get the lead off the premises, but they were also apprehended by the police that very night.

1. He is old enough to know the difference between right and wrong.
2. He has been forced to seek companionship amongst the gang element.
3. Since his previous offence, he has been treated as if he were untrustworthy in all respects.
4. A deliberate decision was made by him to break into the factory.
5. The offence involved damage to property.
6. He is always amongst the first to be questioned if an offence is committed.
7. He was aware of the consequences of being caught.
8. Seen by others simply as a delinquent, he is forced to behave as one.
9. He takes the blame for many things of which he has no knowledge.
10. Protection of property has to be given due regard.

Case Study D
Charlie White, Birdfield Avenue, Farnton (age 15)

Charlie comes from an area of Farnton in which there is considerable anti-social behaviour and frequent confrontation between the police and the local criminal element. Charlie associates with many of those who have been in trouble with the police and with one of them committed the offence which constitutes the present ground for referral.

Mike, Charlie's friend, had remarked that he was short of money and needed some to buy new clothes. Charlie suggested that they could 'raise' the money by stealing some goods from the local Woolworth's store, then selling them. To many of their friends, the department stores offered many opportunities for theft with little risk of being caught. They decided that they would take a tape recorder since it was light enough to carry and was likely to be in demand by various unscrupulous buyers. They then worked out a plan for executing the theft.

According to the social worker who was given the account, Charlie was to act as a decoy while Mike was to be the one who actually stole the tape recorder. It was to be from Woolworth's because, unlike the other larger stores, the arrangements for the protection of goods were known by them to be very poor. They went into the store and while Mike made his way to the appropriate counter, Charlie asked the attendant if he could see the record players on the pretence that he wanted to buy one. Meantime, Mike had begun to handle the cassette tape recorders and when he was sure that he was not being observed and that Charlie had managed to distract the attendant's attention sufficiently, he slipped one inside his denim jacket. He then walked out. When Charlie saw this, he 'decided' that he did not like the record players shown to him and also made his way out. However, both boys had in fact been watched on a concealed closed circuit television and were caught at the door.

It seems that Charlie has acquired his distrust of authority from his father, a building labourer, who has himself been in trouble with the police. When Charlie was younger, his father used to live away from home because his work at that time involved travelling. Mrs White was left on her own to look after Charlie, but, because she was also working, there were many occasions when he was allowed to do simply as he pleased. When his father was at home, he was more inclined to punish Charlie physically than was Mrs White who used to bribe her son with sweets or extra pocket money. This pattern of inconsistency is reported in a social work report as being general throughout Charlie's upbringing, as a result of which he is inclined to act on impulse and from selfishness. It was during his adolescence that he began to associate with the delinquent element of the area in which he lived, and during which his distrust of authority was strengthened.

Most of his participation in crime has been aimed at obtaining the benefits of material possessions, as well as winning for him high esteem in the eyes of his friends who see his flaunting of authority as something to be admired. The fact that there exist law enforcing agencies does little to modify his belief that crime pays. Rather, he now views his criminal activities as a source of material and personal reward. He scorns the police and it is likely that his future will be one of frequent contact with the law. If it is not impressed on him that, in the long run, anti-social behaviour does not pay, he will be tempted to participate in more serious behaviour in the belief that he will for the most part escape the consequences.

1. Though aware of the consequences of being caught, he felt he
   could escape them.

2. His parents were inconsistent in disciplining him in childhood.
3. He was well aware that what he was doing was against the
law.
4. The area in which he lives has a high incidence of anti-social
behaviour.
5. Charlie himself suggested that he be a decoy in the theft.
6. He has lacked the opportunity for learning socially acceptable
behaviour.
7. His attitude of hostility to authority is reinforced by contact
with others of similar mind.
8. The item stolen was of some value.
9. The status he enjoys amongst his friends makes him participate even more in crime.
10. Society needs protection from theft.

Case Study E
Brian Brown, 6 London Road, Kirkhaven (age 15)

On the night of the offence, Brian and his gang, of which he
is leader, were walking the streets of Kirkhaven at about 10
o'clock. At this time, the pubs began to empty and a number of
the patrons were walking home. According to Brian, he and a
few of his friends followed two men, who appeared the worse for
drink, over some common ground where there were few lights.
Their aim was to rob the men whom they supposed to be
incapable of defending themselves. When the time seemed
right, they stopped the men and demanded money or else they
would 'do them in'. However, the men refused to hand over the
money despite the threats and started to hit out at the youths.
Some of them ran away but Brian stood his ground and, according to his own report, took out a steel comb which was sharp-
ened at one end, whilst the other was covered with insulating
tape to act as a handle. He then began to fight with one of the
men, inflicting injuries on him which later required several
stitches. He was, however, unable to use the makeshift knife,
but injured the man with his fists and feet.
The account of the fight given by the men included the statement that, while one was chasing what remained of Brian's
gang, Brian was fighting with the other using heavily booted
feet. According to them, he seemed to have lost control of
himself and even when he was being restrained by both men till
the police arrived, he began to struggle violently. They did not

recollect actually seeing the steel comb and it can only be assumed that Brian, not having the opportunity to use it, and well aware of the consequences of possessing it, had hidden it on his person before the police arrived. However, it was found on him during a search in the police station.

Brian's father had died when he was two and his mother had remarried shortly after. Mr and Mrs Brown have three children by this marriage, none of whom display the same aggressive tendencies of their half brother, Brian.

Mrs Brown stated that her first husband, Brian's natural father, was an extremely aggressive man whose temper got him into considerable trouble. She feels that Brian is, in this respect at least, very similar in nature to his father.

Brian had been an extremely demanding baby in that he had cried a lot from his earliest days and needed continual attention from his mother. When he was a toddler, frustration of his immediate desires brought on particularly severe bouts of temper. In later childhood, discipline was never readily accepted by Brian without resulting in expressions of anger and temper tantrums. Mrs Brown feels that she looked after him as well as she could and is convinced that she provided him with sufficient emotional warmth as well as having adequately met his material needs. But she herself received little sign of affection from Brian.

When he was seven, Brian had a pet rabbit which he teased, for no other reason, apparently, than that he enjoyed doing so. Later he began to treat it rather cruelly and actually brought about its death.

At school, his tendency to slip into violent behaviour without much provocation is recorded as having a disruptive effect on the whole class as well as hindering his own development. He has attended remedial classes throughout his educational career. Outside school, his inclination to hostility made him the natural leader of a gang of boys amongst whom his fierce fighting ability was not only respected but feared.

According to the social worker who visited the family, Brian is without shame or remorse for what he did to the victim of his attack and has by all accounts never been known to have shown these emotions in relation to any of his behaviour.

1. The injuries he inflicted on the older man were quite serious.
2. By nature, Brian is extremely aggressive.
3. There is a history of aggression in Brian's childhood.

4. As leader of the gang, it was his decision to attack the men.
5. The public must be protected from such offences.
6. He has inherited his father's aggressive temperament.
7. He is well aware that it is illegal to carry an offensive weapon.
8. Frustration easily arouses his extremely aggressive temper.
9. He has never been known to show remorse or shame.
10. He knew fully the consequences of being caught.

ii) CASE REPORT

Name
Case (indicate by offender's initials)
  SECTION A
1. Briefly, what were the main reasons for the decision?
2. Was the decision influenced by
   a) The availability of suitable resources   Yes/No
   b) Statutory restrictions   Yes/No
      (In both cases delete as appropriate)
3. Did you agree with the actual decision reached?   Yes/No
4. If not, why not?
5. Given ideal resources what would *your* decision have been?
6. For what reasons.
7. Indicate by placing a tick in the appropriate box whether you thought that, for the purpose of reaching a decision in this case, the available reports were Very informative, Fairly informative or Not informative about the offender's background and circumstances.

   Similarly, if any report available to you made a recommendation as to the appropriate disposal of the case, indicate whether, on the whole, *you* Agreed or Disagreed with that recommendation.

Report:	Very Informative	Fairly Informative	Not Informative	Recommendations Agreed	Recommendations Disagreed
Social work					
School					
Psychological					
Psychiatric					
Others					
. . . .					
. . . .					

SECTION B	Very Important	Important	Not Important
Social work report			
Psychiatric report			
Psychological report			
School report			
Child's relationship with father			
Child's relationship with mother			
Child's relationship with siblings			
Family unit as a whole			
Financial position of family			
Child from a broken home			
Child's character			
Area of residence			
Home conditions			
Child's associates			
Either/both parents in trouble			
Child treated as delinquent since he has been in trouble before			
Use of leisure time			
The offence was committed in the company of others			
Parental discipline of child			
Number of previous offences			
Previous disposals			
Child's first offence			
Nature of this offence			
Child aware of what he was doing			
Child aware that it was wrong			
Child aware of consequences of being caught			
His behaviour was intended			
This was a serious offence			
A lot of harm was done			
Society needs to be protected			
This offence is occurring too much			
Father's attitude in the Hearing			
Mother's attitude in the Hearing			
Child's attitude in the Hearing			
Sibling/s in trouble			
Social worker's relationship with family			
Child denied the facts which were established in court			
Relevant facts not included			

iii) INTERACTION SCHEDULE

Observation Schedule

Case: Start: Finish: Adjournments:

Present:

	A	B	C
Social work report			
School report			
Psychiatric report			
Psychological report			
Age			
Religion			
Formative years			
Relations with father			
Relations with mother			
Relations with siblings			
Family as a whole			
Child's character			
Discipline			
Siblings in trouble			
Either/both parents in trouble			
Associates			
Area of residence			
Recreational facilities			
Leisure			
In trouble before			
Treated as delinquent			
History of trouble			
Delinquent by nature			
Schooling			
Intelligence			
Broken home			
Career prospects			
Other			
Aware of his behaviour			
Aware it was wrong			
Aware of consequences			
Knows right from wrong			
Action was deliberate/intended			
Reasons/motives for action			
Circumstances of offence			
Serious/harmful nature of offence			

                                          A   B   C

Societal protection
Prevalence of offence
Nature of offence
No. of previous offences
Previous disposals
Points of law
S W relation to offender/family
Modifying influences
Availability of resources
Legal restrictions
Discharge
Home supervision
Residential
Other

Summing up by chairman:

Decision:

APPENDIX II

SCOTLAND AND ENGLAND

Case Studies

a) All Scores

	Welfare	Social Protect.	Harm	Awareness	Consequences	Intentionality	Pers. Respons.
All cases							
P M	43.36	11.3	11.48	11.64	12.51	9.7	33.85
J M	52.26	9.06	10.33	9.48	11.84	8.29	29.65
Case A							
P M	9.67	2.24	2.21	1.97	2.57	1.33	5.88
J M	10.61	1.87	1.81	1.64	2.71	1.32	5.71
Case B							
P M	7.91	2.33	2.3	2.3	2.73	2.42	7.48
J M	9.74	1.77	1.93	1.87	2.48	2.19	6.55
Case C							
P M	8.64	2.39	2.57	2.52	2.24	1.61	6.36
J M	10.41	2.	2.19	2.	2.06	1.32	5.44
Case D							
P M	8.09	2.48	2.82	2.3	2.12	2.18	6.61
J M	9.58	1.9	2.61	1.97	2.03	1.9	5.9
Case E							
P M	9.03	1.85	1.57	2.54	2.85	2.15	7.55
J M	10.93	1.52	1.48	2.0	2.55	1.54	6.06

b) *t*-values: 'Between' Scores

	Welfare	Social Protect.	Harm	Awareness	Consequences	Intentionality	Pers. Respons.
All cases	*5.49*	*3.851*	*2.532*	*3.38*	1.75	*2.64*	*3.71*
Case A	*2.307*	*3.407*	*2.32*	1.36	0.98	0.08	0.558
Case B	*4.05*	2.02	*3.37*	*2.39*	1.78	1.19	2.26
Case C	*4.2*	2.27	*2.93*	*2.79*	0.93	1.79	*2.95*
Case D	*4.32*	*3.26*	1.13	1.67	0.44	1.51	2.05
Case E	*4.59*	2.05	0.623	*3.03*	1.5	*3.03*	*4.36*

(Significant *t*-values are in italic)

Case Reports

a) Judicial factors treated as important for decision-making: panel and court *t*-values

	Social Protect.	Seriousness	Harm	Awareness	Consequences	Intentionality
>1 charges	0.891	0.1563	*2.168*	n.s.	n.s.	*1.915*
1 charge	*3.1464*	*4.953*	0.712	*2.716*	*2.57*	1.286
Theft	n.s.	*2.09*	1.311	n.s.	*2.434*	*2.2803*
Theft × H.B.	1.407	*1.883*	*1.658*	n.s.	n.s.	1.165
No previous offences	*1.922*	0.705	0.9525	n.s.	0.5006	*1.893*
≥1 previous offences	*2.537*	*2.409*	*1.672*	*1.529*	1.008	*2.074*

(Significant *t*-values are in italic)

b) Reasons for decisions

	Scotland	England
Child-oriented	52	25
Family-oriented	31	18
Parental control	28	21
Home/Area conditions	2	12
Schooling	13	—
Truancy	12	1
Reports	—	8
Suitability/Availability of Resources	2	—
Nature of offence:		
General	4	11
Trivial	8	2
Serious	5	1
Nature of child's involvement	6	2
Previous record	3	5
First offence	4	12
Bring home nature of offence	—	1
To punish	—	1
To deter offender	—	3
To give a short, sharp shock	—	5
Prevent crime	—	11
Protect public	—	3
Past disposals/measures	11	4

BIBLIOGRAPHY

The following abbreviations have been adopted:

A.C.L.R.	American Criminal Law Review
A.J.S.	American Journal of Sociology
A.S.R.	American Sociological Review
B.J.C.	British Journal of Criminology
B.J.D.	British Journal of Delinquency
B.J.L.S.	British Journal of Law and Society
B.J.S.W.	British Journal of Social Work
C.L.R.	Criminal Law Review
H.L.R.	Harvard Law Review
L.Q.R.	Law Quarterly Review
P.S.R.	Pacific Sociological Review
R.K.P.	Routledge and Kegan Paul

Acton, H. B. (ed.) *Philosophy of Punishment*, Macmillan, London 1969.

Adler, M. 'Financial Assistance and the Social Worker's Exercise of Discretion' in *In Cash or Kind*, ed. Nancy Newman, Department of Social Administration, University of Edinburgh 1976.

Adler, R. 'Black on Young Offenders: Policy without Principles or No Policy at All?' *Scolag*, August 1981.

Aichorn, A. *Wayward Youth*, Wayward Press, New York 1936.

Alihan, M. A. *Social Ecology: a critical analysis*, Columbia University Press, New York 1938.

Allen, F. 'Criminal Justice, Legal Values and the Rehabilitative Ideal' in *Punishment and Rehabilitation*, ed. Murphy, J., Wadsworth, Belmont 1973.

Arendt, H. *The Human Condition*, Doubleday, Chicago 1958.

Armstrong, K. G. 'The Retributivist Hits Back', *Mind*, October 1961. Reprinted in Acton, ed. 1969, p.83 ff.

Asquith, S. '"Relevance" and Lay Participation in Juvenile Justice', *B.J.L.S.*, vol.4, no.1, 1977, pp.61-76.

Asquith, S. 'Juvenile Justice and Ordinary Language'. Paper presented at Nordic-Scottish Colloquium on Criminal Justice, Edinburgh 1977.

Asquith, S. 'Legality and the Hidden Politics of Delinquency' in Brown, P. and Bloomfield, T. (eds) *Legality and Community: the politics of juvenile justice in Scotland*, Aberdeen People's Press 1979.

Austin, J. L. 'A Plea for Excuses', *Proceedings of Aristotelian Society*, LVII (1956-7).

Austin, J. L. *Philosophical Papers*, Oxford University Press 1961.

Ayer, A. J. *Philosophical Essays*, Macmillan, London 1954.

Baier, K. 'Is Punishment Retributive', *Analysis*, XVI, 1955, pp.25-57.

Baldwin, J. and Bottoms, A. *The Urban Criminal: a study in Sheffield*, Tavistock, London 1976.

Bales, R. F. *Interaction Process-Analysis*, Addison-Wesley, Massachusetts 1951.

Bales, R. F. 'A set of categories for the analysis of small group interaction', *A.S.R.*, vol.15, 1950, pp.227-33.

Bankowski, Z. and Mungham, G. *Images of Law*, R.K.P., London 1977.

Bannister, D. and Fransella, F. *Inquiring Man: the Theory of Personal Constructs*, Penguin, Harmondsworth 1971.

Bannister, D. and Mair, J. *The Evaluation of Personal Constructs*, Academic Press, London 1968.

Bean, P. *Rehabilitation and Deviance*, R.K.P., London 1976.

Beccaria, C. *On Crime and Punishments*, (1770), Trans. with an introduction by H. Paolucci. Bobbs-Merrill, Indianapolis 1963.

Becker, H. *Outsiders*, New York Free Press 1963.

Beech, H. R. *Changing Man's Behaviour*, Pelican, Harmondsworth 1969.

Bender, L. 'Psychopathic Behaviour Disorders in Children' in Lindner, R. M. and Saliger, R. V. (eds) *Handbook of Correctional Psychology*, New York 1947.

Benn, S. 'Punishment' in *Punishment and Rehabilitation*, ed. Murphy, J., Wadsworth, Belmont 1973.

Benn, S. I. 'An approach to the problems of punishment', *Philosophy*, XXXIII, October 1958.

Benn, S. I. and Peters, R. S. *Social Principles and the Democratic State*, Allen and Unwin, London 1959.

Berger, P. L. and Luckman, T. *The Social Construction of Reality*, Penguin University Books, Harmondsworth 1971.

Berlins, M. and Wansell, G. 'Caught in the Act' in *Children, Society and the Law*, Pelican, Harmondsworth 1974.

Bevan, H. K. *The Law Relating to Children*, Butterworths, London 1973.

Black, D. J. and Reiss, A. J. 'Police Control of Juveniles', *A.S.R.*, vol.35, 1970, pp.63-77.

Blum, A. and McHugh, P. 'On the Failure of Positivism' in *Understanding Everyday Life*, ed. Jack Douglas, R.K.P., London 1971.

Blumberg, A. S. *Criminal Justice*, Quadrangle Books, Chicago 1967.

Bogen, D. 'Justice versus Individualised Treatment in the Juvenile Court', *Journal of Criminal Law and Criminology*, vol.35, 1944, p.250.

Bordua, D. J. *The Police: Six Sociological Essays*, John Wiley, New York 1967.

Boss, P. *Social Policy and the Young Delinquent*, Library of Social Work, London 1967.

Bottomley, K. *Decisions in the Penal Process*, Martin Robertson, London 1973.

Bottoms, A. 'On the Decriminalisation of English Juvenile Courts' in *Crime, Criminology and Public Policy*, ed. Hood, R., Heinemann, London 1974.

Bottoms, A., McLean, J. D. and Patchett, A. W. 'Children, Young Persons and the Courts – a Survey of the New Law', *C.L.R.*, 368, 1970, pp.370-3.

Bowlby, J. *Maternal Care and Mental Health*. Report on behalf of w.h.o. as a contribution to the u.n. programme for the welfare of children, 1951.

Bowlby, J. *Childcare and the Growth of Love*, Penguin, Harmondsworth 1964.

Box, S. *Deviance, Reality and Society*, Holt, Rinehart and Winston, London 1971.

Bruce, N. 'Two Scales of Justice', *Scotsman*, 2 February 1974.

Bruce, N. and Spencer, J. *Face to Face with Families*, MacDonald, Loanhead 1973.

Bruyn, S. T. *The Humanist Perspective in Sociology: the Methodology of Participant Observation*, Prentice-Hall, Englewood Cliffs 1966.

Burt, C. *The Young Delinquent* (4th ed.) University of London Press 1944.

Campbell, C. A. 'Is "Free-will" a Pseudo-Problem?' *Mind*, 1951.

Campbell, T. 'Discretion and Rights within the Children's Hearings System' in *Social Work in the Children's Hearings System*, ed. D. Houston, Glasgow University 1975.

Carlebach, J. *Caring for Children in Trouble*, r.k.p., London 1970.

Carlen, P. 'The Staging of Magistrates' Justice', *B.J.C.*, vol.16, no.1, January 1976, pp.48-55.

Carlen, P. *Negotiating Magistrates' Justice*, Martin Robertson, London 1976.

Carson, W. G. and Wiles, P. (eds) *Sociology of Crime and Delinquency*, Martin Robertson, London 1971.

Carter, Robert J. and Wilkins, L. T. 'Some Factors in Sentencing Policy', *Journal of Criminal Law, Criminology and Police Science*, 58, 4, 1967, pp.503-14.

Catton, K. and Leon, J. S. 'Legal representation and the proposed Young Persons in Conflict with the Law Act', *Osgoode Hall Law Journal*, vol.15, 1977, pp.107-35.

Cavenagh, W. E. and Sparks, R. F. 'Out of Court', *New Society*, vol.146, 1965.

Cavenagh, W. E. 'What Kind of Court or Committee', *B.J.C.*, 1966, pp.62, 123-38.

Cavenagh, W. E. *Juvenile Courts, the Child and the Law*, Pelican, Harmondsworth 1967.

Cicourel, A. V. *The Social Organisation of Juvenile Justice*, Wiley, New York 1968.

Clarke, M. J. 'The Impact of Social Science on Conceptions of Responsibility', *B.J.L.S.*, vol.2, 1, 1975, pp.32-44.

Cloward, R. and Ohlin, L. *Delinquency and Opportunity: a Theory of Delinquent Gangs*, Chicago Free Press 1960.

Cohen, A. *Deviance and Control*, Prentice-Hall, Englewood Cliffs 1966.

Cohen, A. *Delinquent Boys: the Culture of the Gang*, Chicago Free Press 1955.

Curran, J. 'Children's Hearing System: a Review of Research', *Scottish Office Social Research Study*, 1977.

Davis, K. C. *Discretionary Justice, a Preliminary Enquiry*, Louisiana State University Press 1969.

Denzin, N. K. *The Research Act: a Theoretical Introduction to Sociological Methods* (2nd ed.), McGraw Hill, New York 1978.

Devlin, P. A. D. *The Enforcement of Morals*, Oxford University Press 1965.

Donnison, D., Jay, P. and Stewart, M. 'The Ingleby Report: Three Critical Essays', *Fabian Research Pamphlet*, no.231, 1962.

Douglas, J. (ed.) *Deviance and Respectability: the Social Construction of Moral Meanings*, Basic Books, London and New York 1970.

Downes, D. *The Delinquent Solution*, R.K.P., London 1966.

Downes, D. and Rock, P. 'Social Reaction to Deviance and its Effect on Crime and Criminal Careers', *B.J.S.*, vol.22, 1971.

Downie, R. S. *Roles and Values: an Introduction to Social Ethics*, London 1971.

Duster, T. *The Legislation of Morality*, Free Press 1970.

Elkin, W. A. *English Juvenile Courts*, Kegan Paul, London 1938.

Elson, A. 'Juvenile Courts and Due Process' in *Justice for the Child*, ed. Rosenheim, M., Glencoe Free Press 1962.

Emerson, R. M. *Judging Delinquents*, Aldine, Chicago 1969.

Emil, F. 'The Offender and the Court: a statistical analysis of the sentencing of delinquents', *Journal of Criminal Law and Criminology*, XXXI, November-December 1940.

Erikson, K. T. 'Notes in the Sociology of Deviance', *Social Problems*, 9, Spring 1962, reprinted in H. Becker, 1964.

Etzioni, A. *Complex Organisations: a Sociological Reader*, Holt, New York 1961.

Ewing, A. C. *The Morality of Punishment*, London 1929.

Eysenck, H. J. *Crime and Personality*, R.K.P., London 1970.

Farrington, D. 'The Effects of Public Labelling', *B.J.C.*, vol.17, 1977, pp.112-25.

Faust, F. L. and Brantingham, P. J. (eds) *Juvenile Justice Philosophy*, West Publishing Co., Minnesota 1974.

Ferri, E. *Criminal Sociology*, Little, Brown and Co., Boston 1917.

Fitzjames Stephen, Sir James. *History of the Criminal Law of England*, 1883.

Flew, A. 'Crime or Disease', *New Studies in Practical Philosophy*, London 1973.

Flew, A. 'The Justification of Punishment', *Philosophy*, XXIX, no.iii, October 1954. Reprinted in Acton (ed.) 1969, p.83 ff.

Fox, S. J. 'Juvenile Justice Reform: Innovations in Scotland', *A.C.L.R.*, vol.12:61, 1974.

Fox, S. J. 'Juvenile Justice Reform: Some American-Scottish
    Comparisons', in Martin and Murray, 1976.
Friedlander, K. *The Psychoanalytical Approach to Juvenile
    Delinquency*, R.K.P., London 1947.
Gallacher, J. 'Justice for the Child', *Care*, Discussion paper no.2,
    1974.
Garofalo, R. *Criminology* (1914), Boston 1968 edition.
Gaudet, F. *The Sentencing Behaviour of the Judge* in V. Brandon and
    S. Katash, eds Encyclopaedia of Criminology, New York 1949,
    pp.449-661.
George, B. J. *Gault and the Juvenile Court Revolution'*, Institute of
    Continuing Legal Education, Hutchings Hall 1968.
Gibbs, J. 'Conceptions of Deviant Behaviour: the old and the new',
    P.S.R., 9, 1966.
Giddens, A. *New Rules of Sociological Method*, Hutchison, London
    1976.
Giles, F. T. *The Juvenile Courts*, Allen and Unwin, London 1946.
Gillis, J. *Youth and History*, Academic Press, London 1974.
Glasgow Herald, 8 May 1976. Letter to the editor from Boyd Haining.
Glover, E. *Roots of Crime*, Imago, London 1960.
Glover, J. *Responsibility*, International Library of Philosophy and
    Scientific Method, London 1970.
Glueck, S. and Glueck, E. *Unravelling Juvenile Delinquency*, Harper
    and Row, New York 1950.
Glueck, S. and Glueck, E. *Physique and Delinquency*, Harper and
    Row, New York 1956.
Goldstein, J., Freud, A. and Solnit, A. *Beyond the Best Interests of the
    Child*, Free Press, New York 1973.
Gordon, G. 'The Role of the Courts' in *Children's Hearings*, ed. F.
    Martin and K. Murray, Scottish Academic Press, Edinburgh
    1976.
Gordon, G. *Criminal Law of Scotland* (2nd ed.), W. Green and Sons,
    Edinburgh 1978.
Grant, J. 'Protecting the Rights of the Child', in Martin and Murray
    (eds) 1976.
Green, E. *Judicial Attitudes*, Macmillan, London 1961.
Grunhüt, M. *Competence and Constitution of the Juvenile Court*,
    Oxford University Press 1956.
Haksar, V. 'The Responsibility of Mental Defectives', *Philosophical
    Quarterly*, 1963.
Haksar, V. 'The Responsibility of Psychopaths', *Philosophical
    Quarterly*, April 1965.
Hardiker, P. 'Social Work Ideologies in the Probation Service',
    B.J.S.W., vol.7, 1977, pp.131-54.
Harno, A. 'Some significant developments in Criminal Law and
    Procedure in the last Century', *Journal of Criminal Law,
    Criminology and Police Science*, no.4, 1951, pp.427-67.
Harris, B. 'Children's Act in Trouble', *C.L.R.*, 1972, pp.670-83.
Harrison, P. 'Young Offenders', *New Society*, vol.23, no.537, 1973,
    p.126.
Hart, H. L. A. *Punishment and Responsibility: Essays in Philosophy
    of Law*, Oxford University Press 1968.

Hart, H. L. A. 'Prolegomenon to the Principles of Punishment',
    Proceedings of Aristotelian Society, 1959-60. Reprint in Hart,
    1968.

Healey, W. *The Individual Delinquent*, Little, Brown and Co., Boston
    1915.

Hindess, B. *The Uses of Official Statistics in Sociology*, Macmillan,
    London 1973.

Hogarth, J. *Sentencing as a Human Process*, University of Toronto
    Press 1971.

Hoggett, B. 'Dealing with Juveniles – I and II', *Solicitors Journal*, 3
    and 27, 1973, p.117.

Holden, D. A. *Child Legislation*, 1969, Butterworth, London 1970.

Honderich, T. *Punishment: the Supposed Justifications*, Hutchison,
    London 1969.

Hood, R. *Sentencing in Magistrates' Courts*, Stevens, London 1962.

Hood, R. (ed.) *Crime, Criminology and Public Policy*, Heinemann,
    London 1974.

Hood, R. and Sparks, R. *Key Issues in Criminology*, World University
    Library, Weidenfeld and Nicolson, London 1972.

Horney, K. *The Neurotic Personality of Our Time*, London 1947.

Hughes, E. C. 'Dilemmas and Contradictions of Status', *A.J.S.*, vol.L,
    1944.

Ingleby, D. 'Ideology and the Human Sciences', *Human Context*,
    no.11, June 1970.

Jacobs, F. G. 'Criminal Responsibility', *L.S.E. Research Monograph 8*,
    London 1971.

James, T. E. *Child Law*, Sweet and Maxwell, London 1962.

Jarvis, F. V. 'The Probation Services: the Effect of the White Paper',
    B.J.C., vol.6, 1966, p.152-8.

Jay, P. 'A Plan for Family Bureaux' in Donnison et al., 1962.

Johnson, T. *Professions and Power*, Macmillan, London 1972.

Joutsen, M. *Juvenile Justice in Finland*, paper presented to the Ivth
    International Conference on Comparative Studies in Juvenile
    Justice, May 1981.

Jowell, J. 'Law, discretion and bureaucracy', *The Listener*, 2 March
    1978.

Kahan, B. J. 'The Child, the Family and the Young Offender:
    Revolutionary or Evolutionary?', *B.J.C.*, vol.6, 1966, p.159 ff.

Kean, A. W. G. 'The History of the Criminal Liability of Children',
    L.Q.R., vol.53, 1937, pp.364-70.

Kelly, G. A. 'A Brief Introduction to Personal Construct Theory' in
    Perspectives in Personal Construct Theory, Academic Press,
    London 1970.

Kilbrandon, Lord, 'Children in Trouble', *B.J.C.*, vol.6, 1966,
    pp.112-22.

King, M. 'Welfare and Justice' in *Childhood, Welfare and Justice*,
    ed. M. King, Batsford, London 1981.

Kitsuse, J. I. 'Social Reactions to Deviant Behaviour: problems of
    theory and method', *Social Problems*, 9, Winter 1963,
    pp.247-56.

Kitsuse, J. I. and Cicourel, A. V. 'A note on the uses of official
    statistics', *Social Problems*, vol.11, 1963, pp.131-9.

Kogan, M. 'Management Efficiency and the Social Services: a review article', *B.J.S.W.*, vol.1, 1971.

Kraus, J. 'Judicial Labels as a Typology of Offences committed by Male Juveniles', *B.J.C.*, 13, 1973, pp.269 ff.

Kretschmer, E. *Physique and Character*, trans. by D. Scott, Cooper Square, New York 1921.

Langley, M. H. 'The Juvenile Court: the making of a delinquent', *Law and Society Review* (7), 1972.

Lemert, E. *Social Pathology*, McGraw Hill, New York 1951.

Lemert, E. *Human Deviance, Social Problems and Social Control*, Prentice Hall Inc., Englewood Cliffs 1967.

Lemert, E. 'Choice and Change in Juvenile Justice', *B.J.L.S.*, vol.3, 1, 1976, pp.59-75.

Lemert, E. 'The Juvenile Court – Quest and Realities' in Garabedian, P. and Gibbons, D. (eds) *Becoming Delinquent*, Aldine Publishing Co., Chicago 1970.

Lemon, N. 'Training, personality and attitudes as determinants of magistrates' sentencing', *B.J.C.*, 14, 1974, pp.34-48.

Leon, J. 'The development of Canadian juvenile justice – a background of reform', *Osgoode Hall Journal*, vol.15, 1977, pp.71-106.

Lloyd, D. *The Idea of Law*, Pelican, Harmondsworth 1964.

Lombroso, C. *Crime: its Causes and Remedies*, Little, Brown and Co., Boston 1913.

McBarnett, D. 'False Dichotomies in Criminal Justice Research' in *Criminal Justice*,, ed. J. Baldwin and K. Bottomley, Martin Robertson 1978.

McCloskey, H. J. 'The Complexity of the Concepts of Punishment', *Philosophy*, 1962.

McCloskey, H. J. 'A Non-Utilitarian Approach to Punishment', *Inquiry*, 1965.

MacCormick, D. N. 'Responsibility as a Right'. Paper presented to a Franco-Scottish Colloquium on various aspects of the Dangerous and Abnormal Offender, 1974.

McFaden, W. E. 'Changing Concepts of Juvenile Justice', *Crime and Delinquency*, 17, 1971, pp.131-41.

McHugh, P. 'A commonsense conception of deviance', in Douglas (ed.) 1970.

McNeilly, F. S. 'Immorality and the Law', *Proceedings of Aristotelian Society*, LXVI, 1965/66.

Malmquist, C. P. 'Juvenile Detention: Right and Adequacy of Treatment Issues', *Law and Society Review*, 7, 1972.

Mankoff, M. 'Societal reaction and career deviance: a critical analysis', *The Sociological Quarterly*, 12, Spring 1971.

Mannheim, H., Spencer, J. C. and Lynch, G. 'Magisterial Policy', *B.J.D.*, vol.8, 1957, pp.13-33, 119-38.

Mapstone, E. 'The Selection of the Children's Panels for the County of Fife', *B.J.S.W.*, 2.4, 1972, pp.445-69.

Martin, F. and Murray, K. *Children's Hearings*, Scottish Academic Press, Edinburgh 1976.

Martin, F., Fox, S. and Murray, K. *Children Out of Court*, Scottish Academic Press, Edinburgh 1981.

Matza, D. *Delinquency and Drift*, Wiley, New York 1964.

May, D. 'Delinquency Control and the Treatment Model', *B.J.C.*, vol.11, 4, 1971, pp.359-70.

May, D. 'Rhetoric and Reality: Ambiguity in the Children's Panel System', *B.J.C.*, vol.17, 1977, pp.109-227.

May, D. and Smith, G. 'Policy interpretation and the children's panels: a case study in social administration', *Applied Social Studies*, 2, no.2, 1970, pp.91-8.

Midgley, J. 'Children on Trial: a Study of Juvenile Justice', *South African Studies in Criminology*, Cape Town 1975.

Mill, J. S. *Utilitarianism*, Fontana, London 1962, ed. M. Warnock.

Miller, W. 'Lower class culture as a generating milieu of gang delinquency', *Journal of Social Issues*, 15, 1958, pp.5-19.

Mills, C. Wright. 'The Professional Ideology of Social Pathologists', *A.J.S.*, XLIX, September 1942, pp.165-80.

Moberley, Sir W. *The Ethics of Punishment*, Faber and Faber, London 1968.

Moody, S. 'A profile of panel members', Scottish Office, 1976.

Morris, A. 'Scottish Juvenile Justice' in *Crime, Criminology and Public Policy*, ed. by R. Hood, Heinemann, London 1974.

Morris, A. and Giller, H. 'The Juvenile Court: the Client's Perspective', *C.L.R.*, 1977, pp.198-205.

Morris, A., Giller, H., Szwed, L. and Geach, H. *Justice for children*, Macmillan, London 1980.

Morris, A. and McIsaac, M. *Juvenile Justice*, Heinemann, London 1978.

Morris, A. McIsaac, M. and Gallacher, J. 'Needs of the child: needs of the community', *Times Educational Supplement*, 1973.

Morris, T. *The Criminal Area: a study in social ecology*, R.K.P., London 1957.

Mundle, C. W. K. 'Punishment and Desert', *Philosophical Quarterly*, vol.IV, no.16, 1954. Reprinted in Acton (ed.) 1969, pp.65 ff.

Murray, G. and Rowe, A. 'Children's Panels: implications for the future', *Policy and Politics*, vol.1, no.4.

Murphy, J. (ed.) *Punishment and Rehabilitation*, Wadsworth, Belmont, California 1973.

Napley, D. 'A Comment', *C.L.R.*, 1968, pp.474-7.

Natanson, E. *Phenomenology and Social Reality, Essays in memory of A. Schutz*, Martinus Nizhoff 1970.

Nowell-Smith, P. H. *Ethics*, London 1954.

Park, R. E. 'Human Ecology', *A.J.S.*, 42(1), 1936.

Parker, C. F. 'The Right to Reasons for a Decision of Magistrates' Court', *C.L.R.*, 1973, pp.716-27.

Parsloe, P. 'The boundaries between legal and social work concerns in the hearing system' in Houston, D. (ed.) *Social Work in the Children's Hearing System*, 1975.

Parsloe, P. 'Social Work and the Justice Model', *B.J.S.W.*, 6, 1, 1976.

Patchett, A. W. and McLean, J. D. 'Decision-making in Juvenile Cases', *C.L.R.*, 1965, pp.699-710.

Pavlov, I. P. *Conditioned Reflexes*, Oxford University Press 1972.

Pearson, G. *The Deviant Imagination*, Macmillan, London 1975.

Perelman, C. *Idea of Justice and the Problem of Argument*,
    International Library of Philosophy and Scientific Method,
    London 1963.
Perry, F. *Information for the Court*, University of Cambridge 1974.
Peters, R. S. *The Concept of Motivation*, R.K.P., London 1958.
Phillipson, M. *Sociological Aspects of Crime and Delinquency*,
    Students' Library of Sociology, London 1971.
Piliavin, I. and Briar, S. 'Police Encounters with Juveniles', *A.S.R.*,
    vol.35, 1970, pp.63-77.
Pinchbeck, I. and Hewitt, M. *Children in English Society*, vol.1,
    R.K.P., London 1973.
Pitkin, H. F. *Wittgenstein and Justice*, University of California 1972.
Platt, A. 'Prospects for a radical criminology in the U.S.A.', in Taylor,
    I., Walton, P. and Young, J. (eds) *Critical Criminology*, R.K.P.,
    London 1975.
Platt, A. and Friedman, R. 'Limits of Advocacy: Occasional Hazards
    in Juvenile Court', *University of Pennsylvania Law Review*,
    1968, pp.1056 ff.
Pound, R. 'The future of socialised justice', *National Probation
    Association Yearbook*, 1946.
Poveda, J. G. 'The image of the criminal: a critique of crime and
    delinquency theories', *Issues in Criminology*, 5, 1970.
Priestley, P., Fears, D. and Fuller, R. *Justice for Juveniles*, R.K.P.,
    London 1977.
Puckett, T. C. 'Social Science Methods and Social Work Research',
    Applied Social Studies, vol.3, 1971, pp.29-38.
Quinton, A. M. 'On Punishment', *Analysis*, vol.14, no.6, June 1954.
    Reprinted in Acton (ed.) 1969, pp.1047-60.
Radzinowicz, Sir L. 'Ideology and Crime: the Deterministic
    Position', *Columbia Law Review*, 65, 1965, pp.1047-60.
Rawls, J. 'Two concepts of Rules', *Philosophical Review*, vol.LXIV,
    January 1955. Reprinted in Acton (ed.) 1969, p.105 ff.
Rees, S. J. 'Defining Moral Worthiness: grounds for intervention in
    social work', *Social Work Today*, 7, 7, 1976, pp.203-6.
Rickman, J. 'Selected contributions to psychoanalysis', *International
    Psycho-analytic Library*, no.52, London 1957.
Roche, M. *Phenomenology, Language and the Social Sciences*, R.K.P.,
    London 1973.
Rock, P. *Deviant Behaviour*, Hutchison and Co., London 1973.
Rowe, A. 'Children's Hearings', *New Society*, 2 March 1972.
Ruska, M. S. 'Positivism and Criminal Responsibility'. Thesis
    submitted for the degree of LL.M. at University College, Cardiff
    1974.
Ryan, A. *The Philosophy of the Social Sciences*, Macmillan, London
    1970.
Samek, R. A. *The Legal Point of View*, Philosophical Library, New
    York 1974.
Sanders, B. *Lecture notes for magistrates*. Document issued in the
    training of magistrates, 1973.
Sarbin, R. and Miller, J. 'Demonism revisited: the XYY chromosomal
    anomaly', *Issues in Criminology*, 5, 1970, pp.195-207.

Sayers, S. 'Mental Illness as a Moral Concept', *Radical Philosophy*, 1973.

Schlick, M. *Problems of Ethics*, Prentice-Hall, Englewood Cliffs 1939.

Schur, E. *Labelling Deviant Behaviour: its Sociological Implications*, Random House, New York 1971.

Schutz, A. *The Phenomenology of the Social World*, North Western University Press 1967.

Schutz, A. *On Phenomenology and Social Relations*, ed. Wagner, University of Chicago Press 1970.

Schutz, A. 'Commonsense and Scientific Interpretation of Human Action', *Philosophy and Phenomenological Research*, 14 (1), 1953, pp.1-38.

Scotsman, 26 October 1964. Letter to the editor from the Association of Child-Care Officers.

Scotsman, 3 April 1978. Letter to the editor from E. Morrison.

Scott, P. D. 'The Child, the Family and the Young Offender', *B.J.C.*, 6, 2, 1966, pp.105-11.

Shaw, C. R. and McKay, H. D. *Juvenile Delinquency and Urban Areas*, Chicago University Press 1942.

Sheldon, W. *Varieties of Human Physique*, Harper and Row, New York 1940.

Silverman, D. *The Theory of Organisations*, Heinemann, London 1971.

Skinner, B. F. *Beyond Freedom and Dignity*, Penguin, Harmondsworth 1973.

Skolnick, J. H. *Justice without Trial*, John Wiley, New York 1966.

Smith, G. 'The Children Act: what is going wrong', *New Society*, vol.22, no.533, 1972, p.681.

Smith, G. 'Little Kiddies and Criminal Acts: the Role of Social Work in the Children's Hearings', *B.J.S.W.*, 7, 4, 1977.

Smith, G. 'The place of "Professional Ideology" in the analysis of "Social Policy": some theoretical conclusions from a pilot study of the Children's Panels', *Sociological Review*, vol.25, no.4, 1977, pp.843-65.

Smith, G. 'Discretionary Decision-making in Social Work', in Adler, M. and Asquith, S. (eds) *Discretion and Welfare*, Heinemann, London 1981.

Smith, G. and Harris, R. 'Managing Social Need: a study in the reorganisation of British social work'. Unpublished document submitted to the Scottish Office, 1976.

Smith, G. and May, D. 'The Appointment of the Aberdeen City Children's Panel: a comment on the Social Work (Scotland) Act 1968', *B.J.S.W.*, vol.1, 1, 1971.

Snyder, E. C. 'The Impact of the Juvenile Court Hearing on the Child', *Crime and Delinquency*, 17, 1971, pp.180-90.

Solicitor General, Canada. The Young Offenders Act, February 1981.

Spencer, J. *Juvenile Justice – he Demands of Treatment*, Fourth Denis Carroll Memorial Lecture, 1973.

Sprigge, T. L. S. 'A Utilitarian Reply to Dr McClosky', *Inquiry*, 1973.

Stoll, C. S. 'Images of Man and Social Control', *Social Forces* 47 (2), 1968, pp.119-27.

Strauss, A., Schatzman and Bucher, R. *Psychiatric Institutions and Ideologies*, New York 1964.

Sutherland, E. 'White Collar Criminality' in *Delinquency, Crime and Social Process*, ed. D. Creasey and D. Ward, Harper and Row 1969.

Sykes, G. and Matza, D. 'Techniques of neutralisation: a theory of delinquency', *A.S.R.*, 22, 1957.

Tappan, P. *Juvenile Delinquency*, McGraw Hill, New York 1949.

Tappan, P. 'Treatment without Trial', *Social Forces*, 24, 1946. Reprinted in Faust and Brantingham (eds) 1974.

Taylor, I., Walton, P. and Young, J. *The New Criminology*, R.K.P., London 1973.

Taylor, I., Walton, P. and Young, J. *Critical Criminology*, R.K.P., London 1975.

Taylor, L. *Deviance and Society*, Michael Joseph, London 1971.

Taylor, L. 'The Significance and Interpretation of Replies to Motivational Questions', *Sociology*, vol.6, 1, 1972, pp.23-40.

Terry, R. N. 'Discrimination in the handling of juvenile offenders by social control agencies' in Garabedian, P. and Gibbons, D. (eds) *Becoming Delinquent*, Aldine, Chicago 1970.

Thomas, D. A. 'The Control of Discretion in the Administration of Criminal Justice' in *Crime, Criminology and Public Policy*, ed. Hood, 1974.

Thomas, D. A. *Principles of Sentencing*, Heinemann, London 1970.

Thomas, D. A. 'Sentencing – the Basic Principles', *C.L.R.*, 1967, pp.455-525.

Trasler, G. *The Explanation of Criminality*, R.K.P., 1962.

Vaihinger, H. *The Philosophy of 'As If'*, Trans. by C. K. Ogden, International Library of Philosophy and Scientific Method, London 1924.

Vold, G. *Theoretical Criminology*, Oxford University Press 1958.

Voss, H. L. and Peterson, D. M. *Ecology, Crime and Delinquency*, Meredith, New York 1971.

Waismann, F. 'Language Strata' in A. Flew (ed.) *Logic and Language*, 2nd series, Basil Blackwell, Oxford 1955.

Waite, E. 'How far can court procedure be socialised without impairing individual rights', *12 Journal of American Institute of Criminal Law and Criminology*, 339, 1921. Reprinted in Faust and Brantingham (eds) 1974.

Walker, N. *Sentencing in a Rational Society*, Pelican, Harmondsworth 1969.

Warburton, B. 'The juvenile courts in England and Wales', *International Journal of Offender Therapy and Comparative Criminology*, 16, 1972.

van Waters, M. 'The Socialisation of Juvenile Court Procedure', *13 Journal of American Institute of Criminal Law and Criminology*, 61, 1922. Reprinted in Faust and Brantingham (eds) 1974.

Watson, D. 'The Underlying Principles: a philosophical comment' in F. Martin and K. Murray (eds) 1976.

Watson, J. A. *The Child and the Magistrate*, Jonathan Cape, London 1965.

Watson, J. A. *Juvenile Court _ 1970 onwards*, Shaw and Sons, London 1970.

West, D. J. and Farrington, D. P. *Present Conduct and Future Delinquency*, Heinemann, London 1969.

Wheeler, S., Bonaich, E., Cramer, M. and Zola, S. 'Agents of Delinquency Control: a comparative analysis' in S. Wheeler (ed.) *Controlling Delinquents*, New York 1968.

Willer, D. and Willer, J. *Systematic Empiricism: Critique of a Pseudoscience*, Prentice-Hall, Englewood Cliffs, N.J. 1973.

Williams, G. 'Criminal Responsibility of Children', *C.L.R.*, 1954, pp.493-500.

Wootton, B. *Social Science and Social Pathology*, Allen and Unwin, London 1959.

Wootton, B. *Crime and the Criminal Law*, Stevens, London 1963.

Wootton, B. *Hansard*, H.L. CCLIV, 815, 1962.

Wootton, B. Letter to *New Society*, 29 July 1965, pp.29-30.

Wootton, B. 'White Paper on Children in Trouble', *C.L.R.*, 1968, pp.465-74.

Wrong, D. 'The oversocialised concept of man in modern sociology', *A.S.R.*, XXVI, 1971, pp.184-93.

Yablonsky, L. 'The Role of Law and Social Science in the Juvenile Court', *Journal of Criminal Law, Criminology and Police*, 53, 1962, pp.426-36.

Official Publications

Longford Study Group. *Crime: a Challenge to us all*, Labour Party, London 1964.

Magistrates' Association. Document on Selection and Training of Magistrates, 1975.

Report of the Children and Young Persons Review Group (Black), HMSO, Belfast 1979.

Report of the Committee on Homeless Children (Clyde), Cmnd.6911, HMSO, 1946.

Report of the Committee on Care of Children (Curtis), Cmnd.6922, 1946.

Report of the Committee on Children and Young Persons (Ingleby), Cmnd.1191, HMSO, 1960.

Report on Children and Young Persons (Scotland), (Kilbrandon), Cmnd.2306, 1964.

Report of Committee on the Prevention of Neglect of Children (McBoyle), Cmnd.1466, HMSO, 1963.

Report of the Departmental Committee on the Treatment of Young Offenders (Molony), Cmnd.2831, HMSO, London 1927.

Report of the Departmental Committee on the Probation Service (Morrison), Cmnd.1650, HMSO, 1962.

Report of Committee on Protection and Training (Morton), HMSO, 1928.

Report of the Departmental Committee on Protection and Training (Scotland), HMSO, London 1928.

Royal Commission on Justices of the Peace, Cmnd.7463, 1946-8.

White Papers

The Child, The Family and the Young Offender, Cmnd.2742, HMSO, 1965.

Children in Trouble, Cmnd.3601, HMSO, 1968.

Social Work and the Community, Cmnd.3065, HMSO, 1966.

INDEX